100 BEST CAREERS

FOR THE

21st CENTURY

Shelly Field

WITHDRAWN

WITHDRAWN

MACMILLAN • USA

ARAM PUBLIC LIBRARY
DELAVAN, WIS.

Copyright © 1996 by Shelly Field
All rights reserved including the right of reproduction
in whole or in part in any form

Macmillan General Reference
A Simon & Schuster Macmillan Company
1633 Broadway
New York, NY 10019

An Arco Book

MACMILLAN is a registered trademark of Macmillan, Inc.
ARCO is a registered trademark of Prentice-Hall, Inc.

Library of Congress Cataloging-in-Publication Data
Field, Shelly.
    100 best careers for the 21st century/Shelly Field.
      p. cm.
    Rev. ed. of: 100 best careers for the year 2000.
    ISBN 0-02-860595-0
    1. Vocational guidance.   2. Occupations—Forecasting.   3. Job
vacancies.   I. Field, Shelly.   100 best careers for the year 2000.
II. Title.
HF5381.F476   1996
331.7'02—dc20   95-52518
                                                 CIP

Manufactured in the United States of America

10 9 8 7 6 5 4 3 2

DEDICATION

This book is dedicated to my parents, Ed and Selma, and my sisters, Jessica and Debbie, who encouraged me to follow my dreams, hopes, and aspirations and then helped make them come true.

ACKNOWLEDGMENTS

I thank every individual, company, corporation, agency, association, and union responsible for providing information, assistance, and encouragement for this book.

First and foremost, I acknowledge with appreciation my editor, Linda Bernbach, for providing the original impetus for this book as well as her support and guidance throughout its creation, development, and writing. I gratefully acknowledge the assistance of Ed and Selma Field for their ongoing support in this project.

Others whose help was invaluable include: The Advertising Club of New York; Advertising Council; Advertising Research Foundation; Advertising Women of New York, Inc.; Aerobics Center; Aerobics and Fitness Association of America (AFAA); American Advertising Federation; American Association of Advertising Agencies; American Association for Counseling and Development; American Society for Hospital Marketing and Public Relations; American Association for Music Therapy; American Academy of Actuaries; American Bar Association; American Chemical Society; American Chiropractic Association; American Dance Therapy Association; American Dental Assistants Association; American Dental Association; American Dental Hygienists Association; American Geriatrics Society; American Health Care Association; American Hospital Association; American Association of Certified Public Accountants; American Institute of Chemists; American Meteorological Society; American Optometric Association; American Physical Therapy Association; American Society of Biological Chemists; American Society of Travel Agents (ASTA); Joanne Anderson; Art Directors Club, Inc.; Barbara Ashworth, Beauty School of Middletown; Association of Computer Professionals (ACP); Association of National Advertisers; Allan Barrish; Marguerite Berling, International Chiropractors Association; Eugene Blabey, WVOS Radio; Keith Browne, Environmental Engineer, NYS Department of Environmental Conservation; Theresa Bull; Business/Professional Advertising Association; Liane Carpenter, Executive Director, Advertising Women of New York, Inc.; Mary Cawley; Casualty Actuarial Society; Andy Cohen; Bernard Cohen, Horizon Advertising; Dr. Jessica L. Cohen; Lorraine Cohen; Norman Cohen; Commission on Opticianary Accreditation; Community General Hospital, Harris, NY; Contact, Inc.; Jan Cornelius; Phyllis Cornell, Image Consultant; Crawford Memorial Library Staff; Meike Cryan; Su Perk Davis, Director Clearinghouse Services, Contact Center, Inc.; Council on Chiropractic Education; Barbara Dankulich, Administrative Assistant, Division of Law Enforcement for the NYS Department of Environmental Conservation; Daniel Dayton; W. Lynne Dayton; Linda Delgadillo, Communication Director, Society of Actuaries; Direct Mail/Marketing Association, Inc.; Direct Marketing Educational Foundation, Inc.; Jane Donohue; Scott Edwards; Valerie Esper; Ernest Evans; John Fasciano; Field Associates, Ltd.; Deborah K. Field, Esq.; Gale Findling, RN-Director Harris Home Health Services, Community General Hospital of Sullivan County, NY; Finkelstein Memorial Library Staff; Greg Fotiades, Manager-Radiology Department, Community General Hospital of Sullivan County, NY; John Gatto; Sheila Gatto; Gerontological Society of America; Tina Gilbert, Apollo Plaza; George Glantzis; Kaytee Glantzis; Sam Goldych; Graphic Artist Guild; Gail Haberle; Joyce Harrington, Director of Communications, American Association of Advertising Agencies, Inc.; Hermann Memorial Library Staff; Hope's Corner, Bloomingdale's, New York City; Jan Hopkins, RN, Supervisor—Bio-Chem. Dependency Unit, Community General Hospital of Sullivan County, NY; Patricia Hopkins, Radiology Department, Community General Hospital of Sullivan County, NY; Joan Howard; International Chiropractors Association; Jimmy "Handyman" Jones; Margo Jones; Tom Lagrutta; Liberty Public Library Staff; Lipman Advertising; Ginger Maher; Dorothy Marcus, Grey Advertising; Robert Masters, Esq.; McCann-Erickson; Lois McCluskey, Staff Executive, American Association of Advertising Agencies, Inc.; Werner Mendel, New Age Health Spa; Phillip Mestman; Rima Mestman; Beverly Michaels, Esq.; Monticello Central High School Guidance Department; Monticello Central School High School Library Staff; Monticello Central School Middle School Library Staff; Cindy Moorhead, Recruiter, Community General Hospital of Sullivan County, NY; Sharon Morris; Joseph Napolitano; National Association for Music Therapy; National Association of Alcoholism and Drug Abuse Counselors; National Association of Broadcast Employees and Technicians; National Association of Broadcasters; National Association of Life Underwriters; National Association of Realtors; National Resource Center on Health Promotion and Aging; Earl Nesmith; New York State Department of Environmental Conservation; New York State Employment Service; New York State Nurses Association; Peter Notarstefano; The One Club; Joy F. Pierce, Director of Accreditation, Commission on Opticianary Accreditation; Debra Pless; Robert Pless; Public Relations Society of America; Ramapo Catskill Library System; Doug Richards; Martin Richman, Executive Director, Community General Hospital of Sullivan County, NY; David Rosenberg, Human Resources Manager, Grey Advertising; Genic Ruiz; Saatchi and Saatchi Advertising; Iris Silver, Proprietor/Trainer/Consultant, Computrain; Society of Illustrators; Debbie Springfield; Matthew E. Strong; Sullivan County Community College; Dana Swails, National Association of Life Underwriters; Thrall Library Staff; Anne Thum, R.N., Nurse Manager for Litson Healthcare; Marie Tremper; Leo S. Ullman, Esq.; United States Department of Labor; Karen Waits, Administrative Assistant, Council on Chiropractic Education; Brenda Walker; Carol Williams; John Williams; John Wolfe; Johnny World; WSUL Radio; WTZA-Television; and WVOS Radio.

My thanks also to the many people, associations, companies, and organizations who provided material for this book but wish to remain anonymous.

CONTENTS

APPENDIX: TRADE ASSOCIATIONS, UNIONS, AND OTHER ORGANIZATIONS

PREFACE

This is a comprehensive guide to 100 of the fastest-growing occupations for the 21st century. It is a valuable resource for those planning careers, those just entering the job market, and those hoping to change careers.

Thousands of people aspire to find good jobs or change careers but have no idea how to get a position in their fields of choice. They have no concept of what the career opportunities are, where to find them, or what training is required. *100 Best Careers for the 21st Century* is the single source essential for learning about major job opportunities for the new century.

This book was written to help anyone prepare now for an interesting, exciting, and/or well-paying job. The 100 careers discussed in this book encompass a multitude of interests and fields.

Today's job market requires people with a variety of different talents. The trick to locating the job you want is developing your skills and using them to get in the door of the industry that interests you. Once you take that important first step, you're on your way to career success.

INFORMATION SOURCES

Information for this book was obtained through interviews, questionnaires, and a wide variety of books, magazines, newsletters, television and radio programs, and college catalogs.

Among the people interviewed were men and women in all aspects of business and industry. These include professionals in the corporate and industrial world, colleges, trade associations, nonprofit organizations, newspapers, magazines, radio and television stations, hospitals, health care institutions and agencies, environmental agencies, education, and government. Also interviewed were engineers, accountants, insurance agents, law enforcement and correction officers, individuals working in the computer industry, advertising and public relations agency owners and employees, health care employees, pilots, flight attendants, hotel and restaurant owners and managers, technicians, technologists, owners of home-based businesses, teachers, freelancers, businesspeople, and more. Employment agencies were contacted as well as recruiting firms, schools, personnel offices, unions, and trade associations.

Organization of Material

100 Best Careers for the 21st Century is divided into eleven general employment sections: Medical Technology and Health Care; Geriatrics; Computers; Conservation and the Environment; Advertising, Communications, and Public Relations; Sales and Service; Fitness and Nutrition; Education; Hospitality and the Travel Industry; Science and Engineering; and Home-Based Businesses. Within each section are descriptions of many individual careers.

There are two parts to each job classification. The first part offers job facts in an overview chart. The second part presents descriptive information in a narrative text.

The text details the job description and responsibilities; employment opportunities; expanding opportunities for the 21st century; earnings; advancement opportunities; education and training; experience and qualifications; organizations that offer additional information; and tips for obtaining the specific job.

Names, addresses, and phone numbers of trade associations, organizations, and unions are listed in the Appendix to provide resources for further information.

By reading this book, you are taking the first step toward not only finding a career that will be in demand, but also preparing for it. No matter which facet of the job market you choose to go into, you can find a career that is rewarding and enjoyable. The jobs are out there waiting for you. You just have to go after them.

Shelly Field

INTRODUCTION

The 21st century will bring new employment opportunities that require a wide array of skills, training, education, and experience. Many of these new opportunities will result from today's tremendous growth of technology. Every industry will be affected.

Medical technology, for example, is keeping people alive longer and improving their quality of life. As a result, the health care industry will be one of the major growth areas. Equally important in the employment picture is the geriatrics field. The increase in the population of older Americans not only swells the demand for health care in general, but also for services specific to this age group.

Technology has affected the business world with its computers, modems, fax machines, and cellular phones. Computers can now do more than anyone ever dreamed possible and the extent of their power has not even come close to plateauing. New digital technology will also affect the entertainment industry. There is a constant influx of electronic equipment including VCRs, high-definition televisions, camcorders, laser disks, and compact disk players, and models are constantly being improved.

New technology has similarly affected the way public relations, advertising, and communication messages are relayed to the public. News is now passed on instantaneously via television and radio. No longer are there only three major networks on which to advertise.

Now cable television offers a whole new range of advertising and marketing possibilities. Science and engineering career opportunities will increase in tandem with technological growth. Scientific experiments and tests can now be conducted with computerized equipment. Engineers can use computers to develop plans for roads, bridges, machinery, waste systems, and almost anything that was once handled manually.

Technology has also effectively increased the number of home-based businesses in the country. The affordability and availability of such equipment as computers, fax machines, and modems enable more people to work at home.

High technology has brought some negative changes to the world as well. Greater industrialization has resulted in the abuse and overuse of natural resources. Pollution of water, land, and air has, in turn, led to a growth in the environmental conservation job market.

A great many jobs will be created in education. These jobs will include not only traditional schoolteachers and college professors but also instructors for vocational, technical, and trade schools as well as for adult education classes, bilingual studies, and foreign language studies.

The trend toward two-paycheck families as well as an increase in single heads of households has spurred the growth of sales and service industries in a variety of areas, including health care, personal services, retail trade, business services, hospitality, and travel.

Within each section of this book you will find information to acquaint you with job possibilities for the future. A key to the organization of each entry follows:

JOB DESCRIPTION AND RESPONSIBILITIES

Every effort has been made to give well-rounded job descriptions. As no two companies are identically structured, no two jobs will be precisely the same.

Keep in mind, also, that job titles may vary from company to company. The duties of these jobs are the same; only the names are different.

EMPLOYMENT OPPORTUNITIES

This section lists the possible settings for jobs in each area.

Expanding Opportunities for the 21st Century

Certain occupations are projected to expand faster than others. This section offers trends, explanations, and examples of what areas within the specific industry are expected to grow most rapidly.

EARNINGS

Salary ranges for the job titles in the book are as accurate as possible. Earnings for a job will depend on the size and location of a company as well as the experience, education, training, and responsibilities of the individual.

ADVANCEMENT OPPORTUNITIES

A variety of options for career advancement has been included. However, there are no hard-and-fast rules for climbing to the top of your career. While work performance is important, advancement in many jobs is based on experience, education, and employee attitude.

EDUCATION AND TRAINING

Because the best-qualified people are the most likely to be hired, this section presents the minimum educational and training requirements for each job area. These requirements may include technical and vocational schools, colleges and universities, and on-the-job training.

EXPERIENCE AND QUALIFICATIONS

This section tells which jobs require experience and which ones require licensing, registration, certification, or other credentials. It indicates which positions necessitate examinations, interviews, or other specific prerequisites.

FOR ADDITIONAL INFORMATION: This section lists trade associations, organizations, and unions that offer career assistance, advice, or information. Many also provide scholarships, fellowships, seminars, and other beneficial programs. Addresses and phone numbers are located in the last section of the book in the Appendix.

TIPS

This section contains ideas on how to get a job, gain entry into the areas you are interested in, or become more successful in a current position.

This book will help you prepare for a career you will enjoy and find rewarding for years to come. Don't get discouraged. Keep knocking on doors, sending out resumes, and applying for jobs until you find the job you have been waiting for. Good luck!

CHAPTER 1

Medical Technology and Health Care Careers

The fields of health care and medical technology are booming today and the trend is expected to continue. According to the United States Department of Labor, health services will be one of the fastest-growing industries in the economy, with employment increasing dramatically in the 21st century.

Health care encompasses a variety of careers in which health services and technology are the primary concentrations. The reasons for the expansion in this field are twofold. The major cause is the continuing increase in the size of the older population. The other important reason is the tremendous expansion of new technology. Development of advanced equipment in the fields of imaging, laboratory analysis, laser surgery, laparoscopy, and many other areas of instrumentation will not only extend people's lives but also improve quality of life. New developments in pharmacology, organ transplants, and genetic engineering will also offer extensive employment opportunities.

One of the growing trends in health care is providing services for individuals on an outpatient basis. This will create job opportunities for health care practitioners in outpatient clinics, urgi-centers, surgi-centers, and mobile offices as well as hospitals.

While the outpatient services trend is growing at a tremendous rate, the largest employers of health care professionals will be hospitals, nursing homes, and extended-care facilities.

Careers included in this section are:

Physician	Dental Assistant
Podiatrist	Alcohol and Drug Abuse Counselor
Chiropractor	Dietitian
Audiologist	EEG Technologist/Technician
Registered Nurse	Cardiology Technologist
Licensed Practical Nurse	Emergency Medical Technician
Nurse's Aide	Medical Records Technician
Home Health Aide	Physician's Assistant
Dental Hygienist	Clinical Laboratory Technologist

Respiratory Therapist
Health Services Administrator
Dispensing Optician
Pharmacist
Radiologic Technologist
Physical Therapist

Physical Therapy Assistant
Occupational Therapist
Music Therapist
Dance Therapist
Veterinarian
Veterinary Technician

See also: Chapter 2, Geriatrics Careers.

PHYSICIAN

JOB DESCRIPTION: *Diagnose and treat illnesses; perform examinations; offer advice on preventive health care.*

EARNINGS: *$75,000 to $250,000+.*

RECOMMENDED EDUCATION AND TRAINING: *At least three years of college plus medical school and residency or internship.*

SKILLS AND PERSONALITY TRAITS: *Compassion; scientific aptitude; excellent judgment; good diagnostic skills; communication skills; good bedside manner; stamina; ability to work under pressure.*

EXPERIENCE AND QUALIFICATIONS: *All practicing MDs and DOs must be licensed.*

JOB DESCRIPTION AND RESPONSIBILITIES

Almost everyone uses the services of a physician at one time or another. Physicians may be either Doctors of Medicine, commonly called MDs, or Doctors of Osteopathy, called DOs. While both types of physicians use similar treatment methods, DOs believe that good health starts with proper alignment of the body's bones, muscles, ligaments, and nerves.

Doctors have many responsibilities and functions. While some vary depending on specialty, their major function is to help people attain and maintain good health.

Doctors in all fields are expected to perform examinations. The first thing most doctors do is talk to the patient to find out if there are any problems or symptoms. In order to diagnose illnesses, physicians may perform tests in their offices or at a hospital or laboratory.

Once the patient has been diagnosed, the physician will prescribe a treatment. Treatments include medication, therapy, and surgery. In some cases, the physician will refer the patient to a specialist for treatment or a second opinion.

Physicians often counsel patients on better health habits and preventive medicine. They may, for example, advise patients about proper nutrition and exercise.

Depending on their field, specialists may treat broken bones, heart disease, skin problems, mental and emotional difficulties, cancer, or circulatory diseases. Some specialists treat pregnant women or young children, while others perform surgery.

When patients are in the hospital, the doctor is responsible for attending to their medical needs. He or she may order tests, monitor reactions and symptoms, and prescribe medicine. The physician is also responsible for answering the questions of patients and their families.

Private practice physicians have additional duties managing and running their office. They are responsible for hiring receptionists, bookkeepers, nurses, and other staff.

Additional duties of physicians include billing, keeping proper records, and ordering equipment and medical supplies.

Beyond regular office or working hours, doctors may be required to handle emergencies as they occur. While routine medical problems can usually wait until the next day, medical emergencies cannot.

The life of a physician can be a rewarding one. No matter what their specialty, individuals will be helping others lead more comfortable lives.

EMPLOYMENT OPPORTUNITIES

Longer life spans, exposure to harmful chemicals and environmental hazards, and the emergence of new cancers and illnesses mean that there is an increased need for physicians in all fields. Individuals may be in private practice or may work as a partner or an employee in a number of different settings. Some of these include:

- Medical groups
- Hospitals
- Health care facilities
- Nursing homes
- Prisons
- Schools
- Colleges and universities
- Research laboratories
- Long-term care facilities
- Health maintenance organizations
- Urgi-centers
- Clinics
- Public health centers
- Department of Veterans Affairs

Physicians may specialize in fields such as:

- Surgery
- Pediatrics
- Obstetrics and gynecology
- Internal medicine
- Gerontology
- Psychiatry
- Alternative medicine
- Radiology
- Anesthesiology
- Emergency medicine
- Pathology
- General or family practice

Physicians may also have subspecialties.

Expanding Opportunities for the 21st Century

With people living longer, there is a greater need for physicians specializing in gerontology (the study of the aging process).

As a result of the growing demand for healthier lifestyles and alternative methods of healing, another field that is just beginning to experience growth in this country is homeopathy.

Other expanding opportunities will be in preventive care medicine as well as in primary and family care.

EARNINGS

Physicians earn from approximately $75,000 to $250,000 or more annually. Salaries depend on a number of factors including experience, personality, professional reputation, responsibilities, specialty, and type of work situation the individual is involved in. Work situations include private practice; partnership; or employee status in a medical group, hospital, or other setting.

As a group, physicians usually have higher salaries than most other occupations. Those just beginning to develop their practice will usually earn less the first couple of years than doctors who have already built up their patient roster. Physicians who specialize in surgery will generally earn more than individuals in most other specialties. Pediatricians, as a rule, earn less than those in many other specialties.

Residents earn from $30,000 to $50,000 depending on the specific hospital, its size and geographical location, and the doctor's year of residency.

ADVANCEMENT OPPORTUNITIES

Some MDs and DOs advance their careers by opening their own practice and building a large and prestigious roster of patients. Others use specialties as a method of climbing the career ladder.

Some physicians prefer to go into research or teaching.

EDUCATION AND TRAINING

Physicians or osteopathic doctors must attend four years of medical or osteopathic school. In order to get into these programs, individuals must complete at least three years of college. There are some medical schools that have combined college and medical school programs that last only six years.

Competition for medical school entrance is intense. Students must take the Medical College Admission Test (MCAT). Selection is based on scores from the test, letters of recommendation, college grades, participation in extracurricular activities, and personal interviews.

While still in school, students must pass an examination given by either the National Board of Medical Examiners or the National Board of Osteopathic Medical Examiners.

After medical school, medical doctors (MDs) must obtain three years of graduate medical education, which is called a residency. Doctors of Osteopathy serve twelve months of rotating internships.

Additional training is required for MDs or DOs who wish to be board-certified in a specialty. Individuals must take part in up to a five-year residency program in their specialty and pass an examination in order to be board-certified.

As a result of the competition to get into medical schools in this country, many aspiring doctors attend medical schools in foreign countries. Those who wish to follow this course must graduate from the foreign medical school and then take their residency in the United States. In order to be accepted into a residency program, individuals usually must pass a test given by the Educational Commission for Foreign Medical Graduates and receive certification by this commission. Individuals may also have to take the Federation Licensing Examination.

EXPERIENCE AND QUALIFICATIONS

Both MDs and DOs get clinical experience during medical school and during their residency.

All MDs and DOs working in this country and any U.S. territory must be licensed. Licensing requirements include graduating from an accredited medical or osteopathic school, passing a licensing examination, and completing a residency or internship. The residency may consist of one to six years of supervised practice in an accredited graduate medical education program.

FOR ADDITIONAL INFORMATION: Individuals interested in pursuing careers in medicine can contact the American Medical Association (AMA), the Association of American Medical Colleges (AAMC), the American Osteopathic Association (AOA), and the American Association of Colleges of Osteopathic Medicine (AACOM).

TIPS

- Doctors are most needed in less populated areas. Individuals who practice in these underserved areas usually develop a fairly substantial practice quickly.
- One of the best ways for beginning physicians to let people know they are "open for business" is to volunteer at a community health fair.
- Physicians may volunteer to speak at civic clubs and not-for-profit organizations in order to become better known in a community.

PODIATRIST

JOB DESCRIPTION: *Diagnose and treat foot problems; perform therapy and surgery on feet/lower leg.*

EARNINGS: *$35,000 to $150,000+.*

RECOMMENDED EDUCATION AND TRAINING: *Degree from an accredited college of podiatry.*

SKILLS AND PERSONALITY TRAITS: *Manual dexterity; interpersonal skills; compassion; business skills; proficiency in the sciences.*

EXPERIENCE AND QUALIFICATIONS: *State licensing and residency program.*

Job Description and Responsibilities

Podiatrists are doctors who treat foot and lower leg conditions. They are responsible for the diagnosis and treatment of abnormalities, injuries, and diseases of this area of the human body.

While podiatry has been a medical specialty throughout the years, it is currently becoming more widely recognized and generally used. As people live longer there is greater wear and tear on all body parts, especially the feet. The popularity of podiatry, even among the younger population, is enhanced by the current interest in health, fitness, sports, and exercise.

To correct foot problems, podiatrists often prescribe special shoes or shoe inserts. Today, podiatrists use computerized machinery that reads the foot size, shape, and exact dimensions to get a perfect fit for a corrective shoe or insert device. Sophisticated equipment of this type will become even more prevalent in the future.

Surgery is a major function of many podiatrists. Used to correct deformities or problems such as bunions or hammertoes, surgery may be performed in a hospital or in the podiatrist's office.

In many instances, patients make appointments to see podiatrists to have common foot problems treated, such as corns or calluses or ingrown toenails. Patients may also visit podiatrists for foot or ankle pain resulting from accidents or exercise. A variety of therapeutic procedures and treatments may be used by podiatrists to heal ailments.

Other functions of podiatrists include diagnosing and treating foot problems that develop as a result of diabetes, heart disease, and other circulatory problems.

EMPLOYMENT OPPORTUNITIES

Podiatrists may practice in a vast array of settings including:

- Private practice
- Medical groups
- Hospitals and other health care facilities
- Nursing homes
- Clinics
- Health maintenance organizations
- Public health departments
- Sports medicine clinics

Specialties include:

- Surgery
- Orthopedics
- Primary podiatrics
- Sports medicine
- Public health
- Pediatrics
- Diabetics and other disease-related foot care
- Geriatrics

Expanding Opportunities for the 21st Century

An increase in the popularity of sports, fitness, and exercise will create a demand for podiatrists specializing in sports injuries. A demand will also be seen for podiatrists working with the elderly.

EARNINGS

Annual earnings for podiatrists can range from approximately $35,000 to $150,000 or more. Earnings are, to a great extent, determined by the type of situation the podiatrist is working in as well as the experience and reputation of the individual.

Podiatrists who are in private practice in large metropolitan cities and have built good reputations will have earnings on the higher end of the scale. Those who are just starting out will earn considerably less.

ADVANCEMENT OPPORTUNITIES

Most podiatrists climb the career ladder by going into private practice. Others advance by specializing in a specific field of podiatry.

Individuals who prefer to be on staff at a facility might advance by obtaining positions in larger, more prestigious facilities.

EDUCATION AND TRAINING

Podiatrists must graduate from an accredited college of podiatric medicine. As of now, the only seven states with such schools are California, Florida, Illinois, Iowa, New York, Ohio, and Pennsylvania.

The four-year program includes two years of classroom instruction plus two years of clinical rotation in various practical settings.

After receiving a DPM or Doctor of Podiatric Medicine degree, most podiatrists go on to a three-year residency program.

In order to be admitted to an accredited college, individuals must complete at least 90 hours of undergraduate study with a good grade point average. Most people who gain acceptance into one of the schools of podiatric medicine, however, have obtained a bachelor's degree prior to their acceptance. Individuals must also obtain a good score on the Medical College Admission Test (MCAT).

EXPERIENCE AND QUALIFICATIONS

Podiatrists must be licensed in the state in which they work. Licensing requirements, which differ from state to state, usually include graduating from an accredited college of podiatric medicine, passing oral and written examinations, and completing an accredited residency program. In certain states, individuals may take an examination offered by the National Board of Podiatric Examiners in lieu of the state's written examination. Some states may grant reciprocity to individuals licensed in another state.

While podiatrists do not have to be board-certified, it is suggested. The American Board of Podiatric Surgery, The American Board of Podiatric Orthopedics, and the American Board of Public Health all offer certification in their specific specialty.

FOR ADDITIONAL INFORMATION: Additional information about podiatric careers is available from the American Podiatric Medical Association (APMA) or the American Association of Colleges of Podiatric Medicine (AACPM).

TIPS

- If you are just starting your own practice, you might volunteer to be a speaker for meetings of local civic and nonprofit organizations.
- You might find it easier to start a practice in a smaller area in need of a podiatrist rather than in a larger city with a number of practicing podiatrists.

CHIROPRACTOR

JOB DESCRIPTION: *Perform examinations and therapies; prescribe diets, exercises, and self-care.*

EARNINGS: *$30,000 to $195,000+.*

RECOMMENDED EDUCATION AND TRAINING: *Two years of pre-professional college; four years of chiropractic college.*

SKILLS AND PERSONALITY TRAITS: *Interpersonal skills; sympathy; understanding; communication skills; attention to detail; manual dexterity.*

EXPERIENCE AND QUALIFICATIONS: *State licensing; degree from an approved college of chiropractic.*

JOB DESCRIPTION AND RESPONSIBILITIES

Chiropractic is based on a holistic view of health care. Chiropractors treat an individual's entire system rather than focusing on just one specific part or patient complaint. They deal with the body's structural and neurological systems, placing special emphasis on the spine. These professionals feel that if any part of the body is misaligned or compressed it can drastically affect the rest of the body and its functions. Chiropractic stresses natural methods of healing without resorting to drugs or surgery.

People go to chiropractors to attain maximum health. Many individuals have either chronic or acute health problems including headaches, backaches, fatigue, and stiff necks. Other patients use chiropractic as a method of preventive health care.

Chiropractors begin by taking a patient's medical history. They find out about previous problems, pains, and discomforts. They also may learn from the history that the patient has been in an accident, fallen, or injured him- or herself in some manner.

Examinations include postural and spinal analysis used in chiropractic diagnosis. They may also include visual, orthopedic, neurologic or physical examinations, X rays, and lab tests.

The major treatment used by chiropractors is spinal manipulation and adjustment. Other remedies include various physiological therapies such as water, light, ultrasound, massages, and electric and heat treatments. Many chiropractors counsel patients on stress reduction, nutrition, and exercise. In some instances, chiropractors recommend the use of braces, straps, or other supports to correct body alignment.

Chiropractors who are in their own practice have management duties as well. They may hire and oversee a staff, schedule patients, answer phones, and handle billing and bookkeeping.

EMPLOYMENT OPPORTUNITIES

Most chiropractors open up their own practice right out of school. Other employment opportunities include:

- Chiropractic clinics
- Working for other chiropractors
- Alternative health care clinics
- Health spas and resorts
- Faculty member of chiropractic college
- Researcher at chiropractic colleges

Expanding Opportunities for the 21st Century

The growing awareness of chiropractic as an alternative health care system will result in an increased demand for these professionals. There are also expanding opportunities for chiropractors working with the growing older population. Chiropractors have more opportunities for success in small communities where there is little or no competition.

EARNINGS

Factors affecting earnings include the reputation, experience, personality, geographic location, and marketing skills of the chiropractor. Earnings will also be different for salaried employees than for individuals in their own businesses.

Chiropractors who are salaried may earn between $35,000 and $65,000 plus. Individuals who have their own practices can net between $30,000 and $195,000 or more. Individuals just starting out in private practice will have the lowest earnings. Income will increase as they develop a practice.

ADVANCEMENT OPPORTUNITIES

There are a number of ways for chiropractors to advance their careers. Individuals may work for another chiropractor or a chiropractic clinic. After obtaining some experience they may start their own practice. Individuals who are already in their own practice can climb the career ladder by developing a larger patient roster.

Some chiropractors advance by teaching at a chiropractic college or performing research.

EDUCATION AND TRAINING

Chiropractors must complete two years of college and then the four-year course of study at an accredited chiropractic college.

While chiropractic colleges teach courses in skeletal manipulation and spinal adjustments, there are also a broad range of other courses. The program consists of clinical experience as well as classroom and laboratory work in basic sciences such as anatomy, physiology, chemistry, pathology, hygiene, sanitation, and public health.

Individuals must also take courses in clinical science subjects such as physical, clinical, and laboratory diagnosis, gynecology and obstetrics, pediatrics, roentgenology techniques, geriatrics, dermatology, dietetics, toxicology, psychology, and psychiatry.

Candidates must be at least 21 years old to graduate from an approved college of chiropractic. Those who complete the programs are awarded the degree of Doctor of Chiropractic (DC).

EXPERIENCE AND QUALIFICATIONS

Chiropractors must be licensed in the state in which they work. Many states offer reciprocity. Licensing requirements vary from state to state. Most states require individuals to complete two years of undergraduate education plus four years of chiropractic college at a school accredited by the Council on Chiropractic Education. Individuals must also pass a licensing exam and a basic science examination.

In order to maintain their license, chiropractors must take annual continuing education courses.

FOR ADDITIONAL INFORMATION: For additional information, contact the American Chiropractic Association (ACA), the International Chiropractors Association (ICA), and the Council on Chiropractic Education (CCE).

TIPS

- If you are still in school, consider a part-time or summer job in a chiropractor's office as a secretary or receptionist.
- If you are already in practice, you might offer a free examination or adjustment to new patients.
- If you are just opening up a new practice, volunteer to speak to local civic groups about the chiropractic profession.
- If you are new to the field, consider participating in community health fairs often held at shopping centers and malls in the area. This will help get your name and professional specialty known in the community.

AUDIOLOGIST

JOB DESCRIPTION: *Assess those with hearing disorders; develop and implement treatments.*

EARNINGS: *$28,000 to $65,000.*

RECOMMENDED EDUCATION AND TRAINING: *Master's degree in audiology.*

SKILLS AND PERSONALITY TRAITS: *Communication skills; compassion; patience; interpersonal skills.*

EXPERIENCE AND QUALIFICATIONS: *Certification is available.*

JOB DESCRIPTION AND RESPONSIBILITIES

Audiologists work with people who have hearing disorders. They are responsible for assessing the extent to which the patient's hearing is affected.

To do this, audiologists use a number of testing devices to determine the level at which the patient begins to hear sounds, as well as his or her ability to distinguish different sounds. The individual also tests the patient's hearing to find out the degree of hearing loss.

Once tests are completed, the audiologist makes a diagnosis and develops a course of treatment. This can include anything from cleaning the ear canal to fitting a hearing aid. The audiologist may also recommend training in speech, lipreading, or auditory training.

Audiologists may work with other medical personnel including speech language pathologists, physicians, social workers, and psychiatrists. Individuals may also work with family members and teachers to help develop ways of coping with the physical as well as the emotional problems associated with hearing loss.

EMPLOYMENT OPPORTUNITIES

Audiologists can work full time or may find part-time employment. Individuals may work in a variety of settings including:

- Preschools
- Elementary schools
- Secondary schools
- Colleges and universities
- Health clinics
- Hospitals
- Physicians' offices
- Hearing centers
- Home health care agencies
- Long-term care facilities
- Nursing homes

Expanding Opportunities for the 21st Century

Aging people tend to experience a large degree of hearing loss. Expanding opportunities working with the older population will exist for audiologists in the 21st century. Other opportunities will exist in schools working with pre-, elementary, and secondary schoolers.

EARNINGS

Annual earnings for audiologists can range from approximately $28,000 to $65,000. Variables affecting salaries include the experience level and responsibilities of the individual, as well as the specific job and geographical location.

ADVANCEMENT OPPORTUNITIES

Audiologists can advance their careers in a number of ways. Individuals may find similar positions in larger, more prestigious facilities, resulting in increased responsibilities and earnings. Others may move into supervisory positions. Audiologists may also climb the career ladder by entering private practice.

EDUCATION AND TRAINING

Audiologists must obtain a master's degree in audiology to practice. Courses include anatomy and physiology in hearing-related areas. Other courses will cover the development of hearing and hearing disorders. Individuals also go through supervised clinical training.

Forty-three states regulate audiologists and require them to be licensed or certified. In order to obtain this, individuals must have a master's degree, go through 375 hours of supervised clinical experience, take and pass a national exam, and get 9 months of postgraduate professional experience. Many states also have continuing education requirements. Audiologists can obtain a Certificate of Clinical Competence (CCC) offered by the American Speech-Language-Hearing Association by completing these requirements.

EXPERIENCE AND QUALIFICATIONS

Audiologists need to be compassionate, patient people. Individuals should have good communication skills and be able to deal with problems objectively.

FOR ADDITIONAL INFORMATION: For more information regarding a career as an audiologist contact the American Speech-Language-Hearing Association (ASLHA).

Tips

- Many health care facilities, vocational-technical schools, high schools, and community colleges put on "health career days" where interested individuals can learn more about careers in this field.
- Consider sending your resume with a short cover letter to the personnel directors of hospitals, health care facilities, nursing homes, school systems, clinics, and physicians' offices. Remember to request that your resume be kept on file for the future if there are no current openings.
- Jobs may be advertised in the classified section of newspapers under headings such as "Audiologist," "Health Care," and "School Audiologist."

REGISTERED NURSE (RN)

JOB DESCRIPTION: *Care for patients; administer medication; record symptoms; observe progress; supervise LPNs, orderlies, and aides.*

EARNINGS: *$30,000 to $72,000+.*

RECOMMENDED EDUCATION AND TRAINING: *Associate degree, bachelor's degree, or diploma from an approved school of nursing.*

SKILLS AND PERSONALITY TRAITS: *Compassion; desire to help others; reliability; communication skills.*

EXPERIENCE AND QUALIFICATIONS: *State licensing; clinical experience.*

Job Description and Responsibilities

Registered Nurses have varied responsibilities depending on the setting in which they work. RNs working in nursing homes will have different duties from RNs working in clinics, retirement communities, schools, or other settings. Their main function, however, is to administer medical care to ill or injured individuals.

RNs work beside physicians, assisting in medical care and carrying out the physician's instructions. RNs may be present in the doctor's office when examinations are being conducted and assisting in the exam. They take patients' vital signs and may be responsible for taking blood or performing certain laboratory tests. In some instances, they help the physician perform procedures.

Registered nurses working in hospitals or other health care facilities provide the primary bedside nursing care. This includes changing dressings, cleaning wounds, administering medication, starting intravenous fluids, and monitoring medical equipment. RNs also record patients' symptoms and reactions and chart their progress with regard to medication or course of action prescribed by the physician. In some situations they are responsible for assessing needs of patients and developing treatment plans. This is common in nursing homes and extended-care facilities.

A great deal of the work of an RN is administrative or supervisory. RNs may supervise aides, orderlies, and LPNs in their duties. Registered nurses also handle paperwork such as patient charts.

RNs working in schools, prisons, and clinics have various educational duties. They instruct individuals in preventive health care, nutrition, exercise, etc. They also perform various health screenings, tests, and procedures.

Individuals work varied hours depending on the specific employment situation. They are responsible to either the head nurse or the physician in charge.

EMPLOYMENT OPPORTUNITIES

Registered nurses can work part or full time in a variety of health care situations and environments. Some of these include:

- Hospitals
- Health care facilities
- Physicians' offices
- Clinics
- Schools
- Colleges and universities
- Prisons
- Nursing homes
- Extended-care facilities
- Health maintenance organizations
- Retirement communities
- Rehabilitation centers
- Health departments of corporations
- Home health care
- Surgi-centers
- Urgi-centers
- Diagnostic imaging centers
- Cardiac rehabilitation clinics

Expanding Opportunities for the 21st Century

Hospitals and health care facilities can no longer be reimbursed for patients who are hospitalized beyond the normal time for their specific illness. Many patients are, therefore, sent home before they have fully recuperated. This means that there will be a demand for registered nurses who can administer in-home care.

RNs will be in great demand in geriatric settings such as nursing homes and extended-care facilities. This is due to the growing older population who require long-term care.

Demand for RNs will be especially high in facilities that care for critically and terminally ill patients.

EARNINGS

Earnings vary greatly for registered nurses depending on their experience, education, responsibilities, and geographic location. Other factors affecting earnings include the type, size, and prestige of the facility the individual is working in as well as the particular shift.

Salaries for entry-level RNs range from approximately $30,000 to $38,000. Nurses with more experience may earn up to $54,000 or more with additional training. Those with specialized skills can have annual salaries of up to $72,000.

In addition, most employers offer RNs liberal benefit packages to augment their earnings. Some also offer tuition reimbursement.

ADVANCEMENT OPPORTUNITIES

There are many paths to career advancement for registered nurses, depending on the direction they want to pursue. With experience and additional training, individuals may move into supervisory, management, or administrative positions. They may, for example, become the director of nursing of a facility or a head nurse at a clinic. Other RNs seek positions as nurse practitioners, nurse clinicians, nurse anesthetists, or clinical nurse specialists.

EDUCATION AND TRAINING

Individuals aspiring to become registered nurses may pursue an associate degree in nursing, culminating in an ADN; a bachelor of science degree in nursing, called a BSN; or a diploma program. Associate and bachelor's degree programs are offered in community colleges, junior colleges, and colleges or universities. The diploma program is offered by hospitals.

Length of program varies. ADN degrees usually require two years of schooling while diploma programs last two to three years. The BSN will generally take four years. Any of the three possible programs will qualify individuals for entry-level positions. However, earnings and advancement will be better for those with BSNs.

Nurses' training includes classroom study, supervised training, and clinical experience. Classes include anatomy, microbiology, chemistry, nutrition, physiology, psychology, nursing, and computer usage.

EXPERIENCE AND QUALIFICATIONS

Registered nurses must be licensed in the state in which they work. In order to obtain a license, individuals must graduate from an approved school of nursing and pass a national examination administered by the specific state in which they reside. RNs interested in working in another state must either take another examination or be granted reciprocity.

State nursing licenses must be renewed. Some states require continuing education for renewal.

FOR ADDITIONAL INFORMATION: Individuals interested in becoming registered nurses can obtain additional information by contacting the National Student Nurses' Association (NSNA), the National League for Nursing (NLN), the American Nurses' Association (ANA), the American Hospital Association (AHA), and the American Health Care Association (AHCA).

TIPS

- Many high schools, vocational-technical schools, colleges, and hospitals have health career fairs for people interested in exploring the nursing field.
- Before you make a commitment to nursing, you might want to volunteer in a hospital. This will give you experience in a health care setting. It will also give you an opportunity to see if this type of career is for you.
- Hospitals and other health care facilities often hold teas, luncheons, and dinners to attract new nurses.
- Job openings are advertised in the newspaper classified section under headings such as "Nurses," "RNs," "Registered Nurses," "Hospitals," "Health Care," or the names of specialties.

LICENSED PRACTICAL NURSE (LPN)

JOB DESCRIPTION: *Perform nursing duties under the supervision of physicians and registered nurses.*

EARNINGS: *$15,000 to $33,000.*

RECOMMENDED EDUCATION AND TRAINING: *Completion of a practical nursing program accredited and approved by the state.*

SKILLS AND PERSONALITY TRAITS: *Compassion; stamina; communication skills; ability to follow directions.*

EXPERIENCE AND QUALIFICATIONS: *Experience in a supervised clinical health care setting.*

Job Description and Responsibilities

Licensed practical nurses perform a variety of nursing duties under the supervision and direction of physicians and registered nurses. Individuals in this particular field are commonly referred to as LPNs or licensed vocational nurses (LVNs).

No matter what the job title, one of the main functions of an LPN is to make patients as comfortable as possible. LPNs help patients bathe, brush their teeth, and handle other personal hygiene needs.

A major responsibility of LPNs is taking vital signs on a routine basis or at the direction of physicians. Vitals include a patient's temperature, pulse, and blood pressure. The individual must be sure to record the information accurately on the patient's chart.

If an emergency occurs, the LPN should be able to perform CPR (cardiopulmonary resuscitation). Other responsibilities include preparing and administering injections prescribed by a physician. In some instances, where allowed, LPNs will be required to give prescribed medicines to patients. However, not all states allow LPNs to handle this task.

The LPN may work in any unit in the hospital including maternity, intensive care, recovery, skilled nursing, pediatrics, and medical-surgical.

Employment Opportunities

LPNs may work in a number of different health care settings including:

- Hospitals
- Rehabilitation centers
- Nursing homes
- Group homes
- Senior citizen homes
- Extended care facilities
- Physicians' offices
- Clinics
- Private homes (for private duty)
- Temporary nursing agencies

Expanding Opportunities for the 21st Century

There is a great need for LPNs in all health care settings. With new rules and regulations shortening the length of stay patients can have in a facility, there will be a great demand for private duty nurses. Expanding opportunities will also open up in nursing homes and other long-term health care facilities as our older population increases.

EARNINGS

Annual earnings for LPNs can range from approximately $15,000 to $33,000. Factors affecting income include the specific facility as well as its size, prestige, and geographic location. Other determining factors include the experience and responsibilities of the LPN.

ADVANCEMENT OPPORTUNITIES

Licensed practical nurses may look for career advancement through increased earnings. To accomplish this, individuals can locate similar positions in larger or more prestigious facilities where higher salaries are offered. Others obtain supervisory duties over nursing assistants and nurse's aides.

An LPN might also climb the career ladder by completing the additional education necessary to become a registered nurse.

EDUCATION AND TRAINING

LPNs must complete a state-approved practical nursing program. Generally, in order to enroll in such a program, individuals must be high school graduates. However, there are a number of states in the country that allow candidates into their nursing program after completing one or more years of high school.

Practical nursing programs are usually one year in duration. They are offered through hospitals, community colleges, trade schools, vocational schools, and technical programs. In addition to classroom work, most programs require experience in a supervised clinical setting.

EXPERIENCE AND QUALIFICATIONS

As noted previously, LPNs must have experience working in a supervised clinical setting. They must also pass a national written examination in order to get their license.

FOR ADDITIONAL INFORMATION: Individuals interested in becoming Licensed Practical Nurses may contact a number of organizations and associations for more information. These organizations include the National Federation of Licensed Practical Nurses, Inc. (NFLPN), the National League for Nursing (NLN), the National Association for Practical Nurse Education and Service, Inc. (NAPNES), the American Hospital Association (AHA), and the American Health Care Association (AHCA).

TIPS

- Openings for LPNs are usually advertised in the classified section of the newspaper, under headings such as "Nurses," "Licensed Practical Nurses," "LPNs," "Health Care," "Hospitals," "Private Duty," or "Temporary Nursing."
- Send your resume and a short cover letter to the personnel directors of hospitals, health care facilities, temporary nursing agencies, private duty agencies, rehabilitation centers and extended-care facilities. With the shortage of qualified people, you should expect calls for interviews.
- Large cities have employment agencies specializing in jobs in the health care industry.

NURSE'S AIDE

JOB DESCRIPTION: *Assist nurses in providing patient care.*

EARNINGS: *$11,000 to $25,000.*

RECOMMENDED EDUCATION AND TRAINING: *High school diploma and nurse's aide training.*

SKILLS AND PERSONALITY TRAITS: *Compassion; cheerfulness; comfort working with ill or infirm; ability to follow orders; physical stamina.*

EXPERIENCE AND QUALIFICATIONS: *No experience necessary for many positions.*

JOB DESCRIPTION AND RESPONSIBILITIES

Nurse's aides assist nurses in providing patient care. They may work in any unit of a health care facility including surgical, medical, obstetrics, emergency, outpatient, and pediatrics. Nurse's aides, also referred to as nursing assistants, have a vast array of responsibilities depending on the specific job and unit they are working in.

Nurse's aides work under the direct supervision of registered nurses and licensed practical nurses in order to fulfill their duties. They handle routine tasks related to patient care such as taking and recording the patient's vital signs.

Nurse's aides are expected to answer patients call lights or buzzers. After determining what the patient needs, the aide may either take care of the difficulty or relate the problem to a nurse or physician who will attend to it.

Nurse's aides assist patients with bathing and other personal hygiene needs. They bring and empty bedpans or urinals and help patients to the bathroom. If specimens are requested by a physician, the nurse's aide will be required to collect them and bring them to the lab for testing. If tests are ordered, the aide will be responsible for transporting the patient to the correct unit.

Other duties include changing bed linens and keeping patients rooms neat and orderly, replenishing a patient's water supply, arranging flowers, or helping patient's prepare for visitors. They help patients prepare for meals and assist in feeding, give patients backrubs, and help them out of bed into wheelchairs.

One of the more fulfilling duties for many nurse's aides is talking with patients. They calm a patient's jittery nerves, lift their spirits, or just keep them company.

Nurse's aides usually work a forty-hour week on a shift basis.

EMPLOYMENT OPPORTUNITIES

Nurse's aides work in various units in a variety of health care facilities. Some of these include:

- Hospitals
- Nursing homes
- Extended-care facilities
- Rehabilitation centers
- Psychiatric hospitals

Expanding Opportunities for the 21st Century

With people living longer, there will be an increased number of nursing homes and extended-care facilities in the country. This will result in a need for more nurse's aides. Expect expanding opportunites in private psychiatric facilities and community mental health centers.

EARNINGS

Nurse's aides earn approximately $11,000 to $25,000 annually. Factors affecting earnings include education, experience, and responsibilities as well as the specific type of facility, size, prestige, and geographic location.

Generally, nurse's aides who have completed a training program and are certified will earn more than those who haven't. Individuals working in health care facilities will usually have their earnings augmented by fringe-benefit packages.

Advancement Opportunities

Nurse's aides can advance by obtaining the additional education necessary to become a licensed practical nurse or a registered nurse.

Education and Training

Educational requirements vary from job to job. Some positions do not require a high school diploma or other prior training. Instead, these facilities offer on-the-job training.

As earnings are often determined by an individual's education, and many jobs do prefer a high school diploma, it is recommended that individuals complete high school. There are also training courses for nurse's aides offered in high schools and vocational centers as well as in community colleges. Many facilities offer training courses in hopes of filling jobs with qualified people they have trained themselves.

Experience and Qualifications

As noted previously, experience, while useful, is not required for many jobs. To be successful in this field, individuals must be compassionate and they must be comfortable working with ill or infirm people.

FOR ADDITIONAL INFORMATION: Individuals interested in obtaining further information on becoming nurse's aides may contact the American Hospital Association (AHA) or the American Health Care Association (AHCA). Both organizations provide literature on careers in this field.

Tips

- Contact health care facilities in your area to find out if they offer educational programs for people interested in becoming nurse's aides.
- Many health care facilities hold career days in conjunction with schools, community colleges, or vocational centers. These are a good way to learn more about the field and make contacts.
- Positions for nurse's aides are advertised in local newspaper classified sections under headings such as "Nurse's Aides," "Nursing Assistants," "Health Care," "Hospitals," "Extended Care," "Nursing Homes," or "Psychiatric Centers."

HOME HEALTH AIDE

JOB DESCRIPTION: *Provide care for elderly, incapacitated, ill, and disabled; provide emotional support.*

EARNINGS: *$6 to $25+ an hour.*

RECOMMENDED EDUCATION AND TRAINING: *Formal training program is usually necessary.*

SKILLS AND PERSONALITY TRAITS: *Compassion; interpersonal skills; responsibility; physical stamina.*

EXPERIENCE AND QUALIFICATIONS: *Individuals must be literate; experience is helpful but not required.*

JOB DESCRIPTION AND RESPONSIBILITIES

Home health aides assist elderly, ill, disabled, injured, or incapacitated clients by performing a variety of home care services. Home health aides are vital to many people who would not be able to live at home without help. Duties and responsibilities depend on the client they are working with and specific disabilities and circumstances.

Some home health aides visit clients daily. Others make visits once a week or every other day. If clients require extensive care, aides may work with them exclusively for an extended period of time.

Home health aides are usually assigned to clients by supervisors such as nurses or social workers in the agency. Supervisors will explain the services needed by each client to the home aide and discuss the scheduled times of visits.

Home health aides are usually responsible for transporting themselves to and from each visit. In areas that do not have public transportation, home health aides must possess a valid driver's license and have access to a car.

After visits with clients, home health aides may be required to file reports detailing the services accomplished during the visit and the condition of the client. If there are changes in the individual's condition, either mental or physical, the aide is responsible for reporting these changes to supervisors.

Home health aides assist clients with personal care tasks such as bathing and dressing. In many instances, the home health aide is expected to do light housekeeping such as laundry and changing the linens. Some help clients prepare weekly menus, shop for food, and prepare meals for clients or their families.

Home health aides may also perform simple medical procedures such as checking and recording vital statistics, changing nonsterile dressings, and assisting with medications.

One of the major functions of home health aides is providing psychological and emotional support. Individuals will often make a client feel better just by being there, drinking a cup of tea, and talking. There are many different situations. For example, the home health aide may be assigned to a home where the husband has Alzheimer's disease and the wife is taking responsibility for caring for him. In addition to assisting the wife with the health care needs of her husband, the aide may also be responsible for tending to the emotional needs of the wife.

Home health aides working for agencies are responsible to their supervisor. Those who are self-employed will be responsible to either their client directly or the family of the client. Hours vary in this job, depending on the specific employment situation.

EMPLOYMENT OPPORTUNITIES

Home health aides may be employed either full time, part time, or on a shift basis by a variety of different agencies and facilities including:

- Public home health agencies
- Private home health agencies
- Homemaker home health agencies
- Visiting nurse associations
- Hospitals
- Public health departments
- Public welfare departments
- Temporary help agencies
- Self-employment

Home health aides may also specialize in working with clients who have various diseases, disabilities, or problems.

Expanding Opportunities for the 21st Century

The need for home health aides will continue to increase tremendously. A major reason for this is the expanding population of older adults who do not need twenty-four hour supervision, but may require help with medication, bathing, meals, shopping, etc. By using the services of home health aides, individuals can continue to live on their own.

Another factor that boosts the demand for home health aides is the trend toward home health care. Changes in reimbursement to hospitals for health care costs have forced these facilities to shorten stays. In many instances, hospitals can no longer keep patients for extended periods. While patients may be well enough to leave the hospital, they may still require some type of home health care. Home health aides fill this need. The service is often paid for by Medicaid, Medicare, health maintenance organizations (HMOs), and private insurance.

One of the greatest needs for home health aides in the future will be caring for AIDS patients in hospices and private homes.

EARNINGS

Earnings for home health aides vary depending on the type of agency the individual is working for, geographic location, and the degree of need for people in this occupation. Other factors include the individual's responsibilities, duties, education, and experience. Annual earnings will also depend on whether the home health aide is employed full time or part time.

Home health aides are usually paid by the hour. Hourly rates can start at approximately $6.00 and may go up to $25.00 an hour or more. The majority of home health aides receive between $6.00 and $15.00 per hour. Some agencies offer employees benefit packages.

ADVANCEMENT OPPORTUNITIES

Some home health aides discover that they truly enjoy this type of work and decide to obtain additional education and training and become nurse's aides, LPNs, or RNs.

EDUCATION AND TRAINING

There are no educational requirements for home health aides. While a high school diploma may be preferred, it is not required. According to new regulations implemented by the federal government, however, individuals who provide care that is reimbursed by Medicare must go through a seventy-five-hour training program. At least sixteen hours of training must be classroom study and sixteen hours must be practical training supervised by an experienced registered nurse. Various states add additional training requirements.

Courses covered in these programs include basic nutrition; personal hygiene and grooming; communication skills; observation, reporting and documentation of patient status, and the care of services furnished; basic infection control procedures; basic elements of body function and changes; reading and recording of vital signs; maintenance of clean, safe, and healthy environments; recognition of and procedures for emergencies; physical, emotional, and developmental characteristics of patients; and normal range of motion and positioning. Many agencies also schedule workshops, seminars, and lectures on specialized topics including caring for patients that have Parkinson's disease, Alzheimer's disease, or AIDS.

Recommended training programs are approved by the Health and Human Services Department and are offered by many home health agencies, hospitals, vocational-technical schools, community colleges, and the American Red Cross.

EXPERIENCE AND QUALIFICATIONS

While experience is not usually required for this position, it is helpful. Some people have gained valuable experience prior to their job by taking care of children, grandparents, spouses, friends, or relatives who were ill, injured, or incapacitated.

FOR ADDITIONAL INFORMATION: Additional information can be obtained by contacting the National Association for Homecare (NAH) or local home health agencies.

TIPS

- Home health agencies often offer training programs free or at a minimal charge to entice prospective employees.
- Job openings are advertised in the newspaper's classified section under headings such as "Home Health Aide," "Home Health Care," "Home Care," "Aides," "Homemaker Home Health Aides," etc.
- You might also look in the yellow pages of the telephone book under "Home Health Agencies" or "Home Care" to find agencies to contact.

DENTAL HYGIENIST

JOB DESCRIPTION: *Provide preventive dental care; clean teeth; handle curettage.*

EARNINGS: *$17,000 to $38,000+.*

RECOMMENDED EDUCATION AND TRAINING: *Graduation from an accredited school of dental hygiene.*

SKILLS AND PERSONALITY TRAITS: *Interpersonal skills; good communication skills; compassion; manual dexterity.*

EXPERIENCE AND QUALIFICATIONS: *State licensing; graduation from an accredited school of dental hygiene; written and clinical examinations.*

Job Description and Responsibilities

Almost everyone has had an opportunity to utilize the services of a dental hygienist during his or her lifetime.

One of the main functions of most dental hygienists is to clean teeth. Cleaning may be scheduled on an annual, biannual, or quarterly basis, depending on the state of the patient's teeth and gums. The hygienist may also scrape plaque, perform gumline curettage, and apply fluoride or sealers to help retard cavities and plaque buildup. The hygienist will instruct the patient on tooth and gum care and illustrate the correct way to brush and use floss.

Some states allow the hygienist to perform the preliminary examination of the patient's mouth looking for cavities, broken or cracked teeth, gum disease, and oral cancer. The hygienist may also prepare a patient for X rays and take and develop films.

In certain states, dental hygienists assist dentists in removing sutures or applying dressings and administering anesthesia, if they have the required education in that specialty.

Dental hygienists may be responsible for keeping records of patient care. They might also schedule appointments, handle billing, answer patient's questions, and run the office.

Dental hygienists may work full or part time. In many instances, the individual will work part time in a number of dental offices. Hours in some offices are very flexible, while others may be the traditional nine to five. The hygienist is directly responsible to the dentist in charge of the office.

Employment Opportunities

While individuals may work in a variety of settings, some jobs require additional education. Dental hygienists may work for:

- Private dentist offices
- Group dental practices
- Public clinics
- School systems
- Hospitals
- Dental hygiene schools
- Health maintenance organizations
- Nursing homes
- Extended-care facilities
- State and federal health departments

Expanding Opportunities for the 21st Century

As more people become aware of the importance of preventive dental care, there will be a greater demand for dental hygienists in all settings. There will be a special need for hygienists in geriatrics and geriatric facilities as a result of the increase in our aging population.

EARNINGS

Dental hygienists may be paid by the hour, day, week, or number of patients they've worked on. Hygienists may also have their salaries augmented by fringe-benefit packages.

Individuals working full time in this profession can have annual earnings ranging from $17,000 to $38,000 or more, depending on setting and job, geographic location, and method of payment. Other factors affecting earnings include the hygienist's education, responsibilities, and experience.

Individuals with the most education and working in large metropolitan cities will have the highest earnings.

ADVANCEMENT OPPORTUNITIES

Dental hygienists can advance by locating positions in larger, more prestigious offices. They may also climb the career ladder by obtaining additional education and going after positions in research, teaching, and administration in dental hygiene education programs.

EDUCATION AND TRAINING

Dental hygienists must graduate from an accredited school of dental hygiene. Areas of study include basic sciences, dental sciences, clinical sciences, and social and behavioral sciences. Laboratory, classroom, and clinical instruction is required.

Hygienists may seek either a two-year associate degree, a four-year bachelor's degree, or a master's degree. The two-year degree is usually suitable for working in a private dental office. Four-year or postgraduate degrees are required for positions in teaching, research, clinical practice for public or school health programs, and administrative or teaching positions in dental hygiene education.

Minimum requirements to enter dental hygiene schools vary. There are some programs that prefer or require students to have at least one year of college while others require completion of two years.

EXPERIENCE AND QUALIFICATIONS

Dental hygienists usually receive practical experience in school. Individuals in all states must be licensed by the state they are working in.

Licensing requirements include graduation from an accredited dental hygiene school and passing both a written and a clinical examination. The written examination is administered by the American Dental Association Joint Commission on National Dental Examinations. Individuals may also be required to take another examination on legal aspects of dental hygiene practice.

FOR ADDITIONAL INFORMATION: Individuals interested in careers in dental hygiene can obtain additional information by contacting the American Dental Hygienists' Association (ADHA), the American Dental Association (ADA), and the American Association of Dental Examiners (AADE).

TIPS

- One of the great things about being a dental hygienist is the flexibility. This is especially important for people who have school-age children or who are continuing their own education.
- Openings are often advertised in the classified or display section of newspapers under headings of "Dental," "Dental Hygienist," "Dental Office," or "Hygienist."
- If you enjoy working with children, try to locate a pediatric dentist.
- Send your resume and a short cover letter to dentists, clinics, hospitals, and extended-care facilities in your area. Request that your resume be kept on file if there are no current openings.

DENTAL ASSISTANT

JOB DESCRIPTION: *Assist dentist; make patients comfortable; prepare patients for treatment; sterilize instruments.*

EARNINGS: *$14,000 to $25,000.*

RECOMMENDED EDUCATION AND TRAINING: *Dental assisting program or on-the-job training.*

SKILLS AND PERSONALITY TRAITS: *Personableness; eagerness to learn; ability to follow instruction; communication skills.*

EXPERIENCE AND QUALIFICATIONS: *Some positions require experience; certification available but not required.*

JOB DESCRIPTION AND RESPONSIBILITIES

Dental assistants work alongside dentists, assisting them in their work. Responsibilities vary depending on the specific job.

Before a dental assistant brings a patient into the dentist's office, the individual will usually prepare for that patient. This may entail cleaning, sterilizing, and disinfecting equipment; preparing a tray of sterilized dental instruments; and getting the patient's chart from the receptionist.

When patients are brought into the treatment room, the dental assistant will try to make them as comfortable as possible in the chair. The assistant will put a bib on them to protect their clothing and will inform the dentist when patients are ready.

When the dentist is working with the patient, the dental assistant will be responsible for passing the specified instruments or materials. The assistant may also use a suctioning device to help keep the patient's mouth dry during procedures.

Dental assistants, in some situations, take X rays, remove sutures, apply anesthesia, make casts of the mouth or teeth, or handle other tasks under the direction of the dentist.

In some offices, dental assistants manage the office, schedule and confirm patient appointments, handle billing responsibilities, and maintain records.

Hours are determined by the hours the dentist works. The dental assistant is directly responsible to the dentist.

EMPLOYMENT OPPORTUNITIES

Dental assistants may work in any setting in which a dentist is at work. These settings include:

- Private dentist offices
- Group dental practices
- Public clinics
- School systems
- Hospitals
- Dental hygiene schools
- Health maintenance organizations
- Nursing homes
- Extended-care facilities
- State health departments

Expanding Opportunities for the 21st Century

With the great turnover of jobs in this field, there is a demand for dental assistants in most employment settings. As the majority of dentists work in private dental practices, the need is greatest there. Additional opportunities arise as more dentists utilize the services of dental assistants for routine tasks so that their own time may be used more productively.

EARNINGS

Salaries for dental assistants working full time range from approximately $14,000 to $25,000. Factors affecting salary include the specific job and geographical location as well as the experience, education, qualifications, and duties of the dental assistant.

Individuals who have gone through formal training programs and are certified will generally earn more. Salaries will also be higher in areas where there is a special need for dental assistants or in large metropolitan cities where there is a higher cost of living.

ADVANCEMENT OPPORTUNITIES

Dental assistants seeking advancement may try to locate similar positions in more prestigious offices.

Individuals who are interested in working in the field of dental hygiene might consider going back to school to obtain the necessary education.

EDUCATION AND TRAINING

Education and training requirements vary from job to job. In some positions, employers seek individuals who are eager to learn new skills and train them on the job. In others, employers may prefer that their employees go through a formal dental assisting program.

Dental assisting programs are offered throughout the country in vocational, trade, and technical schools as well as in junior or community colleges. Courses of study include classroom, laboratory, and preclinical instruction in dental assisting skills. Many programs also offer practical experience in clinics, dental offices, or affiliated dental schools.

EXPERIENCE AND QUALIFICATIONS

While some jobs require experience, in most dental offices this is an entry-level position. Certification is available through the Dental Assisting National Board but is not required for most jobs. It does, however, indicate that the individual is competent and may give one person an edge over another. In order to obtain certification, dental assistants must be high school graduates and graduate from a training program accredited by the Commission on Dental Accreditation or have at least two years of full-time experience as a dental assistant. They must also pass a certification examination and a course in cardiopulmonary resuscitation (CPR).

FOR ADDITIONAL INFORMATION: Individuals interested in careers in dental assisting can learn more by contacting the American Dental Assistants Association (ADAA), the American Dental Association (ADA), and the Dental Assisting National Board, Inc. (DANB).

TIPS

- Many of the accredited training schools for dental assistants have job-placement services.

- Openings may be advertised in the classified or display section of the newspaper. Look under headings such as "Dental Office" or "Dental Assistant."

- Write to dentists and dental clinics in the area to find out if they have openings. Remember to send a copy of your resume with a cover letter.

ALCOHOL AND DRUG ABUSE COUNSELOR

JOB DESCRIPTION: *Counsel drug or alcohol addicts; run workshops; supervise group therapy sessions; prepare reports.*

EARNINGS: *$14,000 to $40,000+.*

RECOMMENDED EDUCATION AND TRAINING: *Educational requirements and training vary from state to state and job to job.*

SKILLS AND PERSONALITY TRAITS: *Emotional stability; empathy; good interpersonal skills; communication skills; ability to work independently.*

EXPERIENCE AND QUALIFICATIONS: *Experience depends on job; certification or registration may be required.*

JOB DESCRIPTION AND RESPONSIBILITIES

Alcohol and drug abuse counselors work with individuals who have addictions or are substance abusers. They may also work with the patients' families. Counselors have varied duties and responsibilities depending on their specific employment situation.

Some patients want to be helped. Others do not. It is often difficult to help patients who do not want to stop substance abuse or do not think they have a problem. It is up to the counselor to develop motivational techniques to move patients through the various steps of therapy.

Alcohol and drug abuse counselors often work with other health professionals including physicians, psychiatrists, psychologists, social workers, and psychiatric nurses. It is up to the counselor to refer patients to the appropriate medical personnel, agency, or program. If the patient must go through detox, it must be done under close medical supervision. Counselors may discuss patient's needs with physicians or nurses assigned to the case.

Counselors may specialize in certain groups of people. For example, they may work only with children or teenagers. Others may counsel business executives. Individuals may also specialize in counseling individuals who abuse specific drugs such as heroin, cocaine, or alcohol. Special training may be required to work with specific groups.

Alcohol and drug abuse counselors must evaluate and assess each patient separately. They must determine the extent and pattern of an individual's abuse.

Counselors are responsible for providing services to patients and their families. They may work with the patient on a one-on-one basis; with the patient and the family; or in a group counseling situation. During these sessions, they attempt to help the patient to cease using substances. In a group therapy situation, counselors will supervise the group, trying to move it in positive directions.

Counselors ask probing questions and do a great deal of listening. They may do this to evoke certain emotions in the patient and break down psychological walls. Counselors and patients who are in these situations often build a close working rapport.

There is a great deal of paperwork involved in alcohol and drug counseling. Individuals must prepare reports on patients in order to follow their progress. Counselors will often be required to participate in staff team meetings, develop treatment plans, and contribute to the multidisciplinary treatment plan for each patient.

Other duties include assisting with a patient's social welfare needs or those of the family. Counselors may be required to attend family meetings to discuss progress or to explain therapy needs and requirements. It is extremely important for alcohol and drug abuse counselors to maintain patient confidentiality within the scope of the job.

Alcohol and drug abuse counselors work varied hours depending on their employment setting. Individuals are responsible to the supervisor of the department or the physician in charge.

EMPLOYMENT OPPORTUNITIES

Alcohol and drug abuse counselors may work full or part time in a vast array of profit and not-for-profit employment settings, including:

- Hospitals
- Schools
- Prisons
- Colleges and universities
- Private substance abuse centers
- Health maintenance organizations
- Self-employment
- Public substance abuse centers
- Mental health facilities
- Government agencies
- Social services organizations
- Corporate businesses

Expanding Opportunities for the 21st Century

The increase in drug and alcohol abuse will create a tremendous need for counselors. In fact, the number of postions is expected to double in the new century. Individuals in the greatest demand will be those with the most education and training in substance abuse counseling.

EARNINGS

Alcohol and drug abuse counselors earn from $14,000 to $40,000 plus. Earnings depend on the specific employment setting and the size, prestige, and geographic location of the facility. Other factors include the experience and duties of the counselor.

Generally, the more education and experience, the higher the earnings will be. Counselors will also earn higher incomes in prestigious, private facilities.

ADVANCEMENT OPPORTUNITIES

Alcohol and drug abuse counselors can advance by obtaining experience and additional education to increase earnings and responsibilities, counselors may also climb the career ladder by locating positions in prestigious facilities.

Many counselors advance to supervisory or administrative positions.

EDUCATION AND TRAINING

Education and training requirements for alcohol and drug abuse counselors vary from state to state and job to job. With more states starting to certify counselors, it is important for individuals to get a good education.

There are one-year certificate programs as well as two-year associate degrees, four-year bachelor's degrees, and graduate degrees in alcohol and drug technology. Although some jobs just require a one-year certificate program, the minimum education recommended is an associate degree in alcohol and drug technology from an accredited college.

EXPERIENCE AND QUALIFICATIONS

Certification requirements vary from state to state. Alcohol and drug abuse counselors may be certified by the National Association of Alcoholism and Drug Abuse Counselors (NAADAC) or be state-certified in certain states. In order to obtain certification, individuals must generally go through an accredited educational program, pass written and oral examinations, participate in supervised clinical experience, and have a taped sample of their clinical work.

FOR ADDITIONAL INFORMATION: Individuals interested in pursuing careers in drug and alcohol counseling can obtain additional information by contacting the National Clearinghouse on Alcoholism and Drug Abuse Information (NCADI), Alcohol and Drug Problems Association (ADPA), the National Association of Alcoholism and Drug Abuse Counselors (NAADAC), National Association of Substance Abuse Trainers and Educators (NASATE), the National Institute on Alcohol Abuse and Alcoholism (NIAAA), the National Institute on Drug Abuse (NIDA), the American Association for Counseling and Development (AACD), the Council for Accreditation of Counseling and Related Education Programs (ACREP), the National Board for Certified Counselors (NBCC), and the National Academy of Certified Clinical Mental Health Counselors (NACCMHC).

Tips

- You can obtain an entry-level or volunteer position in this field to obtain necessary experience.
- Job openings are often advertised in the newspaper classified section under "Alcohol and Drug Counselor," "Substance Abuse Counselor," "Mental Health Counseling," "Detox Clinics," "Health Care," etc.
- Colleges offering programs in alcohol and drug technology usually have a placement office that is aware of job openings in the field.

DIETITIAN

JOB DESCRIPTION: *Design diets; analyze dietary needs; promote healthful eating habits; research nutritional needs and requirements.*

EARNINGS: *$25,000 to $45,000+.*

RECOMMENDED EDUCATION AND TRAINING: *Minimum education is a bachelor's degree; some positions require a master's degree.*

SKILLS AND PERSONALITY TRAITS: *Interpersonal skills; communication skills; computer capability; attention to detail; administrative skills; scientific aptitude.*

EXPERIENCE AND QUALIFICATIONS: *Credentialing offered by the American Dietetic Association.*

Job Description and Responsibilities

Dietitians are responsible for developing healthy diets by analyzing the nutritional needs of individuals.

In a clinical atmosphere, dietitians are responsible for handling, on a one-on-one basis, the nutritional needs of patients who are ill, injured, or infirm. Clinical dietitians or therapeutic dietitians, as they are sometimes called, work with patients in hospitals, nursing homes, extended-care facilities, clinics, or doctor's offices in an attempt to develop nutritional plans.

Each patient is different. For example, a patient who has high blood pressure would not be on the same diet as a patient suffering from depression or diabetes. The dietitian will also be responsible for answering any questions patients may have, explaining all dietary allowances and restrictions, and coordinating dietary prescriptions with the menus planned by the facility.

In other situations, the dietitian will be required to advise, counsel, and educate individuals on how to stay healthy and prevent disease. Dietitians who handle these types of functions are called community dietitians. They work in clinics, home health agencies, and human service organizations. In this capacity, dietitians evaluate the eating habits of individuals or families and develop an economical nutrition plan for them to follow. They may educate individuals or groups on the nutritional analysis of foods and explain what type of foods are high in saturated fats or what foods are high in fiber. Disease prevention through nutrition is an important function for community dietitians.

Depending on their specific situation, some dietitians analyze the nutritional content of specific foods or combinations of foods. Others prepare literature on the nutritional analysis of foods, dietary needs, and healthful diets.

Dietitians working in large facilities may be called management dietitians. These individuals work in hospitals, health care facilities, prisons, schools, corporate cafeterias, and other large facilities. Management dietitians are responsible for planning all the meals in these facilities for patients, employees, and visitors.

Another area of specialization for dietitians is research. Research is conducted in a number of areas from nutritional analysis of foods to nutritional requirements of individuals with certain diseases. More companies are attempting to develop new products that are nutritionally sound and lower in calories and fat. Individuals working in this field may work in corporate food research labs, medical centers, and educational institutions.

Employment Opportunities

Dietitians may specialize in research, clinical and community nutrition, or may be management dietitians responsible for the planning and preparation of meals for large facilities. Dietitians work in a vast array of settings including:

- Hospitals
- Nursing homes
- Food service companies
- Prisons
- Schools
- Corporate cafeterias
- Community health programs
- Clinics
- Consulting
- Private practice
- Hotel and restaurant chains
- Extended-care facilities
- Corporations (research)
- Health maintenance organizations
- Home health agencies
- Magazines and other publications

Expanding Opportunities for the 21st Century

With the current knowledge of the correlation between food, nutrition, and disease risk, clinical dietitians who specialize in obesity, kidney disease, heart disease, diabetes, and cancer will be in demand. There will also be a great need for dietitians to work in nursing homes and residential care facilities as the population ages dramatically.

EARNINGS

Full-time dietitians earn from $25,000 to $45,000 or more. Factors affecting earnings include the specific type of facility, its size, prestige, and geographic location. Other factors include the responsibilities, experience, and education level of the dietitian.

The average salary for dietitians is around $30,000. Individuals with postgraduate education, experience, and a great deal of responsibility will earn salaries at the higher end of the scale. Those doing research for large corporations will also earn higher salaries than individuals working for hospitals, schools, and public programs.

ADVANCEMENT OPPORTUNITIES

Dietitians can follow a number of paths to career advancement depending on the direction that they want to pursue. Individuals can locate similar positions in larger or more prestigious facilities, resulting in increased responsibilities and earnings. They may also choose specialization as their path to advancement. Clinical dieticians may, for example specialize in fields including obesity, kidney disease, heart disease, diabetes, or cancer. Other fields of specialization include nutrition for pediatrics, critical care patients, or gerontology.

Dietitians may climb the career ladder by becoming supervisors or managers of a dietary department.

EDUCATION AND TRAINING

Dietitians should have a minimum of a bachelor's degree in foods, nutrition, or food service administration. Individuals interested in becoming registered dietitians should complete their education at a college or university accredited by the American Dietetic Association. Courses for dietitians include nutrition, chemistry, microbiology, physiology, math, statistics, psychology, sociology, economics, biology, and computer science and technology.

Some positions may require a postgraduate degree. These include research teaching, and public health positions. As a rule, the more education, the more options that will be open to the individual, both in attaining a job and in career advancement.

EXPERIENCE AND QUALIFICATIONS

Approximately thirty states require dietitians to be licensed, certified, and/or registered. Many employers prefer that their dietitians be professionally credentialed and registered. In order to obtain these credentials, individuals must fulfill the requirements of the American Dietetic Association. These include completion of a bachelor's degree in foods and nutrition or institution management from an accredited program plus clinical experience. Clinical experience may be obtained by attending one of the accredited four-year university or college programs that combine both the academic requirements and the clinical experience. It can also be obtained by fulfilling a 900-hour accredited internship program or an approved preprofessional practice program. One of the reasons many people, especially career changers, opt for the preprofessional practice program is that it can be undertaken on a part-time basis.

FOR ADDITIONAL INFORMATION: Career-related literature can be obtained from the American Dietetic Association (ADA). Additional information regarding specific careers in this field is available from the U.S. Office of Personnel Management and the Department of Veterans Affairs (VA).

TIPS

- Obtain the best education possible. More options will be open to those with postgraduate degrees. If you can't attend graduate school full time, take courses on a part-time basis while working.
- With the current interest in health and fitness, you may be able to find a part-time job as a consultant for a health club or diet center.
- Job openings may be advertised in the newspaper display or classified section under "Dietitian," "Nutritionist," "Health Care," "Community Health," "Public Health," "School Dietitian," etc.
- The federal government often has openings for dietitians. Contact either the Departmnet of Veterans Affairs or the United States Office of Personnel Management to obtain requirements and information.

EEG TECHNOLOGIST/TECHNICIAN

JOB DESCRIPTION: *Operate and maintain electroencephalographs; read and interpret EEG tapes.*

EARNINGS: *$19,000 to $33,000.*

RECOMMENDED EDUCATION AND TRAINING: *High school diploma; on-the-job training or formal training.*

SKILLS AND PERSONALITY TRAITS: *Manual dexterity; personableness; good eyesight; communication skills; electronic aptitude.*

EXPERIENCE AND QUALIFICATIONS: *Many jobs do not require experience; credentialing is available.*

JOB DESCRIPTION AND RESPONSIBILITIES

EEG stands for electroencephalogram. These are records of brain waves that are important in treating and diagnosing many medical conditions. When no brain waves at all exist, people are considered clinically dead.

EEGs are taken with an instrument called an electroencephalograph. These units are used as diagnostic tools to diagnose the amount of injury patients have sustained from strokes, brain tumors, metabolic disorders, epilepsy, etc. EEGs are also used to monitor patients in surgery, to determine causes of behavioral problems and measure the effects of diseases to the brain. The EEG tests not only brain waves, but heart activity too.

EEG technologists and technicians are responsible for operating electro-encephalographs. Generally, individuals who are credentialed in this area are referred to as technologists while those who are not are called technicians.

EEG techs have a variety of duties depending on the specific job and their training. The first thing that must be done is to make sure that all equipment is working properly. Next, individuals are responsible for taking patients' medical history and putting patients at ease.

EEG techs apply electrodes to various spots on the patient's body and head before performing the procedure. The procedure may be performed while the patient is resting, sleeping, or moving about in normal everyday activities. Various stimuli may also be added to determine reactions.

The information recorded from the EEG will be documented on a paper tape and may look very much like a map or chart. After the procedure is completed, the EEG technologist or technician may be responsible for reviewing and reading the paper tape and determining what sections should be shown to the patient's doctor.

The greater the responsibilities of the individual, the more training that will be required. For example, EEG technologists working in operating rooms must be thoroughly familiar with anesthesia's effect on brain waves. Those working in other areas must be versed in other technologies. Throughout every procedure, the EEG technologist or technician must be aware when a major change is occurring so that a physician can be alerted.

Individuals will be responsible to either the physician or the supervisor of the EEG laboratory depending on the specific situation.

EMPLOYMENT OPPORTUNITIES

EEG technologists and technicians are usually employed full time in hospitals. However, individuals may work in a variety of other settings including:

- Neurology laboratories
- Neurologist's offices
- Neurosurgeon's offices
- Group medical practices
- Health maintenance organizations
- Urgent-care centers
- Emergency clinics
- Psychiatric facilities

Expanding Opportunities for the 21st Century

There is a continuing trend for neurologists, group practices, and health maintenance organizations (HMOs) to have their own equipment for these types of tests. While jobs will be plentiful for EEG technologists and technicians in hospitals, there will also be a tremendous need for individuals in this field in outpatient settings.

EARNINGS

Earnings for EEG technologists and technicians range from approximately $19,000 to $33,000 per year. Salaries depend on the geographic area that the individual is employed in as well as the specific type, size, and prestige of the facility. Other factors include experience, responsibilities, and qualifications.

Those who have experience, are registered, and are working in metropolitan areas will be compensated at the high end of the scale.

EEG technologists and technicians usually have their salaries augmented by benefit packages.

ADVANCEMENT OPPORTUNITIES

With experience, an EEG technologist may advance to supervisory positions including Chief EEG technologist, Special Procedures Instructor or Training Program Director. These jobs would result in increased earnings and responsibility.

EDUCATION AND TRAINING

Aspiring EEG technologists or technicians can take two paths regarding education and training. One method is to receive on-the-job training. The other is to take a formal training program in EEG technology.

Formal programs are offered in many community colleges, colleges, universities, vocational or technical schools, hospitals and medical centers. Depending on the specific program, completion may take from one to two years. The Joint Review Committee for the Accreditation of EEG Technology Training Programs approves some but not all programs.

Students in formal training programs will receive classroom instruction and laboratory experience. Individuals completing this training will be awarded either an associate degree or a certificate.

EXPERIENCE AND QUALIFICATIONS

Many positions in this field are entry-level and will not require any special prior experience.

Although it is not usually necessary for those just entering the field, credentialing may be needed for advancement. Individuals may become credentialed through the American Board of Registration of Electroencephalographic Technologists and receive the title of Registered EEG Technologist.

FOR ADDITIONAL INFORMATION: Individuals interested in a career in EEG technology can obtain additional information by contacting the American Society of Electroneurodiagnostic Technologists (ASET), the Joint Review Committee for the Accreditation of EEG Technology Training Programs, the American Board of Registration for Electroencephalographic Technologists (ABRET), or their local hospital.

TIPS

- Most of the formal programs in this field offer placement services.
- Job openings may be advertised in the newspaper's classified section under headings such as "Health Care," "EEG Technologist," "EEG Technician," or "Technology."
- Contact personnel offices of hospital and health care facilities to inquire about job openings or training programs.

CARDIOLOGY TECHNOLOGIST

JOB DESCRIPTION: *Assist physician in cardiac catheterization, balloon angioplasty, and other procedures; prepare patients; position them on examining table; monitor blood gases.*

EARNINGS: *$24,000 to $35,000.*

RECOMMENDED EDUCATION AND TRAINING: *Two-year college program.*

SKILLS AND PERSONALITY TRAITS: *Mechanical ability; personableness; familiarity with medical terminology; communication skills.*

EXPERIENCE AND QUALIFICATIONS: *Experience in the health care field helpful.*

JOB DESCRIPTION AND RESPONSIBILITIES

Cardiac catheterization is an invasive procedure used by physicians to determine whether blockages exist in a patient's blood vessels. This is done by winding a catheter through a patient's blood vessel in the leg to the patient's heart. Cardiology technologists are responsible for assisting physicians in these cardiac catheterization procedures.

The cardiology technologist is responsible for preparing patients for the procedure by making them comfortable and positioning them on the examination table. The individual must then clean and shave the patient's leg and administer local anesthesia.

Other functions of the cardiology technologist include monitoring the patient's blood gases and heart rate during procedures. This is done by using EKG equipment. It is up to the technologist to keep the physician abreast of any problems and let him or her know if there are any changes.

The cardiology technologist may also be responsible for assisting the physician during a procedure known as a balloon angioplasty. This is used for patients who have blocked blood vessels.

Cardiology technologists may assist in preparing patients for open-heart surgery or implanting pacemakers. The individual will be responsible for preparing and monitoring patients during these procedures as well.

Depending on the training the individual has received, he or she may also perform an array of other invasive or noninvasive vascular tests.

In some situations the cardiology technologist may be responsible for scheduling the physician's appointments, keeping the equipment in order, and maintaining the patient's files.

Cardiology technologists may work various shifts, depending on the specific job. They are responsible to the physician in charge.

EMPLOYMENT OPPORTUNITIES

Cardiology technologists can work full time or may find part-time employment. The majority of cardiology technologists in the country work in hospital settings. With the advances in cardiology medicine, however, there are opportunities in other settings, including:

- Medical centers
- Cardiologists' offices
- Cardiac rehabilitation centers
- Health maintenance organizations
- Health clinics
- Long-term care facilities
- Nursing homes

Expanding Opportunities for the 21st Century

Because heart disease is a major problem in this country, new diagnostic procedures are constantly being developed. As the population ages and the incidence of heart disease increases, there will be a greater need for cardiology technologists throughout the country.

EARNINGS

Annual earnings for full-time cardiology technologists can range from approximately $24,000 to $35,000. Variables affecting salaries include the experience level and responsibilities of the individual, as well as the specific facility and geographical location.

Those who have attained some experience will be compensated toward the middle of the scale, while those who perform more sophisticated or complicated procedures will have earnings at the high end of the pay scale. Earnings are also generally higher for individuals working in facilities in metropolitan areas.

Many cardiology technologists have their salaries augmented by liberal fringe-benefit packages.

ADVANCEMENT OPPORTUNITIES

Cardiology technologists can advance by getting more training and moving into specialized positions. Individuals may also climb the career ladder by locating positions in larger or more prestigious facilities, resulting in increased responsibilities and earnings.

EDUCATION AND TRAINING

Cardiology technologists must complete a two-year program in this field at a junior or community college. Basic core courses are taken in the first year. During the second year, individuals take specialized instruction in invasive or noninvasive peripheral cardiology. Certain educational requirements may be waived for individuals who have come from a related allied health profession.

EXPERIENCE AND QUALIFICATIONS

Some cardiology technologists start out working in the health care field as EKG technicians or other professionals. Others have had no experience in the field previous to their education.

Individuals must be personable, with good communication skills. This is important in order to put patients at ease during procedures and to explain what is happening to them.

Voluntary credentialing can be obtained through the Cardiovascular Credentialing International/National Board of Cardiovascular Testing. Credentialing shows professional competence and may give one applicant an edge over another.

FOR ADDITIONAL INFORMATION: For more information, contact the National Society of Cardiovascular Technology/National Society of Pulmonary Technology (NSCT/NSPT) and the Cardiovascular Credentialing International and National Board of Cardiovascular Testing (CCI/NBCT).

TIPS

- If you are still in school, you may consider either doing volunteer work or getting a part-time or summer job in a health care setting.
- Many health care facilities, vocational-technical schools, high schools, and community colleges put on "health career days" where interested individuals can learn more about careers in these fields.
- Consider sending your resume with a short cover letter to the personnel directors of hospitals, health care facilities, nursing homes, and cardiologists' offices. Remember to request that your resume be kept on file for the future if there are no current openings.
- Jobs may be advertised in the classified section of local newspapers under headings such as "Cardiologist Technologist," "Health Care," "Health Care Professional," "Hospitals," and "Cardiac Rehabilitation Center."

EMERGENCY MEDICAL TECHNICIAN

JOB DESCRIPTION: *Provide emergency medical treatment; assess and monitor patient's condition; drive ambulances or vans.*

EARNINGS: *$19,000 to $40,000+.*

RECOMMENDED EDUCATION AND TRAINING: *High school diploma; standard training course in emergency medical care.*

SKILLS AND PERSONALITY TRAITS: *Emotional stability; enjoyment in helping others; good judgment; physical stamina; ability to work under stress.*

EXPERIENCE AND QUALIFICATIONS: *A valid driver's license required; certification/registration available.*

JOB DESCRIPTION AND RESPONSIBILITIES

Emergency medical technicians provide emergency medical help. EMTs may be called in to deal with accident victims, heart attacks, stab or gunshot wounds, drug overdoses, poisonings, etc. While EMTs are not doctors, they are highly trained in emergency lifesaving techniques.

There are a number of levels of emergency medical technicians. The entry-level job may be referred to as EMT-Ambulance, EMT-A, or basic EMT. Other levels are EMT-Intermediate, EMT-Paramedic, and EMT-Defibrillator.

Levels of the job are based on the amount of training the individual has received and will affect the procedures they can perform. For example, in most states, EMT-Intermediates are allowed to treat trauma patients with intravenous fluids, anti-shock garments' and airway management techniques. EMT-Ambulance personnel are usually not permitted to provide these additional services.

EMT-Paramedics are trained in advanced life support skills. These individuals often work under the direction of a physician using radio communication and administering oral or intravenous drugs, performing endotracheal intubation, and interpreting EKGs. Some EMT-Paramedics may also use defibrillators when required.

EMT-Defibrillators are trained in administering electrical defibrillation, which can be used to resuscitate some heart attack victims. This level of EMT is a relatively new designation. It was designed to provide EMT-Ambulance people with additional training required to administer these procedures.

Once an EMT team arrives at the scene, their first responsibility is to assess the situation. They may work with other emergency departments including police and firefighters to determine priorities for handling the situation.

Once priority decisions are made, EMTs are responsible for providing the appropriate emergency care. Individuals may handle procedures that they have been trained to do or may be in radio contact with medical staff who can give them step-by-step instructions. Depending on the situation, the EMT may perform CPR, treat patients for shock, resuscitate heart attack patients, control bleeding, open airways, assist in the birth of a baby, or handle a vast array of other procedures.

The EMT will transmit information to the dispatcher or hospital regarding the type and extent of emergencies. Individuals may give patient's vital signs, symptoms, and condition. EMTs may be directed to the closest hospital with the appropriate equipment or to a specialty facility, depending on the situation.

After placing a patient in the care of a facility, the EMT must make sure that the ambulance is ready for the next call. Linens, blankets, and bandages may need replacing, and equipment may need to be sterilized.

Other functions of the EMT may include writing reports on patients transported, checking to be sure that the ambulance is in good working order, and supplying the vehicle with the needed equipment.

Working hours will vary for EMTs depending on the specific shift. This is a difficult, challenging, and rewarding job. Most people who are performing this service are saving lives on a daily basis.

EMPLOYMENT OPPORTUNITIES

Emergency medical technicians can work for:

- Hospitals
- Medical centers
- Fire departments
- Police departments
- Rescue squad departments
- Private ambulance companies

Expanding Opportunities for the 21st Century

Financial difficulties are causing many not-for-profit hospitals, municipal police, fire, and rescue squads to cut back on staff and services. These organizations must then contract with private ambulance companies to perform ambulatory services.

It is also important to note that highly trained EMTs will be extremely marketable in the future.

EARNINGS

Earnings for emergency medical technicians vary depending on the specific type of work setting and geographic location, as well as training and experience.

Annual earnings can range from $19,000 to $40,000 or more. Salaries are to a great extent based on the training and level of EMT the individual achieves.

EMTs working for fire departments will usually earn more than those performing similar duties in hospitals or for private ambulance services. Highest salaries will go to paramedics with experience working in large, metropolitan cities.

Advancement Opportunities

Emergency medical technicians can advance by seeking additional training, learning more skills, and obtaining experience. They can move from an EMT-Ambulance to an EMT-Intermediate and up to an EMT-Paramedic.

Education and Training

EMT personnel must hold a high school diploma or equivalent. They must also complete training in emergency medical care techniques. The basic standard training course is offered nationwide by police and fire departments, ambulance corps, health departments, hospitals, medical centers, colleges, universities, and medical schools. The first phase of the nondegree course lasts approximately 110 hours and covers instruction and practice in emergencies and basic life support techniques. It is the training required to become an EMT-Ambulance.

Additional training includes a two-day class in the removal of trapped victims and a five-day course on driving ambulances and other emergency vehicles. Individuals interested in training for the EMT-Defibrillation level must complete an intensive course on defibrillation.

Training for the EMT-Intermediate level includes the basic EMT training as well as some of the EMT-Paramedic course material. Specific training requirements vary from state to state.

Those interested in becoming EMT-Paramedics must go through a program that usually lasts about nine months. Programs are accredited by the American Medical Association's Committee on Allied Health Education and Accreditation.

Experience and Qualifications

Qualifications vary for emergency medical technicians. As a rule, individuals must be at least 18 years old and hold a valid driver's license.

Emergency medical technicians may be certified by either the specific state's certifying agency or the National Registry of Emergency Medical Technicians. While this is not always a requirement, it is certainly recommended.

To earn the title of Registered EMT-Ambulance, individuals must graduate from an approved EMT training program. They must also obtain a certain degree of experience and pass both a written and practical examination administered by either the National Registry of Emergency Medical Technicians or the specific state's certifying agency. In order to keep this certification, individuals must be employed in the field, continue their education, and pay a fee at regular timed intervals.

Those interested in being registered as an EMT-Intermediate must be registered EMTs, pass an examination, take 35 to 55 more hours of classroom study, obtain a certain amount of clinical experience, and go through a field internship.

Requirements for EMT-Paramedics include current registration or state certification as an EMT-Ambulance, completion of the EMT-Paramedic training program, six months of field experience, and taking and passing both a written and practical examination.

FOR ADDITIONAL INFORMATION: For more information contact the National Registry of Emergency Medical Technicians (NREMT), the National Association of Emergency Medical Technicians (NAEMT), or the Emergency Medical Service Director in your particular state.

TIPS

- A good way to make sure this is the career for you is volunteering to work on your local ambulance corps.
- Job openings may be advertised in the newspaper classified section under headings such as "Emergency Medical Technicians," "EMTs," "Emergency Medical Service," "Ambulance Technicians," "Rescue Squad," "Health Care," etc.
- Send your resume and a short cover letter to medical centers, hospitals, private ambulance companies, and municipal fire, police, and rescue squads. Request that your resume be kept on file if there are no current openings.
- If you are or were a medic in the armed forces, you already have valuable experience in this field.

MEDICAL RECORDS TECHNICIAN

JOB DESCRIPTION: *Assemble and organize medical records; code procedures and diagnoses; tabulate data.*

EARNINGS: *$19,000 to $33,000.*

RECOMMENDED EDUCATION AND TRAINING: *Associate's degree from an accredited program in medical records technology.*

SKILLS AND PERSONALITY TRAITS: *Reliability; fastidiousness; computer capability; good communication skills.*

EXPERIENCE AND QUALIFICATIONS: *Knowledge of medical terms.*

Job Description and Responsibilities

Hospitals and other facilities dealing in health care must maintain a vast number of medical records. These records include patients' medical history, symptoms, test results, diagnoses, medications, admission dates, discharge dates, names of attending physicians, and physician notes.

Medical records technicians handle the organization and assembly of these medical records. They work with others in the medical records department to establish files for every patient who visits the facility. It is extremely important to health care facilities to handle this in an accurate and timely manner in order to be reimbursed properly and adequately.

Medical records technicians may also be responsible for tabulating and analyzing data. This information could be used for many purposes. It may, for example, be used to check quality assurance or to determine the plausibility of adding a new type of health unit to the facility.

Medical records technicians may have supervisory responsibilities over clerks working in the department. They are responsible to the medical records supervisor.

Employment Opportunities

With the great demand for qualified people in this profession, there is often flexibility in working hours. Medical records technicians may find full- or part-time employment in a variety of settings such as:

- Hospitals
- Nursing homes
- Health maintenance organizations
- Private or public health clinics
- Physicians' offices
- Home health agencies

Expanding Opportunities for the 21st Century

With the rise in health care costs, hospitals will be in great need of accurate medical records in order to obtain government, health care agency and insurance reimbursement. Providing this accurate information is the job of medical records technicians.

Other expanding opportunities in this field include employment in HMOs, extended-care facilities, and home health agencies.

Earnings

Annual earnings for medical records technicians range from approximately $19,000 to $33,000. Those who have supervisory positions will earn more. Factors affecting salary include the individual's experience and responsibilities. Other factors include the specific facility, its size, prestige, and geographic location. Individuals working in health care facilities will usually have their earnings augmented by benefit packages.

ADVANCEMENT OPPORTUNITIES

Medical records technicians can advance by specializing in a particular area of medical records technology.

Some climb the career ladder by teaching. This method of advancement will usually require a master's degree in either health administration or education. Others become supervisors or managers of either the entire medical records department or a specific area within the department.

EDUCATION AND TRAINING

There are two ways of obtaining the training necessary to become a credentialed medical records technician. One is to complete a two-year course and obtain an associate's degree from a college offering an accredited program in medical records technology. The other is to graduate from an independent study program offered by the American Medical Record Association. In order to participate in independent study, an individual must have 30 hours of credit in areas prescribed by the AMRA.

Once the educational requirements are met, medical records technicians may become credentialed by passing a written examination sponsored by the American Medical Record Association. While credentials are not mandatory, most employers prefer that technicians have them.

EXPERIENCE AND QUALIFICATIONS

Medical records technicians should have a complete knowledge and understanding of medical terminology and procedures.

FOR ADDITIONAL INFORMATION: Individuals interested in learning more about careers in medical records technology should contact the American Medical Record Association (AMRA). Information regarding the Independent Study Program may be obtained from the American Health Information Management Association.

TIPS

- Once you obtain basic experience working as a medical records technician, try to learn extra skills so that you can specialize. This will help you advance and increase your income.
- Take computer courses or workshops. This will put you a step above others who do not have this skill.

- If you are still in school, work summers or part time in a health care facility as a medical records clerk. This will give you hands-on experience.

SURGICAL TECHNOLOGIST

JOB DESCRIPTION: *Set up operating room; prepare patients for surgery; assist in operations.*

EARNINGS: *$21,000 to $32,000+.*

RECOMMENDED EDUCATION AND TRAINING: *Formal training programs vary, lasting from 9 to 24 months and leading to a certificate, diploma, or associate's degree.*

SKILLS AND PERSONALITY TRAITS: *Compassion; emotional stability; conscientiousness; organizational skills; familiarity with medical terminology.*

EXPERIENCE AND QUALIFICATIONS: *Voluntary certification is available.*

JOB DESCRIPTION AND RESPONSIBILITIES

Surgical technologists work under the supervision of surgeons and registered nurses assisting in the operating room. Their functions can encompass duties before, during, and after an operating procedure.

Surgical technologists are responsible for preparing, or "prepping," patients before surgery. This includes washing, shaving, and disinfecting the sites near where the incision will be made. As part of this responsibility, the technologist must help make patients feel calm and comfortable. Once prepped, the technologist transports patients to the operating room, positions them on the operating table, and covers them with sterile drapes.

The surgical technologist is responsible for setting up the operating room before an operation. This includes putting out surgical instruments, equipment, linens, saline, glucose, and the like. The individual must also check all nonsterile equipment to make sure that it is working correctly. The technologist may also help surgeons, surgeon assistants, nurses, etc., scrub and put on sterile gloves, gowns, and masks.

During surgical procedures, the surgical technologist will be expected to pass instruments and supplies to surgeons.

Individuals may also be responsible for observing patients' vital signs, checking charts, and so forth. Depending on their degree of responsibilities, technologists may also bring specimens to the lab for analysis; apply dressings; operate equipment; cut sutures; count needles, sponges, etc.; or maintain supplies of plasma and blood to the patient. After surgical procedures are completed, surgical technologists are responsible for transporting patients to the recovery room.

EMPLOYMENT OPPORTUNITIES

Full- and part-time jobs are available for qualified surgical technologists throughout the country. Individuals can work in a variety of health care situations, including:

- Hospitals
- Clinics
- Surgi-centers
- Private physicians' offices

Expanding Opportunities for the 21st Century

Employment for surgical technologists is growing due to technological advances, as well as to the increase of the older population, which generally requires more surgical procedures.

With the new and escalating shift to outpatient and ambulatory surgery, expanding opportunities will be located in surgi-centers, clinics, and private physicians' offices.

EARNINGS

Annual earnings for full-time surgical technologists range from approximately $21,000 to $32,000 plus, depending on the prestige, size, and geographic location of the health care facility in which the individual is working. Other factors include the responsibilities, experience, and training of the technologist. As a rule, the more specialized the training of the individual, the higher the salary.

ADVANCEMENT OPPORTUNITIES

Surgical technologists can advance their careers by obtaining additional training. Some individuals become first assistants. Others specialize in a particular area of surgery. This may include transplants, neurosurgery, or open-heart surgery.

EDUCATION AND TRAINING

In order to become a surgical technologist, an individual must go through a formal accredited program. There are over 100 such programs throughout the country. Programs vary in length, but usually last between 9 and 24 months and can lead to a certificate, diploma, or associate's degree.

Classes include anatomy, physiology, microbiology, pharmacology, and medical terminology. In addition, individuals receive supervised clinical experience and learn how to sterilize equipment as well as the correct methods of handling drugs, solutions, supplies, and equipment.

EXPERIENCE AND QUALIFICATIONS

Surgical technologists may seek voluntary professional certification from the Liaison Council on Certification for Surgical Technologists. To become certified, individuals must complete and graduate from a formal educational program as well as pass a national certification exam. Continuing education and/or reexamination is required to stay certified.

FOR ADDITIONAL INFORMATION: There are a number of organizations and associations that provide career information for surgical technologists. These include the Association of Surgical Technologists (AST) and the Liaison Council on Certification for Surgical Technologists.

TIPS

- If you think you might be interested in this type of career and are still in school, take classes in biology, chemistry, health, and math.
- Job openings are frequently advertised in the newspaper classified section under headings such as "Surgical Technologist," "Health Care," and "Operating Room Technician."
- Get the best education you can. After you have obtained general training, you can improve your career opportunities by continuing to take courses in specialized fields.
- Contact the Association of Surgical Technologists to obtain a list of accredited programs.

PHYSICIAN ASSISTANT

JOB DESCRIPTION: *Take medical histories; examine patients; order lab tests; treat minor medical problems.*

EARNINGS: *$32,000 to $60,000.*

RECOMMENDED EDUCATION AND TRAINING: *Degree from an accredited PA program.*

SKILLS AND PERSONALITY TRAITS: *Caring; compassionate; emotionally stable; dependable.*

EXPERIENCE AND QUALIFICATIONS: *State certification exam may be required.*

Job Description and Responsibilities

Physician assistants work under the supervision of licensed physicians. Their responsibilities may be determined by either a supervising physician or the state's regulatory agency. In some states, therefore, individuals will be able to perform duties that cannot be carried out by physician assistants in other states.

The services of a physician assistant free up the physician's time to handle other important functions. In many situations, physicians are not always available and the assistant can provide necessary services. The physician assistant may work with the doctor when available or on a telephone to consult when there is no physician at the scene.

Physician assistants may be responsible for treating minor medical emergencies including cuts, bruises, abrasions, and burns. They may also handle both preoperative and postoperative patient care. Those who have the training may work in operating rooms. Others are responsible for taking patient medical histories and performing physical examinations. Some physician assistants do the examinations required by insurance companies for college-bound students.

Physician assistants may also examine patients who are ill. Sometimes PAs are required to make a preliminary diagnosis of a patient's illness and in doing so, may order laboratory tests. Depending on the state, some physician assistants prescribe treatments and recommend medication and drug therapies.

PAs may work in general medicine in private practice offices, hospitals, clinics, or in specialty areas. They may work under physicians who specialize in family medicine, pediatrics, internal medicine, general surgery, emergency medicine, or many other areas.

PAs work a variety of hours depending on their employment situation. They are responsible to the physician with whom they work.

Employment Opportunities

P.A.'s work in most of the same settings as physicians. These include:

- Physicians' offices
- Medical groups
- Hospitals
- Health maintenance organizations
- Public health clinics
- Prisons
- Nursing homes
- Extended-care facilities
- Rehabilitation centers
- Facilities for the disabled
- Facilities for the mentally retarded
- Schools, colleges, universities

Expanding Opportunities for the 21st Century

Currently, most physician assistants work in private medical practices and hospitals. However, trends indicate there will be a growing demand for these professionals in a variety of other facilities that use the services of physicians. These include nursing homes, public health clinics, and health maintenance organizations (HMOs).

One of the greatest opportunities for physician assistants will be in those areas that have difficulty attracting enough physicians. Such areas include rural settings as well as inner-city clinics.

EARNINGS

Physician assistants have earnings ranging from $32,000 to $60,000, depending on the individual's experience, responsibilities, qualifications, and training.

Other factors affecting earnings include the specific facility the individual is working in, its size, prestige, and geographic location. Most physician assistants' earnings range from $50,000 to $55,000. PAs with more experience working in large metropolitan cities will move to the top of the pay scale faster.

ADVANCEMENT OPPORTUNITIES

After obtaining experience, physician assistants can advance into positions in larger or more prestigious settings.

Other physician assistants climb the career ladder by getting additional education so that they can specialize in fields such as emergency medicine, surgery, or neonatology.

EDUCATION AND TRAINING

Recommended educational requirements for physician assistants include graduation from an accredited program. Accredited PA programs lead to a certificate, an associate degree, a bachelor's degree, or a master's degree.

Physician assistant programs are usually two years in duration and include classroom instruction and clinical experience. Subjects cover human anatomy, physiology, microbiology, biochemistry, nutrition, clinical pharmacology, clinical medicine, geriatric and home health care, medical ethics, and disease prevention.

The clinical experience portion of the program covers areas including family medicine, general surgery, inpatient and ambulatory medicine, obstetrics and gynecology, geriatrics, emergency medicine, internal medicine, pediatrics, and ambulatory psychiatry.

Postgraduate residencies are available in a number of specialties.

EXPERIENCE AND QUALIFICATIONS

Qualifications for physician assistants depend on the state in which they work. Some states require individuals to pass a certifying exam in addition to completing an accredited educational program. In order to remain certified, PAs must complete approximately 100 hours of continuing medical education every two years as well as taking and passing a recertification exam evey six years.

FOR ADDITIONAL INFORMATION: Individuals interested in learning more about careers as physician assistants can obtain additional information by contacting the American Academy of Physician Assistants (AAPA), the Association of Physician Assistant Programs (APAP), and the National Commission on Certification of Physician Assistants, Inc. (NCCPA).

TIPS

- Prior experience working in the health care field is a plus for getting into an accredited program.
- Even if physicians are not advertising for physician assistants, it does not mean they would not consider hiring one. Send your resume and a short cover letter to physicians' offices, hospitals, health care facilities, and clinics.
- Part-time work or flexible scheduling is often available for physician assistants.
- Join your volunteer ambulance squad to obtain helpful experience.
- Write for the free pamphlet "Physician Assistants, Partners in Medicine" from the American Academy of Physician Assistants.

CLINICAL LABORATORY TECHNOLOGIST

JOB DESCRIPTION: *Perform laboratory tests; examine blood, tissue, and other body substances; make cultures of body fluid and tissue samples; type and cross-match blood samples.*

EARNINGS: *$19,000 to $40,000+.*

RECOMMENDED EDUCATION AND TRAINING: *Bachelor's degree in medical technology or life sciences.*

SKILLS AND PERSONALITY TRAITS: *Manual dexterity; normal vision; communication skills; ability to work under pressure; computer skills; analytical skills.*

EXPERIENCE AND QUALIFICATIONS: *State licensing; credentialing required for some jobs.*

JOB DESCRIPTION AND RESPONSIBILITIES

Clinical laboratory technologists perform a variety of medical tests on patients. These may include chemical, biological, hematological, microscopic, immunologic, and bacteriological laboratory tests. Technologists use microscopes, chemical analyzers, and computers to perform these tests and analyze the results.

All tests must be ordered by a physician and may be used for a variety of reasons. They may indicate diseases or infections. They might also detect specific illnesses, help with diagnosis and treatment, or be used to determine the status of an individual's health.

Lab technologists' responsibilities and duties depend on the specific job, the employment setting, and the individual's education and experience.

Technologists draw blood, and collect samples of tissues or other body substances to be analyzed and examined. In some situations, technologists take specimens and make cultures in order to analyze them. They may examine the cultures with a microscope, looking for parasites, microorganisms, fungi, or bacteria.

Clinical lab technologists may be required to analyze samples for chemical content. For example, they might prepare slides with body tissue, blood, or fluid to determine abnormalities such as cancer cells. Another duty of the clinical lab technologist includes typing and cross-matching blood samples for transfusions.

Individuals may specialize in clinical laboratory testing. Those who prepare slides of body cells and examine them for abnormalities are called cytotechnologists. Clinical chemistry technologists prepare specimens and analyze the chemical and hormonal content of body fluids. Microbiology technologists examine and identify bacteria and other microorganisms. Blood bank technologists collect, type, and prepare blood for transfusions. Immunology technologists examine elements and responses of the immune system to foreign substances.

Clinical laboratory technologists work various hours depending on their shift. Individuals are responsible to either the chief medical technologist, the laboratory manager, or the physician in charge.

EMPLOYMENT OPPORTUNITIES

Employment possibilities include:

- Hospitals
- Physicians' offices
- Medical centers
- Group medical practices
- Independent laboratories
- Clinics
- Health maintenance organizations
- Pharmaceutical companies
- Public health agencies
- Research institutes
- Extended-care facilities
- Urgi-centers
- Surgi-centers
- Commercial laboratories

Expanding Opportunities for the 21st Century

There will be a great demand for lab technologists as a result of innovative technology leading to newer and more powerful diagnostic tests.

Laboratory technologists will also find new opportunities in research labs working to find treatments and cures for cancer, AIDS, and other deadly diseases.

With an increase in home medical tests, pharmaceutical companies will require a greater number of laboratory technologists to develop products. More expanding opportunities will be found in independent medical laboratories and in physicians' clinics and offices.

EARNINGS

Earnings for clinical laboratory technologists range from approximately $19,000 to $40,000 or more. Factors affecting earnings include the specific employment situation and geographic location as well as the responsibilities, experience, and training of individuals.

Technologists just starting out will have earnings ranging from $19,000 to $27,000. Those with more experience and responsibilities earn between $27,000 and $40,000 plus. Individuals working in metropolitan areas will earn more than their counterparts in less urban areas.

ADVANCEMENT OPPORTUNITIES

Clinical laboratory technologists can advance their careers in a number of ways including additional experience and education. Some individuals locate similar positions in larger or more prestigious facilities. Technologists might also land supervisory positions or administrative jobs such as laboratory manager or chief medical technologist.

EDUCATION AND TRAINING

It is recommended that clinical laboratory technologists have a bachelor's degree with a major in either medical technology or one of the life sciences.

Many colleges and universities, as well as a number of hospitals affiliated with colleges or universities, offer majors in medical technology. It is important that the college, university, or hospital be accredited by the Committee on Allied Health Education and Accreditation, in cooperation with the National Accrediting Agency for Clinical Laboratory Sciences.

The programs in medical technology consist of classroom and lab work in chemistry, microbiology, biological sciences, math, computers, management, business, and clinical laboratory skills.

Graduate programs in medical technology and clinical laboratory sciences are also available.

EXPERIENCE AND QUALIFICATIONS

Clinical laboratory technologists may be required to be state-licensed, depending on the state in which they are working.

Certification is required for certain positions. Individuals may receive certification from a number of organizations including the Board of Registry of the American Society of Clinical Pathologists in conjunction with the American Association of Blood Banks, the American Medical Technologists, the National Certification Agency for Medical Laboratory Personnel, and the Credentialing Commission of the International Society for Clinical Laboratory Technology. Requirements for certification vary with the specific organization.

FOR ADDITIONAL INFORMATION: There are a number of organizations individuals can contact for more information about careers in clinical laboratory technology. These include the American Society of Clinical Pathologists (ASCP), American Medical Technologists (AMT), American Association for Clinical Chemistry (AACC), the American Association of Blood Banks (AABB), the American Society of Cytology (ASC), the National Certification Agency for Medical Laboratory Personnel (NCAMLP), the International Society for Clinical Laboratory Technology (ISCLT), the Committee on Allied Health Education and Accreditation (CAHEA), and the National Institutes of Health (NIH).

TIPS

- Opportunities for clinical laboratory technologists are often available in Department of Veterans Affairs medical centers.
- Federal jobs may be available with the National Institutes of Health.
- Job openings may be advertised in the newspaper's classified section under headings such as "Health Care," "Hospitals," "Laboratories," "Clinical Laboratory Technologists," "Lab Technologists," etc.
- Send your resume with a short cover letter to the personnel directors of hospitals, physicians' offices, medical centers, independent laboratories, etc. Request that your resume be kept on file if there are no current openings.
- Colleges and universities offering degree programs in medical technology usually have placement services for their graduates.

RESPIRATORY THERAPIST

JOB DESCRIPTION: *Test capacity of lungs; treat and care for individuals with breathing problems.*

EARNINGS: *$23,000 to $50,000+.*

RECOMMENDED EDUCATION AND TRAINING: *Formal training through accredited program.*

SKILLS AND PERSONALITY TRAITS: *Personableness; compassion; sensitivity; mathematical problem-solving skills; manual dexterity.*

EXPERIENCE AND QUALIFICATIONS: *State licensing required in some states; voluntary certification available.*

JOB DESCRIPTION AND RESPONSIBILITIES

Respiratory therapists help people with breathing disorders to breathe more easily. They may treat a variety of patients including premature infants, people with chronic asthma or emphysema, or people who have experienced shock, heart failure, strokes, or near-drowning.

Respiratory therapists are responsible for evaluating patients to determine what course of action should be taken. They are then expected to implement treatment. Respiratory therapists must first determine the capacity of the lungs and then analyze the oxygen and carbon dioxide concentration as well as the hydrogen potential in the blood. To do this, they ask patients to breathe into something that measures the volume and flow of air. The therapist must then analyze the levels to determine how best to help the patient to breathe easier.

Depending on their training, respiratory therapists may be responsible for performing chest physiotherapy on individuals to remove mucus from their lungs. Therapists may be responsible for administering aerosol medications and for teaching patients how to inhale the aerosol properly.

Respiratory therapists may also use oxygen or oxygen mixtures to treat patients. They may connect patients to ventilators or place oxygen masks on patients. Therapists are expected to check on patients and the equipment. They may also be responsible for inspecting and cleaning equipment and making sure it is used properly.

Respiratory therapists may work under stress when dealing with emergencies.

EMPLOYMENT OPPORTUNITIES

Respiratory therapists may work in a variety of settings. The majority of jobs are in hospitals. Other settings include:

- Medical equipment rental companies
- Home health agencies
- Nursing homes

Expanding Opportunities for the 21st Century

Careers in respiratory therapy will expand in the new century as the population ages, and more people will be experiencing respiratory ailments and cardiopulmonary diseases. Another increasing need for respiratory therapists will be working with AIDS patients. Trained individuals working in neonatal care as well as in cardiopulmonary care also will experience expanding opportunities for the 21st century.

EARNINGS

Respiratory therapists working full time can have annual earnings ranging from $23,000 to $50,000 or more. Factors affecting earnings include the setting and job as well as the geographic location.

Other factors affecting earnings include education, responsibilities, and experience of the individual.

ADVANCEMENT OPPORTUNITIES

Respiratory therapists can advance by obtaining experience and additional training. Individuals may climb the career ladder by taking care of critical patients instead of general care patients. Respiratory therapists may also move into supervisory or managerial positions in respiratory therapy departments.

EDUCATION AND TRAINING

Respiratory therapists must graduate from an accredited program. Training is offered at colleges, universities, and trade and vocational-technical schools, as well as in hospitals and medical schools. Areas of study include courses in anatomy, physiology, chemistry, biology, microbiology, physics, and mathematics. Technical courses are also offered to help individuals learn to deal with procedures, equipment, and clinical areas.

Respiratory therapists may seek either a two-year associate's degree or a four-year bachelor's degree program. Individuals with a four-year degree in other fields may also study to become respiratory therapists. Individuals in this situation must go through supervised clinical experience.

EXPERIENCE AND QUALIFICATIONS

Certain states require respiratory therapists to be licensed. Voluntary certification and registration are available to graduates of accredited programs. While certification is voluntary, employers prefer applicants for most positions to be certified and registered. Individuals may become Certified Respiratory Therapy Technicians (CRTT) or Registered Respiratory Therapists (RRT) by taking examinations offered by the National Board for Respiratory Care, Inc.

Individuals in this line of work must have good mathematical problem-solving skills and manual dexterity. They should be compassionate and sensitive.

FOR ADDITIONAL INFORMATION: Individuals interested in careers in respiratory therapy can obtain additional information by contacting the American Association for Respiratory Care (AARC), The National Board for Respiratory Care, Inc., and the Joint Review Committee for Respiratory Therapy Education.

TIPS

- If you are still in high school, take classes in health, biology, math, chemistry, and physics.
- Openings are often advertised in the classified or display section of newspapers under the headings "Health Care," "Respiratory Therapist," and "Respiratory Care Practitioner."
- The more extensive your education, the more marketable you will be. A four-year degree will help in advancement.
- Send your resume and a short cover letter to hospitals, home health agencies, and nursing homes. Request that your resume be kept on file if there are no current openings.

HEALTH SERVICES ADMINISTRATOR

JOB DESCRIPTION: *Overall management of health care institution; assess the need for services; hire personnel; supervise assistant administrators.*

EARNINGS: *$40,000 to $175,000+.*

RECOMMENDED EDUCATION AND TRAINING: *Master's degree in health services administration, hospital administration, or business administration.*

SKILLS AND PERSONALITY TRAITS: *Leadership ability; managerial skills; communication skills; ability to deal with press and media.*

EXPERIENCE AND QUALIFICATIONS: *Experience necessary; state licensing required for administrators of nursing homes and extended-care facilities.*

Job Description and Responsibilities

Health services administrators are responsible for overseeing the operation and management of health care facilities. Specific duties and responsibilities vary depending on the size of the facility.

In smaller facilities or agencies, administrators are responsible for the overall direction and financial management of the institution or agency. Administrators in these situations may also be called the CEO or chief executive officer.

In larger facilities, the CEO may delegate duties to other administrators. For example, financial management will be delegated to a chief fiscal officer; personnel requirements to a personnel director; planning to a planning officer; public relations and marketing to a PR director, and supervision of various other patient services and ancillary departments to associate or deputy administrators.

The top health services administrator is expected to supervise all assistant and deputy administrators. Day-to-day decisions are also handled by assistant and deputy administrators or directors who are assigned projects within the scope of their job.

Depending on the type of facility, administrators may have a great deal of direct contact with patients or this contact may be limited. For example, administrators of nursing homes or extended-care facilities will usually have more patient contact than their counterparts working in hospitals.

There is a great deal of responsibility in this type of job. For instance, administrators must prepare for periodic inspections by government agencies, insurance companies, and third-party reimbursers. These visits are extremely important to health care facilities. A negative report can mean fines, loss of public confidence, or the loss of revenue.

Health services administrators work long hours, often under tremendous pressure and in stressful situations. As all operational occurrences in the facility fall into their area of responsibility, they are always on call.

Employment Opportunities

Health services administrators may work as chief or executive administrators, assistants to the administrator, assistant administrators, or associate administrators. They work in a variety of health care settings including:

- Hospitals
- Nursing homes
- Extended-care facilities
- Health maintenance organizations
- Urgi-centers
- Surgi-centers
- Rehabilitation facilities
- Psychiatric facilities
- Large medical groups

Expanding Opportunities for the 21st Century

Because of the growing population of older Americans, the demand for more facilities dealing with both the aging population and long-term care is expected to increase significantly.

In addition, the anticipated availability of some type of universal health insurance will create unprecedented access to health care for those currently uninsured or underinsured.

Expanding opportunities will be found in home health agencies and HMOs.

EARNINGS

Earnings of health services administrators can vary tremendously depending on a number of factors. These include the specific facility or agency, size, prestige, location, and type of ownership. Other factors are the responsibilities, duties, education, and experience.

Annual earnings for health services administrators can range from $40,000 to $175,000 or more. Individuals with limited experience working in small facilities or agencies will earn salaries ranging from $40,000 to $50,000. Those working in larger facilities will have earnings from $50,000 to $70,000. Health services administrators with a great deal of experience and responsibility, working in very large facilities or multihospital systems can earn from $70,000 to $175,000 plus.

In addition to salaries, most health services administrators receive liberal benefit packages to augment their earnings.

ADVANCEMENT OPPORTUNITIES

Health services administrators can advance their careers in a number of ways. Assistants to the director or administrator may become the assistant director or associate director.

Health services administrators can also progress by locating similar positions in larger, more complex facilities. This will result in increased responsibilities and earnings.

EDUCATION AND TRAINING

Health services administrators are usually required to have a master's degree in hospital administration, public health, or health administration. Master's degree programs in these areas are two to three years in duration and often include supervised administrative experience.

In order to be admitted to graduate school, individuals must have their bachelor's degree. Undergraduate majors may be in areas of business administration, health administration, liberal arts, and social sciences.

EXPERIENCE AND QUALIFICATIONS

Health service administrators gain experience through internships, in jobs as department heads, or in other managerial capacities.

State licensing is necessary for health service administrators working in nursing homes and long-term care facilities. In order to obtain a state license, individuals must complete a state-approved training program, continue their education and pass a licensing examination. Some states also have additional requirements.

FOR ADDITIONAL INFORMATION: Individuals interested in learning more about health care facility administration can obtain additional information from the American College of Healthcare Executives (ACHE), the Association of University Programs in Health Administration (AUPHA), the American College of Health Care Administrators (ACHCA), and the American Association of Homes for the Aging (AAHA).

TIPS

- Colleges and universities offering degrees in this field usually have job-placement services.
- Many cities host employment agencies specializing in careers in health care.
- Headhunters are another option for finding the perfect job.
- Job openings are often advertised in the classified sections of newspapers. Look under "Health Care," "Long-Term Care," "Facility Management," "Health Services Administrator," "Nursing Homes", "Health Care Management," and "Health Care Administration."

DISPENSING OPTICIAN

JOB DESCRIPTION: *Fill eyeglass prescriptions; assist customers in choosing frames; adjust finished glasses.*

EARNINGS: *$20,000 to $35,000.*

RECOMMENDED EDUCATION AND TRAINING: *Apprenticeship; associate degree in ophthalmic dispensing.*

SKILLS AND PERSONALITY TRAITS: *Manual dexterity; math and science skills; communication skills.*

EXPERIENCE AND QUALIFICATIONS: *State licensing.*

JOB DESCRIPTION AND RESPONSIBILITIES

The primary function of a dispensing optician is to prepare eyeglass or lens prescriptions provided by either optometrists or ophthalmologists.

Corrective lenses are made by grinding down special lens glass in a specific, measured, scientific manner. The prescription will tell a technician exactly how to prepare the lenses. Each prescription performs a different function. The goal is for the individual to see better by correcting the dysfunction with the prepared glasses.

When a customer comes into an optical store, the optician will either start a new patient chart, if the individual has never been there before, or pull that patient's chart out if he or she has previously used the store's services. Charts indicate prescriptions that have been filled before, and types of frames purchased.

The optician will also take measurements of the distance between the centers of the pupils of the eyes to determine where and how lenses should be placed.

In choosing frames, the customer's occupation, hairstyle, and features must be considered. Other selection indications include the weight and thickness of the corrective lenses. The dispensing optician will help customers try on frames until they find one that looks good and feels comfortable. In some cases, especially with children or people who have never worn glasses, choosing frames can be a traumatic experience. The optician must put the customer at ease and be patient.

Once frames have been chosen, the optician will process a work order to give to the ophthalmic laboratory. This will include information on the lens prescription, size, and color as well as the frame type. In some cases dispensing opticians, trained in this area, may do the actual lab work.

When the glasses are ready, the optician checks the power of the lenses with various instruments to make sure that they are what has been prescribed and adjusts the frames to the customer's head so that the fit is perfect.

Opticians may also fit contact lenses for customers. Individuals must take specific measurements and prepare work orders much the same as they do with glasses. However, a great deal of skill and accuracy is needed when taking these measurements. Opticians must examine the contact lenses in the customer's eyes to make sure that they fit properly.

Other functions of the dispensing optician may include keeping records and charts up to date, filling out forms and referring customers to ophthalmologists or optometrists.

Dispensing opticians work various hours depending on the hours of the store or business and are responsible to either the owner, manager, or optometrist in charge.

EMPLOYMENT OPPORTUNITIES

Dispensing opticians may be employed by:

- Optical chains or franchise stores
- Optical departments in department stores
- Optical departments in pharmacies

- Ophthalmologists
- Optometrists
- Privately owned optical shops

Expanding Opportunities for the 21st Century

As a result of the expanding middle-age and older adult population who usually need some type of corrective lenses, there will be a growing demand for dispensing opticians.

The greatest number of job opportunities will be located in large, metropolitan cities where there are more and larger optical shops and optical chain stores.

The biggest trend in this field is the one-stop shops for optical care where customers can have their eyes examined, choose frames, and have the glasses made within an hour.

EARNINGS

Earnings for dispensing opticians vary from approximately $20,000 to $35,000. Apprentices may earn approximately $15,000 while in training. Factors affecting salaries include the credentials, responsibilities, and experience of the individual. Other variables are the specific store, size, prestige, and geographic location where the dispensing optician works.

Individuals usually receive the highest salaries in states that require licensing. Dispensing opticians will also earn more working in larger, metropolitan areas.

ADVANCEMENT OPPORTUNITIES

Dispensing opticians can advance by obtaining additional training and experience. They may start out as apprentices and become full-fledged dispensing opticians. Others locate similar jobs in larger, more prestigious stores paying higher salaries.

Many dispensing opticians become managers of optical stores. Some become sales representatives for wholesalers or manufacturers of glasses, lenses, or frames. There are also individuals who go into business for themselves.

EDUCATION AND TRAINING

Education and training requirements for dispensing opticians vary from job to job and state to state. A great deal of the training is done on the job in the form of apprenticeship.

Formal training programs in opticianry are offered in community colleges, colleges, and universities. Only some of these programs are accredited by the Commission on Opticianry Accreditation. Schools that are accredited award two-year associate degrees in ophthalmic dispensing.

Some dispensing opticians receive basic training through programs designed for ophthalmic laboratory personnel. These are offered by many vocational-technical schools and trade schools throughout the country. Duration varies from just a few weeks to a year. After completion, individuals may become dispensing optician apprentices.

Many people in this field are trained totally on the job. In states where licensing is required, individuals must usually register with the state as apprentices and train for two to five years. On-the-job training may be informal or consist of structured programs that include technical training as well as office management, bookkeeping, and sales.

Individuals who go through accredited programs in states requiring licensing may be allowed to take licensing exams soon after graduation. This allows states to eliminate all or most of the two-to-five-year apprenticeship.

EXPERIENCE AND QUALIFICATIONS

Experience requirements vary from employer to employer. Trainee positions generally do not require any experience while higher level jobs do.

Qualifications also vary depending on the state. Some require dispensing opticians to be licensed. In order to obtain this license, individuals must usually go through an apprenticeship program and take an examination. To keep the license, dispensing opticians may have to take continuing education courses.

FOR ADDITIONAL INFORMATION: Individuals interested in careers as dispensing opticians can contact the Opticians Association of America (OAA), the National Academy of Opticianry (NAO), and the Commission of Opticianry Accreditation (COA) for more information.

TIPS

- Large chain stores may offer structured, apprentice training programs. These provide excellent opportunities for individuals to receive good training.
- Jobs may be advertised in the newspaper's classified section under headings such as "Dispensing Optician," "Eye Care," "Optical Department," "Fashion Eye Glass Shop," "Eyewear," or the names of optical stores.
- Send your resume with a short cover letter to the owner or manager of optical shops, optical chains or franchise stores, ophthalmologists, or optometrists.
- Walk into optical shops and optical chain or franchise stores and ask if there are any openings.

PHARMACIST

JOB DESCRIPTION: *Dispense prescribed medication; advise on use and side effects of medicines; recommend over-the-counter medicines; maintain accurate records of prescribed customer medications.*

EARNINGS: *$30,000 to $60,000+*

RECOMMENDED EDUCATION AND TRAINING: *Degree from accredited college of pharmacy.*

SKILLS AND PERSONALITY TRAITS: *Knowledge of drugs and interactions; interpersonal skills; reliability; computer skills.*

EXPERIENCE AND QUALIFICATIONS: *Practical experience or internship; state licensing.*

Job Description and Responsibilities

Pharmacists usually work in pharmacies. They are responsible for dispensing medicines and drugs that have been prescribed by physicians, dentists, and other health practitioners.

When filling prescriptions for customers, pharmacists usually explain procedures for using the drug, possible side effects, and other medications, foods, or elements to avoid when taking the medication. For example, some medications cause side effects if taken with milk. Others may lose their effectiveness when alcohol is consumed. The pharmacist must be aware of everything to avoid when taking a medication as well as all the side effects.

Pharmacists keep a record of patient's prescriptions on a computer or in a card file. This allows the pharmacist to determine which medications are being taken to see if they can be combined. This is especially important when a number of different physicians are all prescribing medicines.

Pharmacists may assist customers in choosing over-the-counter medicines for a variety of ailments including the common cold, athlete's foot, tooth pain, headaches, and backaches. Many times pharmacists refer customers to a physician for further assistance. They may also answer many health-related questions themselves. It is important that the pharmacist be aware of all the health care supplies and medical equipment sold in the store and be able to advise customers on which product best suits their needs.

They must keep accurate records of all prescriptions filled and payments received. Pharmacists may be responsible for billing insurance companies and health maintenance organizations. This must be done on a timely basis in order to obtain reimbursement.

In some states there are mandatory inventories of all narcotics, needles, and syringes. Depending on the situation they are working in, pharmacists may be responsible for ordering drugs, medical supplies, and equipment.

Other functions of pharmacists working in stores may include managing the pharmacy and the store, supervising store personnel, displaying items, taking cash for purchases, and talking with sales reps. Individuals working in hospitals or health care facilities might also be responsible for evaluating the use of certain drugs in patient care, offering patient education programs, teaching students, and performing administrative duties.

Pharmacists' hours vary depending on the setting they are working in. Some work nights and weekends. Those who own stores will usually work longer hours than employees. Pharmacists may be responsible to either the manager or owner of a store or the head of the pharmacy department if they are working in a hospital. Those who own their stores are responsible to themselves. However, they must keep their customers happy or the customers will go elsewhere. Pharmacists must follow all rules and regulations of the state and federal governments regarding the dispensing of pharmaceuticals.

EMPLOYMENT OPPORTUNITIES

Pharmacists can work in a variety of settings including:

- Pharmacies (community and chain stores)
- Pharmacy departments in supermarkets
- Pharmacy departments in department stores
- Hospitals
- Health maintenance organizations
- Home health agencies
- Clinics
- Nursing homes
- Extended-care facilities

There are also pharmacists who specialize in various fields. These include the radiopharmacists who prepare and dispense radioactive pharmaceuticals. Another field of specialization is called pharmacotherapy. Pharmacists in this area work with physicians to determine drug therapy.

Expanding Opportunities for the 21st Century

Employment of pharmacists will grow faster than average for all occupations in the new century.

Pharmacists will be required in more settings as a result of research and technological advances that are resulting in new drugs to prevent and treat diseases.

Because senior citizens use nearly twice as many prescription medications as younger people, the increase in the number of senior citizens will result in a greater demand for pharmacists. The need for pharmacists will be especially great in states hosting a large aging population.

EARNINGS

Pharmacists earn from $30,000 to $60,000 or more with an average salary of $40,000 to $50,000. Pharmacists who own their own store or belong to a partnership will have higher earnings.

Earnings vary greatly depending on the individual's experience, duties, and responsibilities as well as the specific type of position. Size, prestige, and geographical location of the pharmacy are also factors.

ADVANCEMENT OPPORTUNITIES

Pharmacists can advance in a number of different ways. They may gain experience and obtain jobs in larger or more prestigious settings. Others land supervisory positions such as store manager or pharmacy supervisor. Advanced positions in hospitals and health care facilities include director and assistant director of pharmacy services.

Many pharmacists move ahead by becoming owners or part owners of pharmacies.

EDUCATION AND TRAINING

Pharmacists must graduate from a college of pharmacy accredited by the American Council on Pharmaceutical Education. The minimum requirement for pharmacists includes at least five years of college resulting in a Bachelor of Science or a Bachelor of Pharmacy degree.

Some individuals choose to obtain a Doctor of Pharmacy degree or Pharm. D. A bachelor's degree is not required to enter this type of program. Instead, the aspiring pharmacist will go through six years of school in a combined bachelor's and doctoral program. (A bachelor's degree is not awarded.) Those who choose to obtain a bachelor's first may also go on for a doctoral degree, but it will usually take longer.

Individuals can also obtain a Master of Science degree in pharmacy if they are interested in research, teaching, or administrative positions.

Entrance requirements to colleges of pharmacy vary. Some schools require individuals to take the Pharmacy College Admissions Test (PCAT). Others require up to two years of prepharmacy education in an accredited two-year school, college, or university. Some schools will admit students after graduation from high school.

EXPERIENCE AND QUALIFICATIONS

All pharmacists must be licensed in the state in which they are working. Most states offer reciprocity. Individuals applying for a license must be at least 21 years old and demonstrate good character. Other requirements include graduating from an accredited college of pharmacy, passing a state board examination, and obtaining either a certain amount of practical experience or going through an internship under the supervision of a licensed pharmacist.

In order to renew the license, many states mandate continuing education.

FOR ADDITIONAL INFORMATION: Individuals interested in becoming pharmacists can obtain additional information by contacting the American Association of Colleges of Pharmacy (AACP), the American Society of Hospital Pharmacists (ASHP), and the National Association of Boards of Pharmacy (NABP).

Tips

- You might talk to pharmacists to learn more about their job and the field in general.
- Interview for several jobs before accepting one. Duties and responsibilities will be different in various settings.
- Large chain stores and major health care facilities often offer better benefits than small community pharmacies.
- Positions are often advertised in the classified sections of the newspaper under the headings "Pharmacist," "Medical," "Health Related," "Health Care Facility," or "Hospital."

RADIOLOGIC TECHNOLOGIST

JOB DESCRIPTION: *Operate radiologic and imaging equipment; prepare patients for procedures; adjust equipment.*

EARNINGS: *$19,000 to $43,000.*

RECOMMENDED EDUCATION AND TRAINING: *Formal training varies; most common training is a 24-month program leading to an associate degree.*

SKILLS AND PERSONALITY TRAITS: *Compassion; communication skills; understanding of medical terminology; personableness.*

EXPERIENCE AND QUALIFICATIONS: *Licensing necessary in some states; certification and registration preferred.*

Job Description and Responsibilities

Not many years ago, radiologic technologists used mostly X-ray equipment to determine broken bones and the extent of injuries, and to diagnose various illnesses. Today, modern technology has increased the kinds of radiologic and imaging equipment and techniques used in health care to include ultrasound machines, magnetic resonance scanners, positron emission scanners, and more. As a result, the role of radiologic technologists is expanding.

The radiologic technologist is responsible for preparing patients for radiological tests, explaining the technique to be used, and answering any questions the patient may have. The technologist is responsible for making sure that patients have removed all jewelry or other metal objects that would interfere with X rays or other radiologic pictures.

For some procedures, the technologist will prepare a contrast medium for the patient to drink before having a procedure. When the patient drinks the medium, the radiologist can follow its flow through the body with images created on a screen. The radiologic technologist will assist the physician during this procedure by readjusting the patient's body and taking radiographs at the appropriate times.

The radiologic technologist is responsible for determining the correct distance and angle of the equipment in relation to the patient's body as well as the desired exposure time. Because too much radiation can be dangerous, it is important to use only as much as necessary to create a clear picture. Once images have been taken, the radiologic technologist is responsible for processing the film and getting it ready for the radiologist to read.

Other methods of imaging use ultrasound waves. Radiologic technologists who administer this type of procedure may be called sonographers or ultrasound technologists. The sonogram is widely used on pregnant women to determine the position, size, and health of the fetus. It is used for other procedures as well, such as diagnosis of tumors and cysts.

Another method of imaging uses magnetic fields instead of radiation or sound waves. This is called magnetic resonance imaging (MRI). This process is becoming increasingly popular for diagnosis of various illnesses.

The radiologic technologist must have a physician's order to perform any imaging techniques or procedures. The individual must keep records of all patients seen and procedures completed.

Radiologic technologists are usually responsible to the director of the radiology department if they are working in a health care facility or a physician if they are working in a doctor's office setting.

EMPLOYMENT OPPORTUNITIES

Full- and part-time jobs are available for qualified radiologic technologists throughout the country. Individuals can work in a variety of health care situations including:

- Hospitals
- Mobile imaging clinics
- Physicians' offices
- Health maintenance organizations
- Diagnostic imaging centers
- Radiological groups
- Nursing homes
- Extended-care treatment facilities

Expanding Opportunities for the 21st Century

As a result of the growing number of older people in this country, there will be a need for radiologic technologists who have specialized training working with the nonradioactive imaging techniques such as MRIs and ultrasound. Many diseases more prominent in aging people use these techniques for diagnostic purposes.

There will also be a need for radiologic technologists trained in radiation therapy.

With increased emphasis on outpatient care, radiologic technologists will find a great many new jobs in physicians' offices, clinics, and diagnostic imaging centers.

EARNINGS

Annual earnings for full-time radiologic technologists range from approximately $19,000 to $43,000, depending on the specific health care facility as well as its size, prestige, and geographic location. Other factors include the responsibilities, experience, and training of the technologist. As a rule, the more specialized the training of the individual, the higher the salary.

ADVANCEMENT OPPORTUNITIES

Radiologic technologists can advance by obtaining additional or more specialized training. Individuals may then move into positions of specialization in the facility that they are currently working in or another larger or more prestigious facility.

Radiologic technologists may also advance their careers by assuming supervisory positions.

EDUCATION AND TRAINING

Education and training programs vary with the specialty. Prerequisites usually include a high school diploma or equivalency. The most common training program for radiologic technologists specializing in X-ray technology usually consists of a twenty-four-month course of study in radiography leading to an associate degree in applied science. There are, however, four-year programs that lead to bachelor's degrees or shorter programs that award certificates upon completion.

Radiologic technologists interested in specializing in sonography may take a one-year program in diagnostic medical sonography and receive a certificate.

Radiologic technologists who would like to specialize in the field of magnetic resonance imaging (MRI) may be trained by the equipment manufacturer of the MRI machine. Some hospitals also provide training programs for this specialty.

There are also one-year certificate programs that individuals already working in the health care field can use to obtain specialized training.

EXPERIENCE AND QUALIFICATIONS

The necessity of the licensing is determined by the specific state in which individuals are working.

Professional credentials or registration in the field may be preferred for some jobs. Registration for radiological technologists is done by the American Registry of Radiologic Technologists (ARRT). Individuals specializing in sonography may be certified by the American Registry of Diagnostic Medical Sonographers (ARDMS).

FOR ADDITIONAL INFORMATION: There are a number of organizations and associations that provide career information for radiologic technologists. These include the American Society of Radiologic Technologists (ASRT), the Society of Diagnostic Medical Sonographers (SDMS), the Division of Allied Health Education and Accreditation of the American Medical Association, the American Registry of Radiologic Technologists (ARRT), and the American Registry of Diagnostic Medical Sonographers (ARDMS).

TIPS

- All hospitals do not have MRI equipment. If the facility you are working in does not have the machinery, you might want to contact a manufacturer to learn about training opportunities.
- Job openings are frequently advertised in the newspaper classified section under the headings: "Radiology," "Radiologic Technologist," "X Ray," "Sonographers," "Ultrasound," "Mobile Imaging Clinics," "Health Care," "Health Maintenance Organizations," "Diagnostic Imaging Centers," etc.
- After you have obtained general training, you can improve your career opportunities by continuing to take courses in specialized fields.
- Many cities have employment agencies specializing in the health care field.

PHYSICAL THERAPIST

JOB DESCRIPTION: *Evaluate patients' physical therapy needs; perform physical therapies.*

EARNINGS: *$20,000 to $58,000+.*

RECOMMENDED EDUCATION AND TRAINING: *Bachelor's degree in physical therapy, master's degree, or certificate program.*

SKILLS AND PERSONALITY TRAITS: *Mechanical aptitude; physical stamina; patience; communication skills.*

EXPERIENCE AND QUALIFICATIONS: *Experience in physical therapy setting helpful.*

JOB DESCRIPTION AND RESPONSIBILITIES

Physical therapy is used for a number of purposes. These include helping people to ease pain and recover from injuries, accidents or illness. Therapy can also help people regain the use of body parts. Patients may be born with physical disabilities or become disabled through strokes, heart attacks, accidents, or sports injuries.

Physical therapists evaluate and assess the therapy needs of patients and then develop, prescribe, and perform these procedures.

After evaluating a patient and performing a range of procedures, the physical therapist must reevaluate the therapy and revise it if necessary. The therapeutic plan of care may take a few weeks, a few months, or many years, depending on the severity of the problem.

During the course of his or her work, the physical therapist will come in contact with a variety of rehabilitative personnel including physiatrists, physical therapy assistants, and physical therapy aides. In some situations, the therapist will give instructions to assistants and aides to carry out. In others, he or she will illustrate therapies directly to the patients or their families so that they can be done at home.

Physical therapists are responsible for keeping records and other documentation on patients. These records chart progress and therapies used.

Other duties of the physical therapist may include participating in conferences with the patient and his or her family, and the nursing staff and/or a social services department representative. If the therapist is in a supervisory position, he or she may also be required to order necessary equipment, schedule daily work loads, assess departmental needs, and assist in the maintenance of the physical environment of the therapy department.

As most facilities schedule appointments during the day, physical therapists will usually work fairly normal hours. There are, however, some facilities that have therapists on staff 24 hours a day. Others may schedule sessions during the evening hours or on weekends.

Physical therapists report to a number of superiors, depending on the specific facility and its organization. These include the head physical therapist or physical therapist supervisor, the facilities physiatrist, or the director of rehabilitative services.

Employment Opportunities

Qualified physical therapists will be able to find employment opportunities in almost every type of health care facility including:

- Hospitals
- Rehabilitation centers
- Nursing homes
- Extended-care facilities
- Sports medicine clinics
- Private practice
- Independent physical therapy centers

Expanding Opportunities for the 21st Century

The need for physical therapists will grow in the new century as a result of advances in medical technology, expanding senior population, and prevailing interest in health promotion. Trends indicate that there will be an especially high demand in hospitals and extended-care facilities. Opportunities will also increase for physical therapists working in the field of sports medicine.

Earnings

Earnings for physical therapists vary greatly, depending on the specific facility, its size, prestige, and the geographical location in which an individual is working. Other variables include the responsibilities, experience, and education of the physical therapist.

Annual salaries range from $20,000 to $58,000 plus. Compensation is usually augmented by liberal benefit packages.

Advancement Opportunities

One way physical therapists can advance their careers is by becoming physical therapy supervisors. Another is to locate a similar position in a larger, more prestigious facility. This will result in increased earnings and responsibilities. Some physical therapists enter private practice as a method of climbing the career ladder.

Education and Training

A physical therapist is required to be a graduate of an approved school of physical therapy. Requirements vary for the type of degree the therapist must hold, depending on the position and state regulations. Individuals may need a bachelor of science degree or a master's degree with a major in physical therapy or a certificate from a licensed school. Many career changers who have bachelor's degrees in other subjects opt for the certificate program. Physical therapists must pass an examination after graduation to be registered and licensed.

EXPERIENCE AND QUALIFICATIONS

Experience working in a physical therapy setting is useful. This experience may be obtained by working as a physical therapy assistant or aide. Hands-on experience in school is also useful.

Many states require that physical therapists be licensed. Check with individual states to determine specific licensing requirements.

FOR ADDITIONAL INFORMATION: The American Physical Therapy Association (APTA) provides educational guidance and support for people in the physical therapy field.

TIPS

- Openings for physical therapists are advertised in the classified section of newspapers under headings such as "Physical Therapy," "Therapists," "Health Care," "Hospitals," and "Sports Medicine."

- Send your resume and a short cover letter requesting an interview to the personnel department of hospitals and other health care facilities. Ask that they keep your resume on file if a position is not currently available.

- Contact the placement office of the college you are attending (or have attended) to find out about job possibilities.

- There are a number of employment agencies around the country specializing in the health care industry. Before you use one of these agencies be sure to find out who pays the fee when you get a job, you or the employer.

PHYSICAL THERAPY ASSISTANT

JOB DESCRIPTION: *Assist physical therapist; administer therapy; handle paperwork.*

EARNINGS: *$15,000 to $28,000.*

RECOMMENDED EDUCATION AND TRAINING: *Associate degree from an accredited college.*

SKILLS AND PERSONALITY TRAITS: *Compassion; positive attitude; enthusiasm; ability to follow instructions.*

EXPERIENCE AND QUALIFICATIONS: *Health care experience is useful, but not required.*

Job Description and Responsibilities

Physical therapy eases pain and helps people recover from injuries, accidents, and illnesses. It also helps those with physical disabilities or those who become disabled by strokes, heart attacks, accidents, etc.

Physical therapists are responsible for evaluating and assessing the therapy needs of patients and then developing, prescribing, and performing these procedures or therapies. Physical therapy assistants are the paraprofessionals who work with the health care professional, assisting them in fulfilling their functions. They work under the supervision of physicians, physical therapists, physiatrists, and rehabilitation specialists.

One of the functions of a physical therapy assistant is to help the physical therapist or physiatrist evaluate new patients. The PT assistant may be given orders to put a patient through a specific battery of tests to learn the extent of the injury or problem.

One of the jobs of the physical therapy assistant is to help a patient not only ease the pain, but also learn how to deal with it. This may be accomplished by providing various treatments including heat therapy or hydrotherapy such as whirlpool baths or wet packs. After working with patients, the physical therapy assistant may help the physical therapist reevaluate them.

The individual will be required to handle a great deal of the paperwork including patient records concerning problems, capabilities, treatments, and progress.

Physical therapy assistants work fairly normal hours. Therapy sessions are usually scheduled during the day; however, some facilities require evening or nighttime shifts. The individual is responsible directly to the head physical therapist, physiatrist, or rehabilitation specialist depending on the institution he or she is working in.

Employment Opportunities

Due to a nationwide shortage of qualified physical therapists and physical therapy assistants, employment opportunities can be located almost anywhere in the country on a full-time or part-time basis. Most health care institutions have more than one physical therapy assistant on staff. Opportunities for physical therapy assistants are available in a variety of health care facilities including:

- Hospitals
- Rehabilitation centers
- Nursing homes
- Extended-care facilities
- Sports medicine clinics
- Independent physical therapy centers
- Private practice

Expanding Opportunities for the 21st Century

Jobs in this field are abundant and projections indicate that the strong demand will continue in the future. Expanding opportunities for the new century will be in hospitals, nursing homes, and extended-care facilities.

EARNINGS

Physical therapy assistants earn approximately $15,000 to $28,000 annually. Most full-time employees also receive benefits.

Variables affecting salaries include the specific size and prestige of the facility, and the geographic location an individual is working in as well as how great the demand for people in this field is at the time. Other factors affecting earnings include the PT assistant's education, experience, and responsibilities.

ADVANCEMENT OPPORTUNITIES

Opportunities for advancement are excellent for physical therapy assistants who want to continue their education. Individuals taking an additional two-year training program at a school with an accredited program in physical therapy can become full-fledged physical therapists.

EDUCATION AND TRAINING

The minimum educational requirements for most physical therapy assistants is an associate's degree from an accredited college offering a physical therapy or physical therapy assistant program.

EXPERIENCE AND QUALIFICATIONS

PT assistants must have the physical stamina to lift and move equipment and people. It is also imperative that people in this field feel comfortable working in a health care facility and around people who are ill. Before getting involved in a career in physical therapy, some individuals get volunteer or part-time experience working in health care facilities.

FOR ADDITIONAL INFORMATION: Additional information for people interested in a career as a physical therapy assistant is provided by the American Physical Therapy Association (APTA). This organization provides educational guidance and professional support for people in the physical therapy field.

TIPS

- The placement office of an accredited college offering a program in physical therapy may be aware of openings.
- Openings for physical therapy assistants are often advertised in the classified section in the newspaper or professional trade journals. Look under headings such as "Physical Therapy," "Physical Therapy Assistant," "Therapists," "Paraprofessional," "Health Care," "Hospitals," or "Sports Medicine."

- Send your resume with a short cover letter to the personnel director of health care facilities in the geographic areas you want to work in.

OCCUPATIONAL THERAPIST

JOB DESCRIPTION: *Evaluate patients; develop activities to help make patient more independent.*

EARNINGS: *$31,000 to $50,000+.*

RECOMMENDED EDUCATION AND TRAINING: *Bachelor's degree, certificate program, or master's degree in occupational therapy.*

SKILLS AND PERSONALITY TRAITS: *Imagination; patience; emotional stability; communication skills; adaptability; creativity.*

EXPERIENCE AND QUALIFICATIONS: *Experience in health care setting helpful.*

JOB DESCRIPTION AND RESPONSIBILITIES

Occupational therapy is used for a number of purposes, including helping patients learn to live more independent and productive lifestyles. Patients may have mental, physical, emotional, or developmental disabling conditions. Occupational therapists evaluate and assess the therapy needs of patients. Therapists then develop activities to help patients develop and maintain daily living and work skills.

In some cases a patient may have permanently lost basic motor functions or reasoning abilities. The therapist must then come up with ways to compensate for this loss of function. In other situations, patients may have only temporarily lost these skills and need to relearn them or adapt during an illness or recovery period.

Therapists may use a variety of activities including dressing, cooking, and eating to increase strength and dexterity. Simple games may be used to improve vision, hand-eye coordination, etc. Time-management skills, budgeting, shopping, and the like may be taught to patients with mental or emotional problems who need to learn how to live more independently. Occupational therapists may also help patients look for, find, and keep a job.

Other functions of occupational therapists may include adapting, designing, or making equipment to help those with permanent function disabilities, such as those with cerebral palsy or muscular dystrophy. Individuals may be expected to teach patients to operate computer-operated wheelchairs or communications devices.

After evaluating a patient and teaching a range of skills, occupational therapists must reevaluate to see if their methods are working. Occupational therapists must keep records and other documentation on patients. These records chart progress and therapies used.

Other duties of the occupational therapist may include participating in conferences with the patient and/or his or her physician, family, teachers, and/or a social services department representative.

Occupational therapists usually find their jobs very rewarding when they see patients responding, learning new skills, and leading happier, more productive lives.

EMPLOYMENT OPPORTUNITIES

Qualified occupational therapists will be able to find employment opportunities in almost every type of health care facility, including:

- Hospitals and other health care facilities
- Rehabilitation centers
- Home health agencies
- Nursing homes and other extended-care facilities
- Adult day-care facilities
- Schools
- Sports medicine clinics
- Private practice

Expanding Opportunities for the 21st Century:

The need for occupational therapists will grow in the new century as a result of the prevailing interest in rehabilitation and long-term care services, as well as in the growing aging population. Trends indicate that there will be an especially high demand in hospitals, nursing homes, extended-care facilities, and HMOs. Other expanding opportunities will be for those in private practice.

EARNINGS

Annual salaries can range from $31,000 to $50,000 plus. Earnings for occupational therapists vary greatly depending on a number of factors. These include the prestige, size, and geographic location of the facility in which an individual is working. Other variables include the responsibilities, duties, experience, and education of the occupational therapist. Therapists who are self-employed usually earn more than their salaried counterparts.

ADVANCEMENT OPPORTUNITIES

One way an occupational therapist can advance his or her career is by becoming an occupational therapy supervisor. Another is to locate a similar position in a larger, more prestigious facility. This will result in increased earnings and responsibilities. Some occupational therapists enter private practice as a method of climbing the career ladder.

EDUCATION AND TRAINING

Occupational therapists are required to have a minimum of a bachelor's degree. There are close to 70 colleges offering bachelor's degree programs in this field. There are also a number of post-bachelor's degree certificate programs offered to students holding a degree in an area other than occupational therapy. Master's degree programs are also available throughout the country.

EXPERIENCE AND QUALIFICATIONS

Experience working or volunteering in any type of health care setting is useful. Courses in high school biology, physics, health, art, chemistry, and social sciences will be helpful.

Many states require a license to practice occupational therapy. This can be obtained by having a degree or a post-bachelor's certificate from an accredited program, as well as by passing a national certification exam offered by the American Occupational Therapy Certification Board. Individuals passing the test and meeting these requirements become registered occupational therapists.

FOR ADDITIONAL INFORMATION: The American Occupational Therapy Association (AOTA) provides educational guidance and support for people interested in this field.

TIPS

- Openings for occupational therapists are advertised in the classified section of newspapers under headings such as "Occupational Therapy," "Therapists," "Health Care," "Hospitals," and "Education."

- Contact the placement office of the college you are attending (or have attended) to find out about job possibilities.

- Send your resume and a short cover letter requesting an interview to the personnel department of hospitals, other health care facilities, and school systems. Ask that they keep your resume on file if a position is not currently available.

- You should also send your resume to nursing homes and other extended care facilities, adult day-care centers, independent living centers, and home health agencies.

- There are a number of employment agencies around the country specializing in the health care industry. Before getting involved with one of these agencies, check to see who pays the fee when you get a job—you or the employer.

MUSIC THERAPIST

JOB DESCRIPTION: *Use music to treat physical, mental, and/or emotional disabilities.*

EARNINGS: *$16,000 to $45,000+.*

RECOMMENDED EDUCATION AND TRAINING: *Minimum of a bachelor's degree in music therapy; many positions require a master's degree.*

SKILLS AND PERSONALITY TRAITS: *Ability to play a musical instrument and sing; compassion; comfortable working with handicapped and/or emotionally disturbed patients.*

EXPERIENCE AND QUALIFICATIONS: *Internship in music therapy.*

JOB DESCRIPTION AND RESPONSIBILITIES

Music therapists use music and musical activities to treat physical, mental, and/or emotional disabilities. Music therapy is often used with other alternative expressive art therapies to make a breakthrough with a patient when other therapies have failed.

The music therapist works with other health professionals including physicians, nurses, teachers, physical therapists, dance therapists, psychologists, and psychiatrists. Depending on the specific job and patient, the music therapist may have varied duties. Those who work in hospitals, nursing homes, or extended-care facilities may be responsible for bringing a group of patients together to sing for the facility staff and other patients. The goal with this type of exercise is to encourage patients to come out of their shells and build self-confidence.

The music therapist may be responsible for planning musical activities for one patient at a time or for a group. He or she may teach patients new tunes or play tapes to help withdrawn patients reminisce, remember, and get involved. The therapist may work with handicapped patients, attempting to give them a renewed sense of accomplishment.

As with most therapy, music therapists must realize that progress may be slow. The slightest amount of progress can mean a great deal to a patient and his or her family.

EMPLOYMENT OPPORTUNITIES

There are more opportunities for music therapists than there are qualified people to fill positions. Music therapists work in a variety of situations including:

- Hospitals
- Rehabilitation centers
- Prisons
- Nursing homes
- Extended-care facilities
- Schools
- Independent expressive arts therapy centers

Expanding Opportunities for the 21st Century

As a result of the increasing aging population, there will be a great demand for music therapists in nursing homes, rehabilitation centers, and extended-care facilities.

EARNINGS

Music therapists just entering the field can earn from $16,000 to $20,000 annually. Those working at larger facilities who have experience may earn from $21,000 to $35,000. Supervisory positions in the field offer annual earnings of $38,000 to $45,000 and up.

ADVANCEMENT OPPORTUNITIES

Therapists can advance by obtaining supervisory or administrative positions. This type of advancement, however, limits the contact a therapist has with patients. Music therapists can also locate a position in research or teaching. Another option to consider is private practice or consulting.

EDUCATION AND TRAINING

Music therapists must have at least a bachelor's degree in music therapy. Some positions require a master's degree. Courses usually include music theory, voice studies, instrument lessons, psychology, sociology, and biology. Those who aspire to work in the public school system must also have a teaching degree.

EXPERIENCE AND QUALIFICATIONS

Music therapists must be licensed in order to work in most positions. Licensing requirements include a six-month internship program. Individuals may gain additional experience by working at health care facilities or schools part time or in voluntary positions.

FOR ADDITIONAL INFORMATION: To learn more about the music therapy field, contact the National Association for Music Therapy, Inc. (NAMT), and the American Association for Music Therapy (AAMT).

TIPS

- Positions for music therapists are available through the federal government. Contact your state's employment service for more information.

- Register with the placement service offered by the National Association for Music Therapy, Inc. and the American Association for Music Therapy.
- Jobs may be advertised in the classified section of newspapers under "Music Therapist," "Health Care," "Expressive Arts Therapist," or "Therapy."

DANCE THERAPIST

JOB DESCRIPTION: *Use dance to treat physical, mental, and/or emotional disabilities.*

EARNINGS: *$18,000 to $55,000+.*

RECOMMENDED EDUCATION AND TRAINING: *Master's degree necessary.*

SKILLS AND PERSONALITY TRAITS: *Dance skills; compassion; ability to work with handicapped and disabled people.*

EXPERIENCE AND QUALIFICATIONS: *Internship required.*

JOB DESCRIPTION AND RESPONSIBILITIES

A dance therapist uses dance, movement, and related activities to treat disabled and handicapped patients. The individual must have extensive knowledge and understanding of body movement and what it can accomplish. Dance therapy is often used with other expressive arts therapies to make a breakthrough with a patient who cannot be reached in any other way.

The function of a dance therapist is to provide a patient with a means of expression. Dance therapists work with doctors, nurses, teachers, physical therapists, musical therapists, psychologists, and psychiatrists to help restore an individual's health.

Working with one patient at a time or a group, the individual may teach a variety of dance forms. The therapist may also have the patient move freely to observe his or her movements and facial expressions. It is important to realize that what works for one patient will not always help another.

This job can be very fulfilling. Watching a patient with an unhealthy emotional or physical status improve through the personal efforts of the therapist is very rewarding.

EMPLOYMENT OPPORTUNITIES

Employment prospects are excellent for dance therapists. There are more positions for qualified individuals than people to fill them. Work settings include:

- Hospitals
- Extended-care facilities
- Schools
- Psychiatric hospitals
- Mental health centers
- Rehabilitation centers
- Nursing homes
- Correctional facilities
- Expressive arts therapy centers

Expanding Opportunities for the 21st Century

As a result of the increasing aging population, jobs will be especially plentiful in extended-care facilities and nursing homes.

EARNINGS

Dance therapists can earn between $18,000 and $55,000 plus. Average yearly salaries in this line of work run between $33,000 and $40,000 and are usually augmented by benefits. Factors affecting earnings include the specific facility an individual is working for, its size, prestige, and geographic location as well as the individual's experience, responsibilities, and educational level.

ADVANCEMENT OPPORTUNITIES

With drive and determination, dance therapists can advance their careers by moving into supervisory positions such as director of recreation therapy or expressive arts therapy.

Therapists may locate similar positions at more prestigious facilities or go into private practice.

EDUCATION AND TRAINING

A dance therapist must hold a master's degree in order to be employed in most facilities. Educational requirements for dance therapists are set by the American Dance Therapy Association. This certifying group has approved the graduate programs of a number of colleges and universities throughout the country. If the individual does not attend one of the approved schools, the ADTA also has alternative education requirements.

Dance therapists hold undergraduate degrees in a variety of areas including liberal arts, dance, psychology, or physical education.

EXPERIENCE AND QUALIFICATIONS

Dance therapists must be registered with the American Dance Therapy Association for most positions. In order to be registered, a dance therapist must fulfill certain educational requirements and obtain practical experience. This is usually achieved through an approved internship program.

FOR ADDITIONAL INFORMATION: The American Dance Therapy Association provides educational and professional support and guidance to members as well as individuals interested in becoming dance therapists. It is also the registering agency for people in this profession.

TIPS

- Job openings are advertised in the classified section of the newspaper under the headings: "Dance Therapy," "Health Care," "Therapists," "Recreation Therapy," "Expressive Arts Therapists," etc.
- The state and federal governments often have openings for dance therapists. These are usually civil service jobs and can be located through your state or federal employment service.
- Make sure you register with your college's job-placement office.

VETERINARIAN

JOB DESCRIPTION: *Prevent, diagnose, and treat illness, diseases, and injuries in animals.*

EARNINGS: *$30,000 to $100,000+.*

RECOMMENDED EDUCATION AND TRAINING: *Doctor of Veterinary Medicine degree from an accredited college of veterinary medicine.*

SKILLS AND PERSONALITY TRAITS: *Compassion; enjoy working with and helping animals; scientific aptitude.*

EXPERIENCE AND QUALIFICATIONS: *State licensing required.*

JOB DESCRIPTION AND RESPONSIBILITIES

Veterinarians work with animals of different sizes and breeds, preventing, diagnosing, and treating illness, disease, and injury. Duties vary depending on the specific type of practice.

Veterinarians performing general veterinary medicine are similar to family practitioners. They handle a number of different types of health problems. The vet may be responsible for giving animals general checkups, administering tests, or giving immunizations. If an owner brings in an animal that is having health problems, the vet must perform an examination to determine the cause and what the treatment should be.

In many cases, vets are called upon to perform surgery to correct a health problem or may perform routine spaying or neutering.

Veterinarians also practice preventive medicine on animals by administering rabies shots, performing heartworm tests, and advising pet owners on feeding, exercising, and grooming.

Vets handling larger animals such as cattle, horses, and sheep usually go to the farm where the animal is located to provide treatment. They perform many of the same functions as those taking care of smaller animals such as examining animals for diseases, treating problems, and administering vaccinations. Veterinarians may be required to visit the farm when an animal is expected to give birth if any problems are anticipated. They also perform tests on animals that provide food products such as milk, eggs, or beef to ensure public health and safety.

While veterinarians usually have set office hours, they may be called to take care of an emergency at any time.

EMPLOYMENT OPPORTUNITIES

There are a vast array of settings for a veterinarian to work in depending on the individual's interests. Some of these include:

- Veterinarian offices, clinics, and hospitals—private practice or in partnerships (working with small animals)
- Veterinarian clinics for large animals (farm animals such as horses, cows, and sheep as well as pigs, chickens, and turkeys)
- Zoos (resident or consulting veterinarian)
- Animal shelters
- Government agencies (including the Department of Agriculture and Public Health Service)
- Research labs (government or private industry)
- Colleges and universities

Expanding Opportunities for the 21st Century

As a result of the expanding pet population in the country, there is an increased need for veterinarians working in clinics and hospitals. Those who specialize in surgery will be especially in demand, as will veterinarians with specialties in toxicology, pathology, and laboratory animal medicine.

EARNINGS

Annual earnings depend on the specific type of work the individual is practicing and the geographic location. Veterinarians who are employed by a veterinary clinic or hospital will be paid from $40,000 to $60,000, depending on their experience and responsibilities.

Newly graduated vets entering private practice might have lower incomes ranging between $30,000 and $40,000. However, as they earn a reputation in the community and begin attracting more clients, their incomes expand considerably. Veterinarians in established private practices can earn between $45,000 and $80,000 or more. Surgeons or researchers in the field can earn $100,000 or more a year.

ADVANCEMENT OPPORTUNITIES

Vets who are in private practice can advance by building up a large roster of clients. Those working for zoos, private industry, shelters, or in government positions can get ahead by locating similar jobs in larger, more prestigious organizations. While some veterinarians take supervisory positions or teach, many choose not to take this path because it takes them away from the day-to-day contact with animals.

EDUCATION AND TRAINING

There are a limited number of colleges of veterinary medicine in the country and competition for entrance is fierce. Individuals must attend six years of college culminating in a Doctor of Veterinary Medicine degree (DVM). This will include a preveterinary course of study before attendance and graduation from an accredited college of veterinary medicine. In order to practice, individuals must also pass state examinations in the state in which they will be working.

EXPERIENCE AND QUALIFICATIONS

Veterinarians must be licensed in the state in which they are working. In order to obtain state licensing, individuals must complete the education requirements and pass the state boards.

FOR ADDITIONAL INFORMATION: For additional information, contact the American Veterinary Medical Association (AVMA) and the American Association of Veterinary Medicine Colleges (AAVMC).

TIPS

- Learn as much as you can about animals. Try to find a part-time or summer job in a vet's office to get hands-on experience. If this is not possible, consider a part-time or summer job in an animal shelter.
- Many large zoos sponsor internship programs.

VETERINARY TECHNICIAN

JOB DESCRIPTION: *Assist veterinarian in care of animals; collect specimens; assist in surgery; monitor improvement.*

EARNINGS: *$18,000 to $35,000.*

RECOMMENDED EDUCATION AND TRAINING: *Associate degree in animal technology or applied science.*

SKILLS AND PERSONALITY TRAITS: *Enjoyment in working with animals; strong stomach; ability to follow orders; scientific aptitude.*

EXPERIENCE AND QUALIFICATIONS: *Experience working with animals helpful; certification or state licensing may be required.*

JOB DESCRIPTION AND RESPONSIBILITIES

Individuals in this position assist veterinarians as nurses do physicians. Specific duties and responsibilities vary depending on the job.

Veterinary technicians handle many of the same tasks as veterinarians with the exception of diagnosing problems, performing surgery, and prescribing medication. Technicians do, however, assist in these functions. Technicians help prepare animals for surgery and assist with the anesthesia and during the surgery itself. They check to see that the animals are coming out of anesthesia properly and that their progress is going according to schedule. Technicians also administer medication under the direction of the veterinarian.

Veterinary technicians are sometimes called animal health technicians. They work closely with the animals, watching them and reporting any problems to the veterinarian. Individuals must keep tabs on the physical symptoms and well-being of the animals as well as their psychological attitude. While performing this task, technicians may comfort them, play with them, and give them extra or special attention.

Technicians may also be responsible for changing dressings, cleaning animals, or holding them while the veterinarian performs procedures. Individuals may be required to draw blood, administer tests, and collect specimens to check for heartworm, fleas, and ticks.

In some instances, technicians assist in managing the facility. Individuals may be required to schedule appointments, obtain case histories, keep records, and handle billing and bookkeeping. Other responsibilities include talking to owners to determine symptoms, explaining pre- or postsurgical care and clarifying instructions for medication, diet, or care.

Veterinary technicians are responsible to the veterinarian in charge of the facility. Hours will vary depending on the facility's schedule.

EMPLOYMENT OPPORTUNITIES

Veterinary technicians can work full or part time in a variety of animal care settings, including:

- Animal hospitals
- Animal shelters
- Private veterinary clinics
- Zoos
- Humane societies
- Sanctuaries
- Horse farms
- Kennels

Expanding Opportunities for the 21st Century

With the increased concern for animal welfare, there will be a demand for veterinary technicians working in animal shelters and humane societies. Additional opportunities will also be found in veterinarian offices where techs will do more of the routine work.

EARNINGS

Veterinary technician's earn between $18,000 and $35,000 annually. Factors affecting salaries include the experience and duties of the individual as well as the type, size, prestige, and geographic location of the facility.

Veterinary technicians with a great deal of responsibility and experience working in facilities in metropolitan areas will have earnings toward the upper end of the scale.

ADVANCEMENT OPPORTUNITIES

Veterinary technicians can advance by locating similar positions in larger or more prestigious facilities where they can receive increased earnings and responsibilities. Individuals may also go back to school and obtain a four-year degree in veterinary technology and become a paraveterinarian.

Education and Training

The recommended education for veterinary technicians is a two-year associate degree in applied sciences with a major in animal technology from an accredited school. There are also four-year programs for individuals who want to earn bachelor's degrees.

Courses in the sciences are a major part of this program. Course work in veterinary physiology, anatomy, animal care and management, radiography, anesthetic nursing and monitoring, animal pharmacology, parasitology, chemistry, biology, and communications will all be included.

Experience and Qualifications

Over thirty states require certification or licensing for veterinary technicians. In order to obtain this, individuals must usually complete an accredited program of study and pass a written exam.

FOR ADDITIONAL INFORMATION: Individuals interested in becoming a veterinary technician can contact the American Veterinary Medical Association (AVMA) for information and literature.

Tips

- Many zoos, animal shelters, humane societies, and sanctuaries have internships. These offer you an opportunity to get hands-on experience working with animals.
- Openings are often advertised in the classified section of the newspaper under "Veterinary Technician," "Animals," "Small Animals," "Zoos," "Animal Shelters," etc.
- Send your resume with a short cover letter requesting an interview to veterinarian clinics, hospitals, and animal shelters.

CHAPTER 2

Geriatrics Careers

An increase in the older population has resulted in the emergence of a multiplicity of careers in the geriatrics field. This growing trend is expected to continue well into the next century.

As noted in the previous chapter, the United States Department of Labor has indicated that some of the fastest-growing occupations through the new century will be health related. The majority of careers in the health care industry have geriatric components. These include geriatricians, dentists, nutritionists, podiatrists, technologists, therapists, and health care facility administrators. Home health care aides can also work exclusively with geriatric patients. Some take the specialization one step further and work exclusively with Alzheimer's patients or stroke victims. Job opportunities will encompass the social service fields as well. These opportunities exist and will continue to exist in a variety of institutional and agency settings as well as in independent practitioner services.

Jobs may also be located in home care situations, senior citizen centers, retirement communities, banking and investment areas, and major corporations.

The careers discussed in this section include:

Geriatric Social Worker
Geriatric Assessment Coordinator
Nursing Home Activities Director
Geriatric Care Manager
Recreational Therapist
Retirement Planner

Individuals interested in geriatric careers should also see Chapter 1, Medical Technology and Health Care Careers.

GERIATRIC SOCIAL WORKER

JOB DESCRIPTION: *Work with aging clients, assessing their situation and problems; counsel clients on economic, social, personal, and psychological matters; refer clients to proper agencies and people.*

EARNINGS: *$24,000 to $48,000+.*

RECOMMENDED EDUCATION AND TRAINING: *Minimum of a bachelor's degree; some positions require a graduate degree.*

SKILLS AND PERSONALITY TRAITS: *Compassion; counseling skills; communication skills; good judgment; dependability; objectivity.*

EXPERIENCE AND QUALIFICATIONS: *State licensing or registration; certification is available.*

JOB DESCRIPTION AND RESPONSIBILITIES

Older people often have unique problems and circumstances to deal with. Geriatric social workers assist aging people and their families when they have difficulties. A big part of their job is to help seniors lead more productive lives.

Geriatric clients may be assigned to social workers for a number of reasons. Individuals may ask for help or be referred by another agency or person. Clients may be ill or have a spouse that is sick. In some cases, the clients don't have any relatives and cannot handle problems on their own. They may need medical or financial help, assistance with food and nutrition, help locating housing, etc. Many geriatric social workers deal with clients who are in nursing homes, extended-care facilities or hospitals. They may also work with clients who are still in their homes and want to remain there.

Geriatric social workers talk to clients, evaluate problems, and assist in finding solutions. They advise the elderly and their families on available services including long-term care, housing, medical help, nutrition, and transportation.

The geriatric social worker may be required to contact a number of different agencies to handle the problems of one patient. For instance, he or she might utilize the local office of the aging, meals on wheels, home health aides, and an adult day care facility. After contacting the appropriate agencies and people, the geriatric social worker must coordinate all services. Individuals are expected to monitor the situation to make sure the client and his or her problems do not fall through the cracks of society.

A great deal of this job revolves around the rights of the elderly client. Geriatric social workers are often expected to investigate cases. For example, the individual may investigate abuse in a nursing home or cases of elderly people who appear not to be getting proper nutrition or individuals who are neglected.

Other duties of geriatric social workers include visiting clients at home, preparing reports on each client, and evaluating programs for the elderly.

This is a job that may be emotionally draining. Geriatric social workers, however, are usually rewarded by the knowledge that they are helping people who very often cannot help themselves.

EMPLOYMENT OPPORTUNITIES

Geriatric social workers can work exclusively in the geriatrics area or may specialize in this field and handle other types of cases as well. They may work full- or part-time. Employment settings include:

- Government agencies
- Social service agencies
- Community organizations
- Religious organizations
- Hospitals
- Nursing homes
- Extended-care facilities
- Home health agencies
- Hospices
- Consulting and private practice

Expanding Opportunities for the 21st Century

While the services of social workers are required by many older people, those most in need are individuals on low incomes and living alone. This segment of the population is expanding and will require the services of geriatric social workers.

EARNINGS

Geriatric social workers can earn between $24,000 and $48,000, depending on a number of factors. These include the education, experience, and responsibilities of the individual as well as the specific employment setting and geographic location.

As a rule, social workers with more education are paid higher salaries. Individuals with experience or those working in metropolitan areas with a high cost of living will also earn more.

ADVANCEMENT OPPORTUNITIES

After obtaining experience and/or additional education, geriatric social workers can advance in a number of ways. Some individuals are promoted to managerial, administrative, or supervisory positions. Others climb the career ladder by teaching in colleges or universities. More options include going into research and opening consulting firms.

EDUCATION AND TRAINING

The minimum education required for most geriatric social workers is a bachelor's degree. The best major is one in social work with an emphasis or specialty in gerontology. Other choices for majors include sociology or psychology with courses in gerontology.

A master's degree in social work may be required for some positions including jobs in research, administration, supervision, or management. A Ph.D. will usually be necessary for teaching and may be required for certain research positions.

EXPERIENCE AND QUALIFICATIONS

Geriatric social workers graduate with a BSW and go through 400 hours of supervised field experience. This prepares them to work right after graduation. The MSW degree has a similar requirement including 900 hours of supervised field instruction or an internship.

Individuals who graduate with other types of degrees may be required to intern or obtain experience in other ways.

Social workers in any field may be required to obtain state licensing or registration. Voluntary certification is available through the National Association of Social Workers.

FOR ADDITIONAL INFORMATION: Additional information is available from the Association for Gerontology in Higher Education (AGHE), the Council on Social Work Education (CSWE), and the National Association of Social Workers.

TIPS

- Internships are especially helpful in this field. Contact social service agencies, the office for the aging, or the department of mental health for details.
- Job openings are often advertised in the newspaper classified section under headings such as "Social Worker," "BSW Needed" (bachelor's in social work), "MSW Needed," "Geriatric Social Worker," etc.
- Many jobs in this field are located in state, county, or municipal government agencies. Contact your local state employment office for information.

GERIATRIC ASSESSMENT COORDINATOR

JOB DESCRIPTION: *Assess the needs of geriatric patients; set up care plan; coordinate health services; handle paperwork.*

EARNINGS: *$30,000 to $60,000+.*

RECOMMENDED EDUCATION AND TRAINING: *Bachelor's degree in social work with an emphasis on geriatrics; some positions require a master's.*

SKILLS AND PERSONALITY TRAITS: *Compassion; interpersonal skills; organizational skills; ability to work with elderly.*

EXPERIENCE AND QUALIFICATIONS: *Experience working with the elderly.*

Job Description and Responsibilities

Geriatric assessment coordinators, serving as part of a multidisciplinary team, meet with geriatric patients to assess their physical, emotional, and mental condition. This is accomplished through examinations, medical tests, and interviews with both the patient and often the patient's family.

Once the patient has been assessed, the geriatric assessment coordinator will be required to determine the needs of the individual and set up a plan of care. This may include coordinating the services of physicians, nurses, nurse practitioners, physical therapists, recreational therapists, occupational therapists, and others. It may also include services such as a hot meal program, senior transportation plans, or adult day care.

It is essential that the patient be included when possible in the decision-making process regarding his or her plan of care. The coordinator will meet with the patient, and sometimes a patient's family, to discuss important decisions. These may include living arrangements and medical problems.

Depending on the specific employment setting and its structure, the geriatric assessment coordinator may be required to provide continuing contact with the patient, checking that the care plan is being followed. The individual may be responsible for reassessing patients as their situations change.

Hours for geriatric assessment coordinators will vary depending on shifts. Individuals are expected to work overtime in crisis situations.

Employment Opportunities

Geriatric assessment coordinators can be employed in a number of settings including:

- Hospitals
- Nursing homes

- Extended-care facilities
- Health maintenance organizations
- Hospices
- Geriatrics clinics

Expanding Opportunities for the 21st Century

Geriatric assessment coordinator is a relatively new career option that will grow as a result of the increasing number of elderly people in society today.

EARNINGS

Geriatric assessment coordinators have annual salaries ranging from $30,000 to $60,000 or more depending on their education, training, expertise, and responsibilities. Other factors affecting earnings include the size, prestige, and location of the specific facility.

Generally, the more education and experience an individual has the higher the salary. Individuals just starting out earn between $30,000 and $38,000. Geriatric assessment coordinators with a great deal of experience and responsibility, working in large or prestigious facilities, will earn the highest salaries.

ADVANCEMENT OPPORTUNITIES

Geriatric assessment coordinators can advance their careers in a number of ways. With additional experience and education, individuals can locate jobs with more responsibility in larger or more prestigious facilities. Individuals may also become the director of a geriatrics program.

Many geriatric assessment coordinators climb the career ladder by expanding the program they are currently working in to include specialties such as adult day care, respite, or care for Alzheimer's or stroke patients.

EDUCATION AND TRAINING

As this is a relatively new career, education requirements vary. The minimum requirement for a geriatric assessment coordinator is a bachelor's degree in social work with courses in gerontology. The best degree to have for this job is either a master's or Ph.D. in gerontology. A master's degree in social work with an emphasis on gerontology is also a good choice.

EXPERIENCE AND QUALIFICATIONS

There is currently no credentialing process for geriatric assessment coordinators. Individuals must, however, have experience dealing with elderly people. This may be obtained through internships or volunteer experience.

FOR ADDITIONAL INFORMATION: Individuals interested in a career as a geriatric assessment coordinator can obtain more information by contacting the National Association of Private Geriatric Care Managers (NAPGCM), the American Geriatrics Society (AGS), or the Association for Gerontology in Higher Education (AGHE).

Tips

- Send your resume and a short cover letter to the personnel directors of hospitals, nursing homes, extended-care facilities, and health maintenance organizations.
- Job openings are often advertised in newspaper classified sections under the headings: "Geriatric Assessment Coordinator," "Geriatrics," "Health Care," etc.
- Colleges and universities offering majors in gerontology usually have placement offices that are aware of openings.

NURSING HOME ACTIVITIES DIRECTOR

JOB DESCRIPTION: *Plan and lead activities; develop care plan; develop budget.*

EARNINGS: *$18,000 to $40,000+.*

RECOMMENDED EDUCATION AND TRAINING: *Requirements vary from job to job.*

SKILLS AND PERSONALITY TRAITS: *Organizational skills; creativity; supervisory skills; communication skills; good interpersonal skills.*

EXPERIENCE AND QUALIFICATIONS: *Credentialing available; state approval may be required.*

Job Description and Responsibilities

Nursing home activities directors are responsible for the daily recreational activities of the residents and patients in nursing homes and other similar facilities.

Activities directors are expected to plan activities in a variety of areas. These activities must be developed for people with various levels of skill and capabilities. When a resident enters a nursing home facility, the activities director is required to develop a personalized care plan. Each resident will be assessed by the activities director to determine an appropriate program of activities. In doing so, it is essential that the activities director finds out past and current interests and present abilities.

The activities director will work with the residents to plan activities in which they would like to participate. Together, they develop a list of activities that are appropriate for the residents. In cases where residents are incapable of planning their own activities, the director is responsible for handling the task.

The activities director meets with an interdisciplinary care team on a regular basis. This team includes nurses, physicians, dietitians, social workers, occupational therapists, physical therapists, recreational therapists, and pharmacists.

The director is required to prepare notes on each resident on a periodic basis, detailing progress. This may be done quarterly or more frequently. Notes might include items such as the manner in which residents are adjusting to the facility and whether they are participating in activities.

Activities may encompass solo projects as well as group events. These may include games, dances, parties, cooking lessons, shopping trips, craft classes, sing-alongs, dance classes, reading time, and exercise classes. Birthday, holidays, and other special events may be celebrated. The extent and complexity of activities will depend on the interest and abilities of residents as well as the budget of the facility.

This type of job can be very rewarding. Individuals can often see the difference in the quality of residents' lives as they become involved in various activities.

EMPLOYMENT OPPORTUNITIES

Activities directors in nursing homes may work in small or large facilities. Individuals may be employed in:

- Private nursing homes
- Public nursing homes
- State-run facilities
- Hospitals
- Extended-care facilities
- Long-term care facilities

Expanding Opportunities for the 21st Century

Careers in all phases of geriatric care are increasing as a result of the large senior population. With more people living longer, there is a greater demand for nursing homes and extended-care facilities. Activities directors are needed to staff these facilities.

EARNINGS

Earnings for nursing home activities directors range from approximately $18,000 to $40,000 or more. Factors affecting earnings include the education, experience, and responsibilities of the individual as well as the size, prestige, and location of the facility. As a rule, individuals with higher education, working in larger facilities, will earn more.

ADVANCEMENT OPPORTUNITIES

Nursing home activities directors can advance by locating positions in larger, more prestigious facilities. This will usually result in increased earnings and responsibilities.

EDUCATION AND TRAINING

Educational requirements for nursing home activities directors can vary. The minimum is a high school diploma and two years experience working full time in a geriatric setting.

Some facilities prefer that their nursing home activities directors hold associate or bachelor's degrees. Possible majors include occupational therapy, geriatrics, recreation therapy, therapeutic recreation, rehabilitation therapy, or social work.

Organizations and trade associations may offer comprehensive training courses, workshops, and seminars.

EXPERIENCE AND QUALIFICATIONS

Experience requirements vary for nursing home activities directors. In many instances, if the individual has a college degree in a related area, experience requirements are waived.

Individuals can obtain experience working as activities staffers or in other facets of geriatric care. Some activities directors work in recreation in other fields before becoming involved in geriatrics.

Individuals may become certified through the National Council for Therapeutic Recreation Certification.

FOR ADDITIONAL INFORMATION: Individuals interested in learning more about careers as nursing home activities directors can contact the National Association of Activities Professionals (NAAP), the National Council for Therapeutic Recreation Certification (NCTRC), the American Health Care Association (AHCA), the American Therapeutic Recreation Association (ATRA), and the National Therapeutic Recreation Society (NTRS).

TIPS

- Send resumes and cover letters to hospitals, nursing homes, adult homes, and extended-care facilities indicating your experience and interest in a job.
- Positions may be advertised in the newspaper classified section under headings such as "Nursing Homes," "Extended-Care Facilities," "Adult Homes," "Long-Term Care Facilities," "Activity Director," "Director of Activities," "Geriatric Activity Director," or "Geriatric Recreation Director."

- Get experience by volunteering at local senior centers, nursing homes, extended-care facilities, or hospitals.

GERIATRIC CARE MANAGER

JOB DESCRIPTION: *Serve as "stand-in relative"; make doctor appointments; assist in an emergency; call or visit the client on a regular basis.*

EARNINGS: *$25,000 to $85,000+.*

RECOMMENDED EDUCATION AND TRAINING: *Educational requirements vary from job to job; see text.*

SKILLS AND PERSONALITY TRAITS: *Attention to detail; communication skills; bookkeeping and accounting skills; ability to deal with elderly; compassion.*

EXPERIENCE AND QUALIFICATIONS: *Experience dealing with the elderly; licensing or certification may be required.*

JOB DESCRIPTION AND RESPONSIBILITIES

The major function of a geriatric care manager is to act as a stand-in family member when the family cannot be around to respond to problems and assist a geriatric relative. Some of the responsibilities of geriatric care managers include simple tasks such as calling clients daily to make sure they are safe and healthy and to see if they require anything. Other care managers are hired to visit the client on a regular basis. During these visits they make sure the geriatric client is eating properly and taking any required medication. The individual might also make appointments for the client to see physicians, therapists, or dentists and be responsible for transporting the client to the appointment.

The geriatric care manager may be required to determine which agencies and services the client is eligible to use. He or she will fill out forms and applications including Medicaid applications, insurance forms, and reimbursements.

Another main responsibility is paying the client's bills and keeping his or her day-to-day finances in order. The individual may be responsible for writing checks for rent, phone, and utility bills, pharmacy and medical bills, and incidentals.

Complex tasks such as estate planning, living wills, and family trusts usually require special training.

Geriatric care managers usually have caseloads of clients. In situations where individuals are working for an agency or firm, they are assigned cases. Those who are self-employed find their own clients. Many clients are referred to the geriatric care manager by others who use the service or by agencies.

Close bonds are often formed between geriatric care managers and their clients. For those who enjoy working with older adults, this type of job can be very fulfilling and rewarding.

EMPLOYMENT OPPORTUNITIES

Geriatric care managers may work full or part time in a number of different settings. These include:

- Private geriatric care management firms
- Home care organizations
- Self-employment
- Consulting
- Hospitals

Expanding Opportunities for the 21st Century

The increase in the mobility of our society and the breakup of the extended family leaves many individuals geographically distant from their aging parents. As a result, they need someone responsible to handle the tasks that their parents can no longer deal with. People are finding that it is often less costly, both financially and emotionally, to hire a geriatric care manager to execute the functions that they would perform if they lived nearby.

EARNINGS

Self-employed geriatric care managers may be paid a monthly retainer, a flat fee for a project, or an hourly rate. This ranges from approximately $25 for handling a simple phone call to $250 or more an hour. A great deal of the individual's earnings depend on the type of services they are performing and how many clients they have. The more complex the tasks, the more the individual will earn. Geriatric care managers who handle very complex tasks such as estate planning, family trusts, or living wills can earn up to $85,000 or more per year.

Those working full time for an employer may earn annual salaries ranging from $25,000 to $60,000 plus, depending on the individual's education, experience, responsibilities, geographic location, and the specific employer.

ADVANCEMENT OPPORTUNITIES

Geriatric care managers may advance by locating similar positions in larger or more prestigious facilities. They also might choose self-employment.

EDUCATION AND TRAINING

Education and training requirements vary, as the position is so new to the job market. Recommended education for this position is a master's in social work, gerontology, or psychology. Many self-employed geriatric care managers have an MBA or a law degree.

Courses in gerontology, business, accounting, bookkeeping, social work, sociology, or psychology will be useful.

EXPERIENCE AND QUALIFICATIONS

Geriatric care managers should have experience dealing with elderly people. This may be obtained by working or volunteering in geriatric situations.

As the individual often deals with client's financial situations, many people prefer that the geriatric care managers be bonded.

Licensing or certification may be necessary in private practice.

FOR ADDITIONAL INFORMATION: Individuals interested in learning more about a career as a geriatric care manager can contact the National Association of Private Geriatric Care Managers (NAPGCM).

TIPS

- Colleges and universities offering degrees in gerontology usually have job-placement offices.
- Jobs may be advertised in the newspaper classified section under "Geriatric Care Manager," "Geriatrics," etc.
- Self-employed geriatric care managers should volunteer to speak at local senior citizen group meetings and nonprofit organizations. This is important in obtaining referrals.

RECREATIONAL THERAPIST

JOB DESCRIPTION: *Develop activities; observe reactions to activities; monitor patient progress.*

EARNINGS: *$22,000 to $45,000.*

RECOMMENDED EDUCATION AND TRAINING: *Bachelor's degree in therapeutic recreation.*

SKILLS AND PERSONALITY TRAITS: *Compassion; personableness; organization; communication skills; creativity; ability to work with elderly and disabled patients.*

EXPERIENCE AND QUALIFICATIONS: *Supervised internship; some states require licensing and/or certification.*

JOB DESCRIPTION AND RESPONSIBILITIES

Recreational therapists work with mentally, physically, and emotionally disabled patients. They attempt to rehabilitate patients through the use of various activities. In some situations, supervised recreational activities help patients forget about their physical, mental, and/or emotional problems and focus on the activities.

Many patients of recreational therapists are older people. Other patients may be mentally disturbed, mentally retarded, or recovering substance abusers. Patients are referred to recreational therapists to increase mental stimulation or physical strength and coordination. They may need to achieve a higher level of confidence or self-esteem. Some need to learn how to express their feelings or manage stress.

When choosing activities, recreational therapists must determine the patients' interests. Choice of activities also reflects the physical and emotional problems of the patients. Activities include craft projects or lessons, exercises, theatrical skits, games, and field trips.

One of the recent activities that many recreational therapists are finding useful, especially in nursing homes, is bringing puppies and kittens to the facility. Therapists have found that even patients with severe problems react well to animals.

Recreational therapists may work with other therapists including music, dance, art, and occupational therapists as well as physicians, psychiatrists, psychologists, and social workers. Together the team of professionals determines how best to treat the patient.

The recreational therapist is expected to talk with the patient, family, and the other professionals involved to find out the mental, physical, and emotional status of the individual. The therapist can then plan appropriate activities.

Recreational therapists oversee the patients as they participate in the various activities. Over a time span, the therapist must determine whether the patient is improving. For example, does the patient interact well with others, gain more self-confidence, become more assertive, express feelings in a more positive manner, or deal with stress better?

If a treatment is not working, the therapist will be expected to develop other activities.

EMPLOYMENT OPPORTUNITIES

While many recreational therapists work with the elderly, there are also opportunities in community-based programs for the disabled or in special education school programs.

Employment settings for recreational therapists include:

- Nursing homes
- Extended-care facilities
- Hospitals
- Adult day care programs
- Community mental health centers
- Correctional facilities

- Residential facilities for the mentally retarded
- Residential facilities for substance abusers

Expanding Opportunities for the 21st Century

As a result of the increasing aging population, there will be a need for recreational therapists in all types of nursing homes, long-term care facilities, adult care centers, and hospitals.

EARNINGS

Earnings for recreational therapists can range from approximately $22,000 to $45,000. Variables affecting earnings include the specific employment setting, its size, prestige, and location. Other factors include the experience, responsibilities, and education of the therapist.

Therapists with more experience and education will earn higher salaries. Individuals just entering the field can earn between $22,000 and $26,000. Those with experience who are working in more prestigious facilities or in geographic locations with higher costs of living can earn between $26,000 and $45,000.

ADVANCEMENT OPPORTUNITIES

With additional experience and education, recreational therapists can be promoted to administrative, supervisory, or management positions. Individuals might also advance their careers by locating similar positions in more prestigious facilities.

EDUCATION AND TRAINING

Education and training requirements vary from job to job. The recommended education is a bachelor's degree in therapeutic recreation, recreational therapy, or recreation with an emphasis on therapeutic recreation.

The course of study includes classroom and clinical work in abnormal psychology, physiology, medical and psychiatric terminology, program design, management and professional issues, helping skills, clinical practice skills, human anatomy, characteristics of illnesses and disabilities, concepts of mainstreaming and normalization, assessment and referral procedures, professional ethics, and the use of adaptive and medical equipment.

A graduate degree may be required for administrative, managerial, or supervisory positions or those in research or teaching.

EXPERIENCE AND QUALIFICATIONS

Recreational therapists must go through a 360-hour internship program in which they obtain the necessary experience to work on their own.

In a number of states, recreational therapists must either be licensed or certified. In order to be licensed, individuals must usually graduate from a regionally accredited program in therapeutic recreation or recreation with an emphasis on therapeutic recreation. Other qualifications include going through a supervised internship and taking and passing a state licensing examination.

Certification is obtained through the National Council for Therapeutic Recreation Certification.

FOR ADDITIONAL INFORMATION: Individuals interested in a career as a recreational therapist can obtain additional information by contacting the National Council for Therapeutic Recreation Certification (NCTRC), the American Health Care Association (AHCA), the American Therapeutic Recreation Association (ATRA), and the National Therapeutic Recreation Society (NTRS).

TIPS

- Jobs are often available in Department of Veterans Affairs medical centers. Contact the Department of Veterans Affairs for more information.
- Job openings are advertised in the newspaper's classified section under "Recreational Therapist," "Therapist," "Gerontology," "Nursing Home," "Activities Director," "Health Care," and "Long-Term Care Facilities."
- Colleges and universities offering programs in therapeutic recreation usually maintain placement offices that are notified of job openings.
- Get on-the-job experience volunteering in a nursing home, hospital, or long-term care facility.

RETIREMENT PLANNER

JOB DESCRIPTION: *Counsel retirees; help people adjust to retirement; explain retirement programs.*

EARNINGS: *$30,000 to $70,000+.*

RECOMMENDED EDUCATION AND TRAINING: *Requirements vary.*

SKILLS AND PERSONALITY TRAITS: *Communication and counseling skills; comfortable dealing with older people; organization; business skills.*

EXPERIENCE AND QUALIFICATIONS: *Requirements vary. See text.*

Job Description and Responsibilities

After working for twenty, thirty, or forty or more years, most people look forward to retirement. The problem is that many people do not have any set plans for what they are going to do after they retire. To deal with this potential difficulty, many companies employ retirement planners. These individuals work with potential retirees to help them develop plans for a healthy, active lifestyle after retirement.

Corporations have found that individuals who do not adjust well after retirement get sick more often than others. This can result in higher health care and insurance claims. Those who are active in their older age usually require less health care. As a result, the cost of retirement planning for employees is less than paying higher health care costs.

Retirement planners meet with employees who are nearing retirement to determine their future goals, aspirations, and dreams. A great deal of the retiree's plans depends on the individual's age, interests, and financial situation. The retiree may be interested in going back to school to obtain a degree. Other retirees look forward to becoming involved in hobbies and a vast array of social activities that they did not previously have time for. Many retirees plan on traveling, relocating, finding a second career, or volunteering.

Once the retirement planner ascertains what the future retirees want to do with their new lives, the planner will help them find ways to implement the plans.

Employees often have several options regarding retirement programs, pensions, and benefit plans. The retirement planner is expected to explain the benefits and drawbacks of each and provide information concerning the provisions and regulations of the company retirement program. An important function of the retirement planner is to assist the retiree with financial plans based on the retirement income. Individuals may also be expected to help the retiree develop a budget.

Retirement planners may work varied hours depending on the specific situation.

Employment Opportunities

Retirement planners may work full or part time in settings that include:

- Corporations in every industry
- Self-employment
- Consulting
- Private retirement planning firms
- Government agencies

Expanding Opportunities for the 21st Century

As corporations begin to realize that active, contented individuals have fewer health problems, more companies will begin to employ either in-house retirement planners or consultants.

EARNINGS

Annual salaries for retirement planners range from approximately $30,000 to $70,000 or more, depending on their responsibilities, experience, education, and location. Other factors affecting earnings include the specific employer and geographic location.

ADVANCEMENT OPPORTUNITIES

There are a number of paths retirement planners can take for career advancement. Some individuals seek similar positions in larger or more prestigious firms. Others become supervisors, managers, or administrators.

Many retirement planners become consultants or open up their own retirement planning company.

EDUCATION AND TRAINING

The job of retirement planner is a relatively new career. As a result, educational requirements have not been set and vary from job to job. Individuals should have at least a bachelor's degree. A master's or a Ph.D. may be preferred. Majors might include social work, business, gerontology, psychology, recreational or occupational therapy, or related fields.

EXPERIENCE AND QUALIFICATIONS

Experience requirements vary for potential retirement planners. Any background in working or dealing with elderly people will be helpful as will any counseling experience.

FOR ADDITIONAL INFORMATION: Individuals interested in becoming retirement planners can learn more by contacting the Center for Creative Retirement (CCR) and the American Association of Retired Persons. (AARP).

TIPS

- You may have to create your own job in this field. Contact corporations and request an interview to discuss employment as their retirement planner.
- Send a short cover letter with your resume to the personnel directors of large corporations.
- Companies seeking retirement planners often contact colleges and universities offering degrees in gerontology. Talk to the placement office.

CHAPTER 3

Computer Careers

According to the U.S. Department of Labor, computer and data processing services are among the fastest-growing industries in today's economy. This is a result of an increasing demand from private businesses, government agencies, and individuals.

A higher quality of work can be accomplished more quickly and efficiently with computers. Their extent of power continues to grow and shows no signs of leveling off. Tremendous amounts of data can now be stored and retrieved in seconds. Offices are becoming automated. Secretaries can now automatically prepare and personalize hundreds of letters a day. Medical records can be transferred almost instantaneously between institutions. Lab tests can be performed, data tabulated, and information analyzed quickly and efficiently.

With CAD (computer aided drafting) programs, engineers can develop plans for systems, bridges, roads, tunnels, and machinery. Architects, clothing designers, and a host of people in other industries are also beginning to depend on computers and CAD programs.

Schools now train children starting in kindergarten about computers and their use. By the time they graduate from high school, these children will be more computer proficient than many of today's adults.

Prices on personal computers have dropped and machines have become accessible to the individual. As a result, home businesses are also profiting from the computer revolution. There are literally hundreds of ways to make money with a home computer including data processing, desktop publishing, word processing, and information brokering. In addition, people are using home computers to keep records, develop promotional material, and handle financial matters.

Telecommuting is projected to be a growth industry for the next century. Many corporations have found it practical to have employees work on a computer at home and send work to the office through the use of a modem. Telecommuting can save money on the rental of office space and, also, on commuter costs. Many companies have found that this system increases productivity and efficiency.

Computer careers require a variety of educational levels, experience, and skills.

Careers covered in this chapter include:

Word Processor Operator   CAD Specialist
Systems Analyst   Computer Salesperson—Retail
Technical Documentation Specialist   Computer Service Technician
Computer Programmer   Computer Trainer

Individuals interested in this area should also review entries in Chapter 11, Home-Based Business Careers.

WORD PROCESSOR OPERATOR

JOB DESCRIPTION: *Process text; prepare and type letters, envelopes, and reports; format documents.*

EARNINGS: *$6.00 to $30.00+ hourly.*

RECOMMENDED EDUCATION AND TRAINING: *High school diploma; training in word processing.*

SKILLS AND PERSONALITY TRAITS: *Word processing skills; typing skills; good grammar, punctuation, and spelling; knowledge of many computer programs.*

EXPERIENCE AND QUALIFICATIONS: *Proficiency in word processing.*

JOB DESCRIPTION AND RESPONSIBILITIES

Until recently, many offices relied on typewriters to process text. Now computers with word processing capabilities are being used almost exclusively. Individuals who work on computers inputting data are called word processors or word processor operators.

Word processing equipment usually includes a keyboard, a video display terminal, and a printer. This equipment has many capabilities that traditional typewriters don't. For example, it can check and correct spelling, grammar, and punctuation. Documents that are typed can be saved and changes can be made. This means that documents do not have to be typed over to correct errors.

Responsibilities of word processor operators may vary with the specific job. The main function of most individuals is to type information into the word processor. Information may consist of any type of document including correspondence, reports, contracts, manuscripts, etc. Anything that can be typed on a typewriter can be done on a word processor.

Once word processors have finished typing the required material, they can save the document in the machine's internal memory or on a computer floppy disk. Word processors run the copy through spelling and grammar checkers to detect and correct errors.

In addition to straight data entry, many word processors format documents. They may space paragraphs, set margins, change type fonts and sizes, and move copy around. Word processors print out copies of documents, proofread them, and give them to the proper people in the organization.

Hours vary depending on the work environment in which the word processors are employed. They are responsible to the office supervisor.

EMPLOYMENT OPPORTUNITIES

Individuals may work in office settings in a vast array of industries, including:

- Public relations
- Schools, colleges, and universities
- Health care facilities
- Advertising agencies
- Temporary agencies
- Banks
- Law offices
- Manufacturers, wholesalers, and retailers
- Construction companies
- Book publishers
- Record companies
- Government agencies
- Insurance agencies
- Real estate companies
- Investment firms
- Shopping centers
- Travel agencies

Expanding Opportunities for the 21st Century

Constant changes in office technology mean costly training and retraining. Word processors that will be most in demand are those who can work on a variety of computers and are familiar with many computer programs.

Many companies are trying to save money by finding ways to cut back on employee benefits. One way is to utilize word processors provided by temporary agencies.

Using home computers and fax machines or modems, employees can handle word processing projects at home. In this instance, many employers do not have to pay full benefits because of the employment structure.

EARNINGS

Word processors may earn between $6.00 and $30.00 an hour or more. Earnings depend on the individual's responsibilities, experience, training, geographic location, and the specific employment situation. Those working in large cities will earn more than their counterparts in less urban areas. Word processors with working knowledge of several computer programs and languages will be paid more than individuals who can handle only one program.

ADVANCEMENT OPPORTUNITIES

Word processors can advance their careers by obtaining more training or learning additional computer skills. Individuals can locate positions in companies with higher earnings if they know more complex computer programs. They might also move into positions in desktop publishing.

Some word processors become trainers, supervisors, secretaries, or administrative assistants, depending on the path they want to take in their career advancement.

EDUCATION AND TRAINING

Generally, most employers prefer high school graduates or those with equivalency diplomas. Individuals should be trained in word processing. Some people learn these skills in high school; others attend vocational-technical schools, business schools, or community colleges. Many temporary agencies also offer training programs covering various computer programs and word processing skills. Some companies have internal training programs to help their employees keep up with new equipment.

It is imperative for individuals who want to work in this field to continue learning new computer programs and languages as technology changes.

EXPERIENCE AND QUALIFICATIONS

Word processors do not generally need experience to obtain a job, as long as they possess the technical skills to perform.

FOR ADDITIONAL INFORMATION: Individuals interested in becoming word processors should contact vocational trade schools or business schools specializing in word processing skills.

TIPS

- There are seminars, workshops, and classes available throughout the country on a variety of word processing programs. The more you know, the more marketable you make yourself.
- There is a vast array of books available in bookstores and libraries on the subject. Make sure you are reading the most current material.
- Temporary agencies, especially in large cities, offer training programs in word processing. Some are free and others have a charge.
- Job openings are advertised in the classifieds under headings for the specific industry the job is in, such as "Education" or "Health Care." They may also be under "Word Processors," "Word Processing," or "Computers."

SYSTEMS ANALYST

JOB DESCRIPTION: *Define goals of computer systems; plan computer systems; determine hardware and software needs; assist in debugging of systems.*

EARNINGS: *$25,000 to $70,000+.*

RECOMMENDED EDUCATION AND TRAINING: *Four-year college degree preferred; some positions require graduate degree.*

SKILLS AND PERSONALITY TRAITS: *Communication skills; attention to detail; analytical mind; familiarity with programming languages; extensive knowledge of computer systems.*

EXPERIENCE AND QUALIFICATIONS: *Experience in computer science and computer programming.*

Job Description and Responsibilities

Systems analysts plan and develop new computer systems. It is their job to make the most of a computer's power by making it perform efficiently.

In order to be effective, systems analysts must be fully knowledgeable about computers, programming, and applications. They must have a full understanding of the capabilities and limitations of all the hardware and software they are dealing with.

In some cases, systems analysts will be required simply to recommend a specific computer. In others, individuals may be asked to design new computer systems or add additional hardware or new software applications.

Systems analysts meet with managers of businesses to determine what they require the computer to accomplish. They must know exactly what types of problems the computer will be expected to handle so that they can break down each task into separate programmable procedures.

They will then design the system and determine the required hardware and software. Systems analysts may also prepare an analysis comparing the cost of the new system to its benefits, as well as the return on the investment. With this information, management can evaluate whether the proposed system is financially feasible, useful, and cost efficient.

One of the major duties of a systems analyst is the debugging of a computer system. The term *debug,* in computer jargon, means to eliminate errors from a system. It often takes a great deal of time and must be checked and rechecked until it is error free. The analyst must determine the cause of the bug and eliminate it from the system.

Analysts usually work fairly normal schedules. Individuals may, however, be required to work overtime when a deadline must be met.

Employment Opportunities

Systems analysts can work for temporary agencies, on a contractual basis or in full-time employment settings. Some of these include:

- Hardware manufacturers
- Software manufacturers
- Aerospace industry
- High-tech companies
- Banks

- Data processing services
- Government agencies
- Insurance companies
- Manufacturers in a variety of industries
- Self-employment

Expanding Opportunities for the 21st Century

The current automation of offices, telecommunications, and countless industries indicates that there will be a growing demand for systems analysts in the future. In addition, many more homes and small businesses are using computers as a result of a drop in prices. Therefore, systems analysts are needed to help these people increase their productivity.

Systems analysts will be required to network different computers so that they can communicate with each other. This is important as more businesses use multiuser systems. This includes businesses that use a large number of personal computers or microcomputers in addition to mainframe systems.

Earnings

Systems analysts can earn approximately $25,000 to $70,000 or more. Factors affecting earnings include the particular industry the individual is working in, the specific employment setting, and location. Other factors include experience, education, and responsibilities.

Generally, the more experience and education individuals have, the higher their earnings. Salaries will be higher for individuals working in metropolitan areas than they are for their counterparts in less urban areas.

Advancement Opportunities

One way systems analysts can advance is by obtaining additional education. Individuals might also seek more complex projects or locate similar positions in more prestigious employment settings that offer higher earnings and responsibilities.

Individuals start out as junior systems analysts. With more experience they can become senior or lead systems analysts. Some individuals are promoted to manager of information systems. Others become chief information officers.

Another option is to open one's own consulting firm in the computer field.

EDUCATION AND TRAINING

Some positions do not require a college degree. However, competition is stiff in this field. If an individual does obtain a job without a degree, advancement may be difficult.

The minimum recommended education for systems analysts is a bachelor's degree. Some positions prefer postgraduate degrees. Required majors for systems analysts differ from job to job. Systems analysts may have degrees in computer science, computer information systems, data processing, or information science. Other individuals have degrees in business management, physical sciences, engineering, or applied mathematics with an emphasis in computer science.

No matter what the degree, systems analysts must have courses in programming languages, computer systems, database management, and computer sciences.

Continuing education in the field is necessary to keep up with new technology. Many employers sponsor classes and training programs. In addition, software vendors, professional societies, and trade associations offer a variety of classes, seminars, and workshops.

EXPERIENCE AND QUALIFICATIONS

Computer experience is usually necessary to get a job as a systems analyst. Individuals can obtain needed experience working as computer engineers or programmers.

While it is not a requirement, systems analysts can be certified by the Institute for Certification of Computer Professionals. In order to obtain this credential, they must have at least five years' experience and pass a number of examinations. Individuals who hold the Certified Systems Professional (CSP) credential may be preferred for positions as it indicates experience and professional competency. Another voluntary certification is offered by the Quality Assurance Institute. In order to hold the designation Certified Quality Analyst (CQA), individuals must complete certain education and experience requirements, pass an examination, and endorse a code of ethics.

FOR ADDITIONAL INFORMATION: Individuals interested in a systems analyst career can obtain additional information by contacting the Association for Systems Management (ASM), the Association for Computing Machinery (ACM), the Quality Assurance Institute (QAI), or the Institute for Certification of Computer Professionals (ICCP).

TIPS

- Large cities often host employment agencies specializing in computer-related positions.
- Newspapers regularly advertise job openings in this field. Look in the classified section of the paper under "Computers," "Systems Analyst," "Programmer Analyst," or specific industry names.

- Jobs are advertised in trade journals. In addition to computer-related trade journals, consider industry journals.
- The placement offices of colleges and universities offering degrees in computer related areas are usually notified of job openings.

TECHNICAL DOCUMENTATION SPECIALIST

JOB DESCRIPTION: *Prepare hardware and software manuals; translate technical information into understandable language.*

EARNINGS: *$24,000 to $65,000+.*

RECOMMENDED EDUCATION AND TRAINING: *Bachelor's degree in computer science, liberal arts, communications, or English.*

SKILLS AND PERSONALITY TRAITS: *Writing skills; knowledge of computers; ability to work under pressure.*

EXPERIENCE AND QUALIFICATIONS: *Writing experience is necessary.*

JOB DESCRIPTION AND RESPONSIBILITIES

Technical documentation specialists write manuals, operating instructions, and other documents for computer hardware and software. These professionals are sometimes referred to as technical writers. They may also prepare copy for computer or software catalogs, sales promotion material, advertising, and marketing campaigns.

Technical documentation specialists have varied duties depending on the specific job. Their main function, however, is to take hard-to-understand jargon and turn it into everyday, understandable language.

They collaborate with programmers, engineers, and other technical people to learn everything there is to know about the software program. The individual might also do research to learn more about the specific subject of the program. Having extensive knowledge of the subject will make it easier to prepare documentation.

Next is the actual writing of the documentation or users' manual. Most manuals offer explanations about what the program can accomplish and then provide step-by-step instructions on how to use the program. Similar functions are required when writing users' manuals for printers, modems, scanners, and other peripheral equipment.

Computer software usage can be either extremely easy or very difficult, depending on the skills of the technical documentation specialist. It is essential that the specialist writes so that the general public can not only read it but also understand and make use of the information.

Employment Opportunities

Technical documentation specialists can work full or part time in a number of different employment situations including:

- Hardware manufacturers
- Software developers and manufacturers
- Self-employment
- Book publishers

Expanding Opportunities for the 21st Century

The need for technical documentation specialists will increase as additional companies emerge with new software programs. Individuals who have writing skills as well as technical knowledge in both computer usage and other specialty subjects will be especially in demand.

Earnings

Annual earnings of technical documentation specialists can range between $24,000 and $65,000 plus. Factors affecting earnings include the specific employment setting and geographic location as well as the experience, education, technical knowledge, and responsibilities of the individual.

Advancement Opportunities

Technical documentation specialists can advance their careers in a number of ways. They can move into positions in other areas of the computer company such as advertising or marketing. Other documentation specialists search out companies that are larger or more prestigious and offer increased earnings and responsibilities. Some individuals become editors of technical documentation projects, or managers.

Education and Training

Most employers prefer or require a college degree. Good choices for majors include liberal arts, computer science, communications, or English.

Experience and Qualifications

Technical documentation specialists usually need a degree of writing experience and technical knowledge. Sometimes individuals are writers who are familiar with computers and programs through personal use. In other situations, they have worked as programmers or technicians.

FOR ADDITIONAL INFORMATION: Interested individuals can contact the Society for Technical Communications, Inc. (STC), the Association of Computer Programmers and Analysts (ACPA), the Association for Computing Machinery (ACM), or the Microcomputer Software Association (MSA).

TIPS

- Get as much writing experience as you can in all areas.
- Jobs in this field are often advertised in trade journals as well as the newspaper classified section under headings including "Documentation Specialist," "Technical Documentation Specialist," "Technical Writer," "Software," "Hardware," "Writer," or "Freelance."
- Send your resume and a short cover letter to software companies and hardware manufacturers.

COMPUTER PROGRAMMER

JOB DESCRIPTION: *Write instructions for a computer to follow; test new programs; write user's manuals.*

EARNINGS: *$20,000 to $60,000+.*

RECOMMENDED EDUCATION AND TRAINING: *Educational requirements vary.*

SKILLS AND PERSONALITY TRAITS: *In-depth knowledge of programming and operating languages; analytical thinking; attention to detail; organization; communication skills.*

EXPERIENCE AND QUALIFICATIONS: *Requirements vary; credentialing is available.*

JOB DESCRIPTION AND RESPONSIBILITIES

Computer programmers are responsible for writing the detailed instructions that a computer follows. These instructions, input in computer language, are known as computer programs or software.

Programmers develop software used for everything from handling hotel reservations to playing computer games. Some work as programmer-analysts, handling the tasks of both the systems analyst and the programmer. Others may also work directly with experts in specific fields developing programs for software companies.

There are two different types of computer programmers. *Systems* programmers maintain software that controls the entire computer system while *application* programmers write programs that handle specific tasks. In many instances systems programmers are called in to assist application programmers with specific programming problems.

Computer programmers work in special computer languages such as BASIC, COBOL, C, Fourth-Generation Languages (4GL), FORTRAN, PASCAL C, DOS, or Artificial Intelligence (AI). Typically, each language is used for different kinds of applications. COBOL, for example, is traditionally used when writing business programs.

Once the programmer has written the desired program, the individual is responsible for testing it to make sure that it runs properly. The process of going over each set of instructions until the program runs error free is called debugging. This is one of the more challenging and time-consuming tasks for a programmer.

The individual may also write instructions to be used by the operator who will be running the program. In some cases, computer programmers may write instruction manuals.

Computer programmers are responsible to the senior or lead computer programmer.

EMPLOYMENT OPPORTUNITIES

Computer programmers may work full or part time. They can also work on a consulting or temporary basis for specific projects. Employment settings include:

- Software companies
- Research organizations
- Robot manufacturers
- Corporate industry
- Data processing services
- Business services
- Banks
- Computer manufacturers
- Educational institutions
- Machinery and equipment wholesalers

Expanding Opportunities for the 21st Century

The most employable computer programmers will be those with a college education who are familiar with a variety of programming and operating languages.

The demand for computer programmers will increase in the future as a result of the automation of almost every industry. Two areas that are growing especially quickly are data communications and computer networking.

EARNINGS

Computer programmers earn from $20,000 to $60,000 plus. Factors affecting earnings include the education, experience, and responsibilities of the individual as well as the specific employment situation and location.

The more education and experience, the higher the earnings will be. Those just entering the field may earn between $20,000 and $23,000. With more experience, programmers can earn between $25,000 and $60,000 or more.

Also, systems programmers generally earn more than application programmers.

ADVANCEMENT OPPORTUNITIES

Individuals starting out as junior programmers may, with experience and education, become senior programmers. They can also obtain managerial, administrative, or supervisory positions such as lead programmer.

EDUCATION AND TRAINING

A four-year college degree in computer science, computer programming, or information science is usually preferred but is not mandatory. Other degrees may be in engineering, physical science, or math. Though not mandatory, the degree may be necessary for advancement.

Many individuals learn computer programming in high school or vocational-technical school. Others choose degree programs in two-year or four-year colleges.

Some employers who hire entry-level programmers offer training classes. Most programmers continue their education throughout their career because of constantly changing technology.

EXPERIENCE AND QUALIFICATIONS

Individuals usually work under close supervision until they obtain adequate experience. While not always a requirement, certification is available. Individuals who are college graduates with little or no experience in the field can be certified as assistant computer programmers. Senior programmers can receive a certificate in computer programming.

The credentialing process is handled by the Institute for Certification of Computer Professionals. In order to obtain the assistant credential, individuals must take an examination. Senior programmers must have experience in addition to passing a core examination plus two more exams in specialty areas. Credential holders may be preferred for some positions as it is an indication of experience and professional competency.

FOR ADDITIONAL INFORMATION: Individuals interested in learning more about careers in computer programming can contact the Association of Computer Programmers and Analysts (ACPA), the Association for Computing Machinery, Special Interest Group on Programming Languages, (SIGPL), the Data Processing Management Association (DPMA), the Microcomputer Software Association (MSA), and the Institute for Certification of Computer Professionals (ICCP).

TIPS

- Look in computer magazines for the names and addresses of major software firms. Send your resume and a short cover letter requesting an interview.

- Jobs are often advertised in the classifieds under the headings "Computers," "Computer Programmer," "Systems Programmer," "Applications Programmer," "Software Designer," "Software Programmer," "Scientific Programmer," etc.
- Job openings are advertised in the trade journals of many industries.
- Many jobs are available in federal or state government in this field. Contact your state or federal employment service for information.

CAD SPECIALIST

JOB DESCRIPTION: *Use computers to design and draft plans, blueprints, etc.; prepare technical illustrations.*

EARNINGS: *$24,000 to $65,000+.*

RECOMMENDED EDUCATION AND TRAINING: *High school diploma plus training in CAD; some positions require college degree.*

SKILLS AND PERSONALITY TRAITS: *Drafting skills; design skills; computer skills.*

EXPERIENCE AND QUALIFICATIONS: *Experience requirements vary.*

JOB DESCRIPTION AND RESPONSIBILITIES

CAD stands for computer aided drafting. CAD specialists are drafters that prepare technical illustrations using computers instead of the traditional paper, pencil, and measuring instruments.

CAD software programs have a variety of symbols, measuring tools, and angles installed within the program. In addition to using CAD, individuals utilize hardware such as digitizers, graphics tablets, cursor pads, light pens, plotters, and printers. Using this equipment, CAD specialists can draft any type of drawing that can be done manually.

CAD specialists may be responsible for developing the actual design or may just be required to draft from the specifications of other designers. They often work with engineers to develop the specifications for various systems, machinery, or structures.

CAD specialists can do almost any type of drafting. They must, however, have the technical skill for the specific industry. For example, CAD specialists who draft clothing patterns must have a basic understanding of fashion, just as drafting electronic machinery requires a knowledge of schematics and wiring diagrams.

CAD specialists usually work fairly normal hours. They may be required to work overtime to finish a project or meet a deadline.

EMPLOYMENT OPPORTUNITIES

CAD specialists can work in a variety of employment settings. These include:

- Construction companies
- Architectural firms
- Machinery manufacturers
- Engineering firms
- Clothing manufacturers
- Electronics firms
- Electrical manufacturers
- Transportation manufacturers
- Communications manufacturers
- Utility companies
- Government agencies

Expanding Opportunities for the 21st Century

The drop in price of CAD programs and systems means that more industries will be utilizing the services of CAD specialists. Robotics manufacturers will have an especially great demand for these individuals.

EARNINGS

Annual earnings for CAD specialists can range from $24,000 to $65,000 or more depending on the experience, training, education, expertise, and responsibilities of the individual. Other factors affecting earnings include the specific employer, industry, and geographic location.

Individuals just starting out will earn between $24,000 and $30,000. With more experience and training, individuals earn from $32,000 to $44,000. Those with a great deal of experience in supervisory or management positions can earn $65,000 or more.

ADVANCEMENT OPPORTUNITIES

CAD specialists just entering the field may work as trainees. They can advance to full CAD specialists at the same company or locate a similar position in a larger or more prestigious firm. With additional experience, training, and education, individuals can also be promoted to supervisory or management positions.

Some CAD specialists go on to become engineers.

EDUCATION AND TRAINING

Some employers require that applicants have a minimum of a high school diploma; others look for employees with a college degree or background.

CAD specialists must be trained in drafting, design, and CAD systems. This training may be obtained in high school, trade or vocational school, a technical institute, or community college. Classes in drafting, drawing, computer technology, computer aided design, and engineering are required.

EXPERIENCE AND QUALIFICATIONS

Requirements vary from job to job. Experience working with computers is helpful. Proficiency in manual drafting and mechanical drawing is also helpful but may not be required.

FOR ADDITIONAL INFORMATION: To learn more about a career as a CAD specialist, contact the Association for Computing Machinery (ACM) or the American Institute for Design and Drafting (AIDD).

TIPS

- Technical, trade, and vocational schools with programs in this field often offer placement services.
- Job openings are advertised in trade journals and the newspaper classified section. Look under headings such as "CAD Specialist," "Computer Drafter," "CAD Designer," or "Computer Designer."
- The state employment service may have openings for government jobs in this specialty.

COMPUTER SALESPERSON—RETAIL

JOB DESCRIPTION: *Sell computers and related hardware and software; answer technical questions; demonstrate products.*

EARNINGS: *$15,000 to $45,000.*

RECOMMENDED EDUCATION AND TRAINING: *Education and training vary.*

SKILLS AND PERSONALITY TRAITS: *Sales ability; good communication skills; complete knowledge of product; dependability.*

EXPERIENCE AND QUALIFICATIONS: *Computer experience necessary; sales experience helpful.*

JOB DESCRIPTION AND RESPONSIBILITIES

There is such a vast array of computers and other hardware and software in the marketplace that it is difficult for customers to know what to purchase. Computer salespeople help these people choose the correct equipment.

Salespeople must know how the equipment works in order to demonstrate the functions to buyers. They must be able to explain the differences between brands of the same type of equipment and be familiar with various computer programs that the store sells.

In some stores, salespeople specialize in one brand or type of equipment. For example, one salesperson may specialize in selling the Apple Macintosh while another sells IBM machines. In other stores, the salesperson may be required to be fully informed about all of the store's merchandise.

As computers represent such a major investment, customers usually require full presentations to explain all the points of a particular machine. Computer salespeople must be fully competent in the use of each piece of equipment they are selling. They are often required to answer technical questions about computers or computer accessories.

Successful salespeople try to find out exactly what the customer's needs are. For example, it is important to determine the price range the customer is considering as well as the brand of equipment, its options, and its projected uses.

In some shops, the salesperson may be required to install the computer and other hardware in the person's home or business. In other situations, the individual may just be required to explain assembly directions. Some computer stores offer free or low-cost lessons to people who have purchased equipment or software.

Other functions of the salesperson may include serving as a cashier, closing sales, totaling up customer's purchases, arranging for layaways, putting through credit card purchases, taking payments for products, and giving change to customers. The salesperson might also have to count merchandise that has arrived, verify the receipt of items on invoices and check that stock arriving is the merchandise ordered.

Computer salespeople are directly responsible to the manager or owner of a computer store, shop, or department. Hours vary and individuals may be required to work overtime during special promotions or when stock comes in.

EMPLOYMENT OPPORTUNITIES

The highest volume of jobs in this area are in major cities hosting a large number of computer stores. Individuals may work in a number of different employment situations including:

- Privately owned computer stores
- Chain and franchise computer stores
- Computer departments of department stores
- Computer departments of office machine and supply stores

Expanding Opportunities for the 21st Century

Computer salespeople, knowledgeable about more than one brand of computer as well as hardware and software, will be in demand throughout the country. Individuals who can demonstrate and explain features in an easy-to-understand manner will be sought out by stores and shops.

EARNINGS

Earnings for computer salespeople range from approximately $15,000 to $45,000. Variables affecting earnings include the ability, experience, and responsibilities of the salesperson as well as the size of the store, the geographic location, and the method of payment.

Salespeople may receive a straight salary, a commission on equipment sold, or a combination of the two.

ADVANCEMENT OPPORTUNITIES

Computer salespeople can advance their careers in a number of ways. Individuals who are being paid on commission may work toward increased earnings as a result of large sales. Salespeople can locate positions in large, prestigious stores that are more popular with customers.

Some computer salespeople are promoted to store managers, department managers, or service managers, depending on their expertise.

Others may move into wholesale computer sales.

EDUCATION AND TRAINING

The minimum education for most full-time jobs is a high school diploma.

Some employers will hire salespeople if they demonstrate proficiency on the equipment sold in the store. Other employers prefer individuals with college backgrounds or degrees. Many stores are beginning to require that salespeople have degrees in computer science.

Classes, seminars, and workshops in computer science, marketing, sales, programming, and computer services are all useful.

EXPERIENCE AND QUALIFICATIONS

Some employers do not require prior sales experience. They opt, instead, for technical knowledge of hardware and software. Other employers prefer individuals who have experience selling computers and computer accessories.

FOR ADDITIONAL INFORMATION: For career information, contact Computer and Business Equipment Manufacturers Association (CBEMA).

TIPS

- Learn as much as you can about all types of computers, software programs, and hardware. This will make you more marketable.

- Many computer companies offer training programs to fully familiarize salespeople with their products.
- You might consider workshops or seminars in selling and marketing.
- Job openings are advertised in the newspaper classified section under "Sales," "Salespeople," "Computer Sales," "Hardware Sales," etc.
- There is a high turnover in this type of position. Send your resume and a cover letter to computer stores and personnel directors of department stores with computer departments. You might also stop in and fill out an employment application.

COMPUTER SERVICE TECHNICIAN

JOB DESCRIPTION: *Repair computers and peripherals; perform preventive maintenance; install equipment.*

EARNINGS: *$20,000 to $43,000+.*

RECOMMENDED EDUCATION AND TRAINING: *High school diploma plus training in electronics; some positions require college training.*

SKILLS AND PERSONALITY TRAITS: *Mechanical and electrical aptitude; communication skills; analytical thinking; manual dexterity.*

EXPERIENCE AND QUALIFICATIONS: *Computer and electronics experience helpful.*

JOB DESCRIPTION AND RESPONSIBILITIES

Computer service technicians are called in when computers or computer equipment are not working properly. They talk to the customer, inspect the equipment, and determine the problem. Technicians may often run diagnostic programs or use testing equipment to locate specific problems. Sometimes the malfunction is in the system or other parts of the hardware. At other times, the problem is the software.

After pinpointing the malfunction, the service technician must repair it. This may be accomplished by replacing semiconductor chips, circuit boards, or other components. Repair may also be handled by fixing the mechanical parts of the computer.

Service technicians inspect the computers and peripherals and adjust, oil, and clean parts as preventive maintenance. They are also responsible for installing new equipment and testing it to make sure it is in working order.

Service technicians who work in the field use their own vehicle or may be provided with a company car or van. Individuals work varied hours depending on their shift and may be called in to handle emergencies. Computer service technicians are responsible to the shift supervisor or service manager.

Employment Opportunities

Some businesses that employ computer service technicians include:

- Wholesalers of computer equipment
- Computer maintenance services
- Equipment manufacturers
- Corporate industry
- Consulting and self-employment
- Retail computer stores

Expanding Opportunities for the 21st Century

Computer service technicians who will be most in demand are those trained and experienced in servicing a variety of models and brands of equipment. Individuals with at least a two-year degree in electronics will be more marketable than their counterparts with no formal education. The increasing number of home offices creates additonal opportunites for servicing and setting up home computer systems.

Earnings

Earnings for computer service technicians range from approximately $20,000 to $43,000 plus. Factors affecting earnings include the specific employment situation and location as well as the education, training, responsibilities, and experience of the technician.

Generally, the more training and education individuals have, the higher their earnings are. Service technicians in management or supervisory positions will earn more than those who handle only service and repair.

Advancement Opportunities

There are a number of ways computer service technicians can advance. Those who started out as trainees can become full-fledged service technicians and then senior technicians. Other individuals might be promoted to supervisory or management positions. Some technicians find increased responsibilities and earnings by locating similar positions with larger or more prestigious companies.

Computer service technicians may also climb the career ladder by opening up their own computer maintenance service.

EDUCATION AND TRAINING

Employers usually require at least a high school diploma plus additional training in basic electronics or electrical engineering and data processing equipment maintenance. Training may be received at a vocational-technical school, college, or university, or through the armed forces.

Many employers offer on-the-job training or formal training programs to new employees.

Computer franchises sponsor workshops, classes, and seminars so that technicians can not only get the proper training but also continue learning new technology. Manufacturers also sponsor similar programs.

EXPERIENCE AND QUALIFICATIONS

Trainee positions may not require any experience. Other positions usually will. These requirements, though, will usually be waived if individuals have formal training.

FOR ADDITIONAL INFORMATION: Additional information can be obtained through the Computer and Business Equipment Manufacturers Association (CBEMA).

TIPS

- Send your resume and a short cover letter to computer manufacturers, computer maintenance firms, and computer retail stores.
- This is an excellent career opportunity for individuals trained in electronics, such as television service technicians.
- If you are still in high school, take as many electronics and computer courses as possible. Some technical high schools offer preparation in computer repair.
- Job openings may be advertised in the newspaper classified section under "Computer Service Technician," "Computer Technician," or "Computers." They may also be advertised in trade journals.

COMPUTER TRAINER

JOB DESCRIPTION: *Train individuals to use computers and/or software; develop curriculum; answer questions.*

EARNINGS: *$20 to $150+ per hour; $20,000 to $45,000+ annually.*

RECOMMENDED EDUCATION AND TRAINING: *Requirements vary.*

SKILLS AND PERSONALITY TRAITS: *Teaching ability; technical skill and proficiency in computers; interpersonal skills; organization; communication skills.*

EXPERIENCE AND QUALIFICATIONS: *Experience using computers and software necessary.*

JOB DESCRIPTION AND RESPONSIBILITIES

The job market for computer trainers is growing tremendously as businesses become fully computerized.

Trainers may teach computer and software usage as well as programming. Some teach computer courses that include not only computer use but also desktop design, desktop publishing, newsletter design, etc. Individuals may specialize in instruction of one particular brand of computer or a variety of brands. The same is true of software packages.

Trainers may teach in their own offices or classrooms, at clients' offices or homes, or at rented facilities. There are training companies that move around the country, rent large conference rooms, and fill them with computers that are used to teach various programs.

Computer trainers use a variety of teaching aides including slides, overhead projections, and videos. Teaching methods depend to a great extent on the size of the class. In a one-on-one situation, trainers will illustrate methods to each student on his or her own computer. In larger classes, trainers may demonstrate methods using overhead charts and other teaching tools.

Trainers must explain complex technical matters in ways that students can readily understand. Getting students to ask questions is an important way of gauging if they are interested and are grasping the concepts.

Individuals may teach one student, a small group or a large audience of people, depending on the subject matter and the teaching methods.

EMPLOYMENT OPPORTUNITIES

Computer and software trainers can work full time, part time, or on a consulting basis. Individuals may be employed in a number of situations including:

- Corporations
- Software manufacturers
- Computer stores
- Computer manufacturers

- Consulting
- Consulting companies
- Self-employed
- Computer training centers

Expanding Opportunities for the 21st Century

There is a growing trend for self-employed individuals who are proficient in the use of computers and popular software packages to offer classes from their home or in students' homes or places of business.

EARNINGS

Computer trainers have a tremendous earning range depending on a number of factors. These include the specific type of employment situation, geographic location, experience, education, and responsibilities of the individual.

Individuals working part time or consulting may earn $20 to $150 or more per hour. Those working full time can have annual salaries ranging from $20,000 to $45,000. Trainers teaching more complex programs or software packages will usually earn more than individuals teaching basic ones.

ADVANCEMENT OPPORTUNITIES

After working for other trainers or training companies, many individuals open up their own facility or become training consultants.

EDUCATION AND TRAINING

Employers usually prefer that their trainers have a minimum of a high school diploma. Many trainers pick up the skills needed to be proficient in this area while using their own equipment. Others attend formal or informal training programs.

Training may be obtained in high schools, vocational-technical schools, junior or community colleges, four-year colleges, and universities. There are also a variety of seminars, workshops, and classes offered by training centers, computer stores, and software manufacturers.

The more software packages and computer skills trainers possess, the more marketable they will be.

EXPERIENCE AND QUALIFICATIONS

Experience requirements vary for trainers. Employers usually require some experience teaching or working with computers. Sometimes both skills are required. Many computer trainers were salespeople in computer stores, software departments, or sales reps for software companies.

FOR ADDITIONAL INFORMATION: Individuals interested in becoming computer trainers should contact the Association for Computing Machinery (ACM) or the Micro-computer Software Association (MSA).

TIPS

- Send your resume and a short cover letter to computer training centers, software manufacturers, and computer stores.
- Learn as much as you can about computers, software, and computer technology.
- If you are starting your own business as a trainer or want to consult, talk to the management of local computer stores. They may recommend your services to their customers.
- Place an advertisement in the business or classified section of the newspaper advertising your services.
- Obtain experience by teaching a class in computers or software in an adult or continuing education program.

CHAPTER 4

Conservation and Environmental Careers

As a result of the public's interest in the preservation and replenishment of the environment, there is a tremendous demand for people in a multiplicity of related careers. Included are environmentalists, engineers, technicians, technologists, and scientists. Other key players are educators, lawyers, physicians, nurses, landscape architects, farmers, horticulturists, public relations and communications specialists, writers, and fund-raisers.

Employment opportunities can be located in government agencies, corporations, private industry, environmental organizations, research laboratories, schools, colleges, and universities.

Individuals may work in a specific area of environmental protection or conservation or in a combination. Qualified people are needed now and will be required in the future to handle the prevention of and solution to pollution and contamination of air, water, and land. Individuals will also be needed to protect wildlife from extinction.

While careers in conservation and the environment require a variety of educational levels, experience, and skills, the one criterion they all have in common is a concern for the environment.

Careers covered in this section include:

Environmental Engineer
Environmentalist
Environmental Technician (water and wastewater)
Hazardous Waste Management Technician

Individuals interested in this area should also review career entries in Chapter 10, Science and Engineering Careers.

ENVIRONMENTAL ENGINEER

JOB DESCRIPTION: *Supervise cleanup of environmental contamination; design "environmentally safe" systems; propose solutions and preventions for environmental concerns.*

EARNINGS: *$30,000 to $85,000+.*

RECOMMENDED EDUCATION AND TRAINING: *Minimum of a bachelor's degree.*

SKILLS AND PERSONALITY TRAITS: *Communication skills; concern for and commitment to environment; scientific aptitude; math skills.*

EXPERIENCE AND QUALIFICATIONS: *State licensing required for certain jobs.*

JOB DESCRIPTION AND RESPONSIBILITIES

Environmental engineers deal with the cleanup or remediation of man-made contamination of the environment. This includes oil spills, chemical spills, and the dumping of toxic and hazardous waste.

They are involved with contaminated water, air, and land. Within these specialties are subspecialties that these individuals may concentrate in. For example, environmental engineers working with contaminated land may encounter a variety of toxins including solid waste, hazardous waste, and radioactive and medical wastes.

Environmental engineers use the skills of environmentalists and of chemical and civil engineers to determine the complexity of the problem and find safe ways to rid the area of the contaminants. For example, when there is an oil spill, a means of cleanup is determined that will do no further harm to the environment. Environmental engineers might also be responsible for finding ways to keep landfills environmentally safe and designing waste treatment systems.

One of the responsibilities of environmental engineers is determining exactly what the problems are and explaining what the consequences could be if they are not rectified. Individuals are also expected to discuss how they intend to solve these problems. In many positions, environmental engineers are required to provide public statements about problems.

Environmental engineers are often involved in fieldwork in areas where there is a high exposure to toxic substances and materials. Depending on the specific employer, individuals may also be expected to go to remote places that are in need of their services.

EMPLOYMENT OPPORTUNITIES

About half of the environmental engineers in the country work for government agencies while the other half work in the private sector. Individuals can work in a number of different employment situations including:

- Government agencies
- Engineering firms
- Manufacturing industry
- Energy industry
- Chemical industrial corporations
- Waste disposal firms
- Private industry
- Public utilities

Expanding Opportunities for the 21st Century

Cleaning up environmental contamination is more difficult and expensive than preventing it. Environmental engineers are needed to develop ways to prevent environmental contamination.

A great many environmental engineers will also be required in the manufacturing industry to determine how better to dispose of waste.

EARNINGS

Environmental engineers earn between $30,000 and $85,000 or more, depending on their employment setting, geographic location, experience, responsibilities, and education.

Generally, the more education and experience the individual has, the higher the earnings. Individuals who hold bachelor's degrees will earn between $30,000 and $42,000. Master's degrees command between $40,000 and $70,000. Those who hold Ph.D.s and are licensed can earn up to $85,000 plus.

ADVANCEMENT OPPORTUNITIES

Environmental engineers can advance their careers with additional experience and education. Individuals may locate positions in larger or more prestigious companies or be assigned to more complex projects.

Some environmental engineers are promoted to supervisory, administrative, or management positions. Others open up their own consulting firms.

EDUCATION AND TRAINING

Environmental engineers are required to have a minimum of a bachelor's degree. The best type of program for this job is a degree in environmental engineering. Other possible majors include environmental studies, civil engineering, chemical engineering, engineering management, or general engineering.

A master's degree is necessary for many senior positions. A Ph.D. is usually required for research or teaching.

EXPERIENCE AND QUALIFICATIONS

Some states require licensing for environmental engineers handling projects such as approving workplans for systems. Licensing is also necessary for individuals working in areas affecting property, health and/or life, or for individuals who offer their services to the public for a fee.

Individuals may receive the credential of professional engineer or PE.

FOR ADDITIONAL INFORMATION: Individuals interested in a career as an environmental engineer can contact the Environmental Industry Council (EICO), the Association of Environmental Engineering Professors (AEEP), Environmental Management (EM), the National Association of Environmental Professionals (NAEP), the National Environmental Health Association (NEHA), and the National Society of Professional Engineers (NSPE).

TIPS

- Contact state employment agencies for job openings in this field.
- Jobs are often advertised in the newspaper classifieds under "Environment," "Environmental Engineer," "Engineer," "Environmental Health," etc.
- Colleges and universities offering degrees in environmental engineering usually have job-placement offices that are notified of openings.
- Join trade associations. Membership is a good way to keep up with trends, meet people interested in the same field, and make important professional contacts.

ENVIRONMENTALIST

JOB DESCRIPTION: *Prevent and control pollution; solve environmental problems; conduct research.*

EARNINGS: *$20,000 to $60,000+.*

RECOMMENDED EDUCATION AND TRAINING: *Bachelor's degree in environmental science or a related field.*

SKILLS AND PERSONALITY TRAITS: *Strong concern for the environment; communication skills; interpersonal skills.*

EXPERIENCE AND QUALIFICATIONS: *Requirements vary.*

JOB DESCRIPTION AND RESPONSIBILITIES

The main function of environmentalists is to prevent pollution of the air, land, and water.

With increased chemical use in industry, the environment has become severely polluted. Environmentalists conduct research to find ways to handle or control pollution that has already occurred as well as to stave off new polluting incursions. Individuals also deal with conserving natural resources.

Environmentalists may specialize in areas including the preservation of wildlife, land and range conservation, contamination of water, removal of hazardous or toxic wastes, etc. They work with environmental, chemical, and civil engineers to deal with the extinction of wildlife, oil spills, and dumping of toxic wastes among other problems.

The duties of environmentalists in certain situations encompass lobbying and testifying in front of legislative committees. Some environmentalists are required to speak to civic groups, not-for-profit organizations, and government leaders concerning preventive measures.

Additional duties of environmentalists include preparing reports, performing inspections of polluted sites, appraising damage, and developing solutions.

Environmentalists report to either the project director, organization director, CEO, chief engineer, or other administrator.

EMPLOYMENT OPPORTUNITIES

Environmentalists can work in a variety of employment settings. These include:
- Government agencies
- Environmental consulting firms
- Private industry

- Mining corporations
- Chemical companies
- Oil companies
- Not-for-profit organizations

Expanding Opportunities for the 21st Century

As a result of widespread pollution, there will be an increased demand for environmentalists in this country and the world. Almost every employment setting will require specialists in this field.

EARNINGS

Environmentalists earn between $20,000 and $60,000 or more depending on an individual's area of expertise, education, experience, and responsibilities. Other factors affecting earnings include employment setting and geographic location.

Generally, the more experience and education individuals have, the higher their earnings are. Those just starting out will have annual salaries from $20,000 to $30,000. Environmentalists working in the private sector will usually earn more than their government counterparts.

ADVANCEMENT OPPORTUNITIES

Advancement opportunities for environmentalists depend to a great extent on the area in which they are working. Individuals starting out as trainees can become full-fledged environmentalists after obtaining a degree of experience. Those working in environmental research can become project directors. Some individuals seek supervisory or administrative positions.

Environmentalists working in not-for-profit organizations may advance their careers by being promoted to the position of the organization's executive director.

EDUCATION AND TRAINING

Environmentalists should have a minimum of a bachelor's degree. Majors depend on the areas individuals want to pursue. Good choices for majors include environmental science, the natural sciences, environmental engineering, environmental studies, civil engineering, chemical engineering, engineering management, or general engineering, liberal arts, or political science.

A graduate degree may be necessary for many senior positions.

EXPERIENCE AND QUALIFICATIONS

Experience requirements vary depending on the specific responsibilities of the position. Some jobs require or prefer experience in the environmental field. Individuals often obtain this through volunteer work or an internship with an environmental organization.

FOR ADDITIONAL INFORMATION: Individuals interested in becoming environmentalists can obtain additional information by contacting the Environmental Protection Agency (EPA), the National Association of Environmental Professionals (NAEP), the Institute of Environmental Sciences (IES), and the Association of Environmental Scientists and Administrators (AESA).

TIPS

- Colleges and universities offering programs in environmental sciences usually have placement offices that are aware of job openings.
- Jobs are advertised in trade journals or the newspaper classified sections under headings including "Environmentalist," "Environment," "Environmental Project Directors," or names of nonprofit environmental groups and organizations.
- Internships are an excellent opportunity to obtain on-the-job training. They also help you make valuable contacts.
- Many individuals seek out volunteer work for not-for-profit environmental groups to learn more about the field.

ENVIRONMENTAL TECHNICIAN (WATER AND WASTEWATER)

JOB DESCRIPTION: *Collect water samples and conduct tests to determine water pollution; operate and monitor equipment; treat pollutants with chemicals.*

EARNINGS: *$20,000 to $34,000.*

RECOMMENDED EDUCATION AND TRAINING: *High school diploma; some positions prefer college degree.*

SKILLS AND PERSONALITY TRAITS: *Concern for the environment; communication skills; scientific aptitude; detail oriented.*

EXPERIENCE AND QUALIFICATIONS: *State licensing and certification may be required.*

JOB DESCRIPTION AND RESPONSIBILITIES

Environmental technicians are responsible for preventing water pollution and treating wastewater. Wastewater might include sewage or it may be water from streams and lakes.

Environmental technicians may be referred to as wastewater technicians, water technicians, or solid waste technicians.

Individuals working in sewage plants take samples of water or sewage and test them to determine if any pollutants are contained. They treat the sewage with chemicals to break it down and then test the water again to make sure that it is pollutant-free before it is discarded.

Individuals may be responsible for operating equipment to control the waste into a plant as well as the equipment for removing the solid waste. Technicians may also be required to monitor equipment, record data, and prepare reports for review by other personnel.

Environmental technicians working in other employment settings may be expected to go out and perform field tests on streams, lakes, industrial wastewater, etc. They collect samples and prepare them for testing.

Environmental technicians may work directly in sewage plants, in laboratories, in the field, or in a combination of settings. Hours will vary depending on the job.

EMPLOYMENT OPPORTUNITIES

Environmental technicians can work in a variety of employment settings including
- Sewage plants
- Equipment manufacturers
- Government agencies
- Companies manufacturing pollution control equipment

Expanding Opportunities for the 21st Century

Increasing numbers of treatment plants will be needed in the future and technicians will be required to work in these plants. Environmental technicians who have associate degrees will be more marketable than their counterparts who just hold high school diplomas.

EARNINGS

Environmental technicians earn between $20,000 and $34,000, depending on their education, training, experience, location, and the specific employer.

Generally, the more education and experience individuals have, the higher their earnings. Environmental technicians working in large cities with a high cost of living will also be paid more than individuals in suburban areas.

ADVANCEMENT OPPORTUNITIES

With additional experience, training and/or education, individuals may be promoted to supervisory, administrative, or management positions.

EDUCATION AND TRAINING

Education requirements vary from job to job. Some positions may require just a high school diploma or equivalency. Others require or prefer a college background.

There are both associate and bachelor's degree programs in environmental technology and wastewater technology. Employers may offer on-the-job training programs. They might also send new employes to in-service courses through the government.

EXPERIENCE AND QUALIFICATIONS

Many entry-level jobs in this field do not require any experience. Others require experience or training. Environmental technician positions require licensing or certification in certain states.

FOR ADDITIONAL INFORMATION: Interested individuals can contact the Water Pollution Control Federation (WPCF), the National Association of Environmental Professionals, (NAEP), the Institute of Environmental Sciences (IES), Environmental Management (EM), and the Environmental Industry Council (EICO).

TIPS

- Schools offering degrees or certificate programs in wastewater technology usually have placement offices that are aware of openings.
- Contact your state employment office for details on government job openings.
- Job openings may be advertised in trade journals or the classified ad section of newspapers. Look under headings such as "Environmental Technician," "Environment," "Sewage Plant," "Waste Management Technician," etc.

HAZARDOUS WASTE MANAGEMENT TECHNICIAN

JOB DESCRIPTION: *Dispose of chemical and nuclear waste; run tests on water and soil samples.*

EARNINGS: *$20,000 to $44,000.*

RECOMMENDED EDUCATION AND TRAINING: *High school diploma plus on-the-job specialized training program.*

SKILLS AND PERSONALITY TRAITS: *Scientific aptitude; communication skills; ability to follow instructions.*

EXPERIENCE AND QUALIFICATIONS: *Requirements vary. Many positions do not require experience.*

JOB DESCRIPTION AND RESPONSIBILITIES

Hazardous waste does not just disappear; it must be disposed of in a safe manner. The people who are responsible for disposing of the waste are called hazardous waste management technicians. This job can be dangerous as technicians work with and around toxic chemicals. Hazardous waste management technicians are usually required to wear protective equipment to make the job safer.

Toxic wastes cannot just be picked up and moved. There are a number of methods of ridding an area of hazardous waste. Over twenty different methods have been approved by the federal government.

After the method of disposal has been determined, the hazardous waste management technician will work with others to eradicate the harmful chemicals. This is often accomplished by moving them to either a processing center or an area where chemicals can safely be disposed of.

Removing the chemicals may be accomplished by pumping them out of water or digging them out of soil or land. Once the chemicals have been removed, technicians will be required to take samples of the water and/or soil and run tests to be sure that the contaminants have been eliminated.

Technicians work varied hours depending on their shifts. Individuals are responsible to either the senior technician or engineer of the project.

EMPLOYMENT OPPORTUNITIES

Hazardous waste management technicians work for a variety of employers in either the private sector or government. Employment possibilities include:

- Hazardous waste consulting engineering firms
- Chemical companies

- Waste disposal companies
- Government agencies
- Independent consulting

Expanding Opportunities for the 21st Century

Hazardous waste management technicians will be in great demand as a result of the increasing quantity of hazardous waste produced by industry. As it has been proved that this waste is dangerous to both the population and the environment, trained individuals will be needed to dispose of it properly.

EARNINGS

Hazardous waste management technicians can earn approximately $20,000 to $44,000 annually depending on their experience, training, responsibilities, geographic location, and specific employer.

Individuals just entering the field will earn from $20,000 to $25,000. Those with more experience and responsibilities will have salaries toward the top of the pay scale.

ADVANCEMENT OPPORTUNITIES

Hazardous waste management technicians who obtain additional experience and training can advance by locating positions in larger companies. They can also be promoted to supervisory or management positions. Some individuals become independent consultants.

EDUCATION AND TRAINING

Hazardous waste management technicians must have a minimum of a high school diploma. Individuals will then go through an on-the-job training program or take training courses offered by the company they work with.

EXPERIENCE AND QUALIFICATIONS

Experience requirements vary for hazardous waste management technicians. Usually, no experience is necessary for trainees. Individuals in other positions may be required to have either experience or training.

FOR ADDITIONAL INFORMATION: Individuals interested in hazardous waste management can obtain additional information by contacting the Hazardous Waste Treatment Council (HWTC) or the Hazardous Materials Control Research Institute (HMCRI).

TIPS

- Contact state employment offices for openings in this field in government agencies.
- Send a short cover letter with your resume to hazardous waste consulting engineering firms, waste disposal companies, and chemical companies.
- Job openings may be advertised in trade journals or the classified section of the newspaper under such headings as "Hazardous Waste Management Technician," "Hazardous Waste," "Toxic Waste," "Chemical Waste," or "Nuclear Waste."

CHAPTER 5

Advertising, Communications, and Public Relations Careers

The advertising, communications, and public relations industries are multibillion-dollar businesses. Almost every type of company, not-for-profit organization, and political and government entity uses the services of these companies in one form or another. As a result, these occupations have been expanding and are expected to continue growing well into the 21st century.

It is difficult in today's society not to be affected by mass communications. Radio, television, print commercials, and billboards as well as articles in newspapers, magazines, and other publications influence what the public thinks and believes. Together the three fields impact on our purchasing, reading, and viewing habits as well as affecting opinions and decision making.

These industries require a wide variety of employees with different talents, skills, education, training, and experience. Secretaries, accountants, computer operators, salespeople, and receptionists are needed as well as advertising and public relations executives, publicists, press agents, copywriters, graphic artists, layout artists, desktop publishers, editors, marketing managers, and others.

Opportunities are available in publishing, radio and television, the corporate world, industry, agencies, sports, entertainment, hospitality and tourism, not-for-profit organizations, politics, and government. Freelance and consulting positions in these areas are just as important.

Careers in advertising, public relations, and communications cover a broad spectrum. Space restrictions limit inclusion of all possible opportunities. Careers included in this section are:

Copywriter
Graphic Artist
Radio/Television Advertising Salesperson
Reporter (Print)
Print Advertising Salesperson
Public Relations Counselor
Marketing Manager

COPYWRITER

JOB DESCRIPTION: *Write effective, creative copy for print ads, television and radio commercials, brochures, newsletters, etc.*

EARNINGS: *$18,000 to $85,000+.*

RECOMMENDED EDUCATION AND TRAINING: *Bachelor's degree.*

SKILLS AND PERSONALITY TRAITS: *Excellent writing skills; creativity; originality.*

EXPERIENCE AND QUALIFICATIONS: *Writing experience.*

JOB DESCRIPTION AND RESPONSIBILITIES

The main function of copywriters is to write copy for print advertisements, broadcast commercials, newspaper and magazine articles, and corporate publications.

Individuals working for advertising agencies are responsible for writing the copy for advertisements or commercials. Like copywriters working in other settings, they may also be responsible for brochures, sales pieces, letters, and internal publications.

Some copywriters are hired to write press releases, feature stories, newsletters, brochures, leaflets, and manuals. Others, such as those working in the corporate world or in not-for-profit agencies, write stockholder reports, annual reports, proposals, speeches, scripts for audiovisual material, instructional booklets, give-away sheets, and promotional materials.

In order to write effective copy, the writer must come up with a creative concept that will sell the product or idea or make it memorable. Copywriters working in advertising agencies, for example, may have to develop a central or motivating theme for a campaign to tie together advertisements for the same product or product family. In some instances the copywriter will have only a few words to accomplish this. In other circumstances such as when writing a report, he or she may have to write pages of copy.

EMPLOYMENT OPPORTUNITIES

Jobs can be located in a vast number of different environments including:

- Advertising agencies
- Public relations agencies
- Direct response agencies
- Not-for-profit organizations
- Television and radio
- Magazines and newspapers
- Corporate industry
- Freelance

Expanding Opportunities for the 21st Century

Copywriters who can develop effective copy for telemarketing and direct response advertising agencies will be in demand as a result of the growing popularity of this sales approach.

EARNINGS

Earnings for copywriters vary greatly depending on the specific job, the company, its size, prestige, and location. Other variables include the responsibilities, duties, and experience of the individual.

In general, those working in larger organizations in more urban areas can command higher annual earnings. Additionally, copywriters working in most not-for-profit organizations will receive lower compensation than their counterparts in advertising and public relations agencies or in corporate industry.

For example, a copywriter in a not-for-profit situation can earn between $18,000 and $28,000 plus annually. Individuals in corporate jobs may start at $18,500 and go up to $45,000 plus. Copywriters in advertising and public relations agencies may earn between $20,000 and $85,000 plus.

ADVANCEMENT OPPORTUNITIES

Copywriters can become copy supervisors, senior copywriters, creative supervisors, or freelancers.

EDUCATION AND TRAINING

Though some positions require only a high school diploma, a four-year college degree is usually expected. Good choices for majors include advertising, marketing, English, public relations, communications, and liberal arts.

Seminars, workshops, and additional courses in advertising, publicity, public relations, psychology, and writing are useful. Seminars dealing with specific types of copywriting such as direct mail/direct marketing, newspaper advertisements, brochures, and sales letters are available throughout the country.

EXPERIENCE AND QUALIFICATIONS

While there are some entry-level positions in this field that require little or no experience, to compete in the workforce individuals should have writing experience.

Summer or part-time jobs in the advertising department of newspapers, magazines, department stores, and radio or television stations offer excellent training. Other experience may be obtained through internships, through trainee programs, or in school through appropriate classes.

Career changers should have experience in journalism, public relations, advertising, or marketing.

FOR ADDITIONAL INFORMATION: Copywriters can belong to a number of trade associations and organizations that offer trade journals, conferences, seminars, workshops, and professional guidance. Addresses can be found in the Appendix.

These include the Public Relations Society of America (PRSA), the American Advertising Federation (AAF), Direct Marketing Creative Guild, the American Marketing Association, the Advertising Club of New York, the Advertising Research Foundation (ARF), Advertising Women of New York, Inc. (AWNY), The One Club, the International Association of Business Communicators (IABC), the American Business Communication Association (ABCA), and Women in Communications (WIC).

Individuals interested in direct marketing or direct response companies may also want to contact the Direct Marketing Association (DMA), the Direct Mail/Marketing Association (DM/MA), Sales and Marketing Executives International (SMEI), the American Telemarketing Association (ATA), and the Mail Advertising Service Association (MASA).

Contact the Writers Guild of America (WGA), a bargaining union for television, radio, and film scriptwriters, for additional information on writing television or radio commercials.

Those aspiring to work for not-for-profit organizations might write to the National Society of Fund Raising Executives (NSFRE) and Council for the Advancement and Support of Education (CASE).

Tips

- Obtain experience and contacts by volunteering to do publicity and write press releases for community or civic groups.
- Openings for copywriters are advertised in the classified sections of newspapers.
- Send your resume and a short cover letter to the personnel, advertising, and public relations departments of radio and television stations, not-for-profit organizations, advertising and public relations agencies, and businesses in corporate industry.

GRAPHIC ARTIST

JOB DESCRIPTION: *Design the graphics for advertisements, catalogs, promotional pieces, etc.*

EARNINGS: *$18,000 to $45,000.*

RECOMMENDED EDUCATION AND TRAINING: *Bachelor's degree with major in art required for many positions; other positions may accept graduation from art school.*

SKILLS AND PERSONALITY TRAITS: *Creativity; artistic; drawing and illustration skills; knowledge of paste-ups, mechanicals, and typography; understanding of advertising industry; computer capabilities.*

EXPERIENCE AND QUALIFICATIONS: *Portfolios are necessary for most positions.*

JOB DESCRIPTION AND RESPONSIBILITIES

Graphic artists are responsible for designing and developing the graphics for a variety of advertising and business needs. Graphics encompass artwork, pictures, and illustrations as well as layout. These artists design material for advertisements, packaging, book covers, record or cassette covers, sales pieces, logos, publications, and more.

Individuals in this position might work for an advertising or public relations agency or be part of the advertising and promotion department within a corporation, publication, or organization in any industry. They might also freelance.

Graphic artists are responsible for developing creative, innovative, appealing, and memorable graphics.

Those working for corporations or advertising agencies may be asked to develop designs for product packaging. As package design is a form of advertising for a product, it is extremely important to all companies. The graphic artist must design a package that catches the eye of the consumer when the product is on the shelf in the marketplace.

Graphic artists working for book publishers may be responsible for creating the entire design of a book from the interior page layout and type style to jackets and promotional displays.

Other functions include designing graphics and art for advertisements, sales pieces, brochures, stationery, envelopes, order forms, labels, sales tags, etc. Individuals might be required to design point-of-purchase advertising promotions, signs, or display racks that are seen in stores.

The individual is usually responsible to the art director of the corporate advertising and promotion department or the art director or account executive of an advertising agency.

EMPLOYMENT OPPORTUNITIES

There are almost always employment opportunities for talented graphic artists. One of the good things about being a graphic artist is that positions can be located throughout the country. Individuals can work in a variety of environments including:

- Advertising agencies
- Public relations agencies
- Corporations
- Record companies
- Television stations
- Magazines
- Newspapers
- Book publishers
- Not-for-profit agencies
- Freelance

Expanding Opportunities for the 21st Century

Talented graphic artists are always in demand. Individuals will be needed in advertising departments of corporations as well as in newspapers and other periodicals. The new century will bring expanding opportunities to freelance graphic artists and to those who are competent designing on computers.

EARNINGS

Graphic artists earn from approximately $18,000 to $45,000 depending on the specific type of job, company size, and geographic location. The reputation, talent, skill, experience, and responsibilities of the individual also greatly affect salary.

Graphic artists working in advertising agencies or large corporations in metropolitan areas earn more than those working in advertising departments of publications.

ADVANCEMENT OPPORTUNITIES

Graphic artists can advance their careers in a number of ways. Individuals may find jobs in large, prestigious companies. They may also become art director or creative director of an advertising agency or art department.

EDUCATION AND TRAINING

Educational requirements for graphic artists differ from job to job. Most corporations and advertising agencies require a four-year college degree with a major in fine or commercial art. There are some jobs that require only a high school diploma and art school training. There are also instances where an applicant's education is not as important as the merits of a creative portfolio.

As computer-generated graphics are being used more and more, computer graphics courses will give an applicant the competitive edge.

EXPERIENCE AND QUALIFICATIONS

Graphic artists must have a portfolio to present. This is a collection of the best and most creative work of the artist. Many individuals who are just entering the job market or are changing careers fill their portfolio with samples of work from college projects, or any other ideas that illustrate their talents.

FOR ADDITIONAL INFORMATION: For more information contact the Graphic Artists Guild (GAG), the Educational Council of the Graphic Arts (ECGA), the American Institute of Graphic Arts (AIGA), or the Society of Illustrators (SOI). These associations provide support, guidance, and helpful seminars for their members.

TIPS

- Many trade associations will critique your portfolio and offer constructive criticism to make it better.
- If you are still in school, try to locate an internship or training program to get hands-on experience.
- Write to the personnel director of corporations, businesses, organizations, and publications inquiring about openings for graphic artists. Send your resume with a short cover letter offering to meet for an interview and show them your portfolio.

RADIO/TELEVISION ADVERTISING SALESPERSON

JOB DESCRIPTION: *Sell space to advertisers for radio or television commercials.*

EARNINGS: *$18,000 to $125,000+.*

RECOMMENDED EDUCATION AND TRAINING: *Minimum requirement is a high school diploma; most positions require a bachelor's degree.*

SKILLS AND PERSONALITY TRAITS: *Aggressiveness; communication skills; sales ability; personable; self-motivated.*

EXPERIENCE AND QUALIFICATIONS: *Sales experience helpful.*

Job Description and Responsibilities

Radio and television stations make money by selling airtime to businesses that want to advertise their products and services. It is the job of advertising salespeople, also referred to as sales reps, to solicit new advertisers and maintain existing accounts.

The station sales manager may assign specific territories to the salesperson or the individual may be free to sell advertisements anywhere. Instead of geographic territories, salespeople are sometimes assigned categories of advertisers such as restaurants or retail shops. Depending on the station's size and structure, the salesperson may be assigned local, regional, or national accounts or may sell to all three.

Whatever the territory, the sales rep's main function is to bring in new business. At times, the salesperson will be working with businesses who call up and are interested in advertising. In other instances, the individual may have to make "cold calls" to businesses who have expressed little or no interest in advertising.

There is a great deal of paperwork in this job. One of the duties of the salesperson is writing sales orders for commercial insertion and moving them on to the appropriate people at the station. The individual will also be required to keep records detailing when advertisements are aired, insertion rates, discounts, and billing names and addresses.

The advertising salesperson is responsible to the station's advertising director. While the salesperson is expected to keep normal business hours, many individuals set up appointments at the convenience of clients even if it means working at night or on weekends.

Employment Opportunities

Without salespeople, radio and television stations would have limited income. Individuals who are aggressive, hardworking, and can sell are always in demand by station advertising departments.

Most stations, even the smaller ones, have at least two salespeople. Some larger stations have twenty-five or more people in this position; networks employ even greater numbers. Employment options include:

- Local television or radio station
- Independent television or radio station
- Network television or radio station
- Cable television station

Expanding Opportunities for the 21st Century

As cable is becoming an increasingly influential force in the broadcast industry, sales departments for this market are expanding and employment opportunities should be plentiful.

EARNINGS

Earnings for sales reps depend on the experience and selling ability of an individual. Other factors affecting take-home pay include the size, location, and prestige of the station. Salaries range from approximately $18,000 to over $125,000. Most stations also offer fringe benefit packages to employees to augment their income.

Television or radio advertising salespeople may be paid in a number of ways.

Options include salary plus a commission on sales, a straight commission, or a draw against commissions.

When commission is a factor, salespeople who sell more, earn more. The percentage of commission varies but is usually between 10 percent and 20 percent.

ADVANCEMENT OPPORTUNITIES

Radio and television salespeople can advance their careers in a number of ways. One method is to locate a position in a large market or prestigious station. Another method is to become a sales manager for a broadcast station.

EDUCATION AND TRAINING

Educational requirements vary from job to job for radio and television salespeople. While the minimum requirement for some jobs is a high school diploma, most stations require a bachelor's degree. Individuals in this line of work may have various majors including advertising, communications, business, marketing, or liberal arts. Useful courses include advertising, sales, business, marketing, speech, math, English, sociology, psychology, writing, and communications.

Successful salespeople also keep up with selling trends and hone skills by taking workshops and seminars offered by trade associations or other organizations.

EXPERIENCE AND QUALIFICATIONS

Any type of selling experience is useful for radio or television salespeople. Individuals just entering the job market might find it easier to break into small- or medium-market radio or television.

FOR ADDITIONAL INFORMATION: Associations and organizations that can provide additional information include the Television Bureau of Advertising (TBA), American Advertising Federation (AAF), the National Association of Broadcasters (NAB), Radio and Advertising Bureau (RAB), or the National Association of Broadcast Employees and Technicians (NABET).

TIPS

- Job openings are often listed in the television and radio broadcast trade papers. If your local library doesn't stock these, contact a local television or radio station to ask if you can review a few issues. You might also contact the trade journal itself to inquire about obtaining a short-term subscription.

- Positions in this field are advertised in the newspaper classified sections under the headings: "Advertising," "Sales," "Salesperson," "Radio," "Television," or "Broadcasting."

- Selling is selling. Remember when you prepare your resume to put down every sales job you have ever held.

- Look in the yellow pages of the telephone book to obtain the names and addresses of television and radio stations in the area. Send your resume and a short cover letter to the personnel manager, station manager, or station owner. Try to address your correspondence to a specific name, not just a title.

REPORTER (PRINT)

JOB DESCRIPTION: *Gather information through interviews and investigation; develop an angle or emphasis; write and edit stories and articles.*

EARNINGS: *$14,000 to $100,000+.*

RECOMMENDED EDUCATION AND TRAINING: *Educational requirements vary from high school diploma to college degree.*

SKILLS AND PERSONALITY TRAITS: *Excellent communication skills; writing skills; creativity; persistence; ability to deal with pressure; word processing.*

EXPERIENCE AND QUALIFICATIONS: *Experience requirements vary.*

JOB DESCRIPTION AND RESPONSIBILITIES

Reporters working in print media are called journalists, columnists, or correspondents. Their main function is to write factual, informative, and interesting articles for newspapers, magazines, and other print markets. Individuals may be general reporters or specialize in fields such as sports, news, current events, family matters, health, politics, police beats, education, foreign affairs, fashion, theater, the arts, consumer affairs, education, business, or investigative reporting.

Once a reporter is assigned a story or topic, the individual must gather information. This is accomplished through interviewing, investigating leads and news tips, talking to people on the scene, and reviewing preexisting documents. It is essential that individuals make sure their information is accurate.

Once reporters have the facts, they develop an angle and/or focus to the story and write their article. They may rewrite it a number of times until it is polished. Reporters must then type the story and give it to the editor for review. Most larger newspapers and magazines now use computers.

All fact-gathering, interviewing, and writing must be done in a timely fashion as publications work under deadlines. Additional responsibilities may include taking photographs, writing captions and headlines, or editing wire service copy and press releases.

Reporters are responsible to either their section editor or the editor-in-chief.

EMPLOYMENT OPPORTUNITIES

Employment settings include:

- Daily newspapers
- Weekly newspapers
- Trade journals
- Magazines

Expanding Opportunities for the 21st Century

It is expected that there will be an increase in the number of small-town daily and weekly newspapers. In addition, new magazines on a variety of subjects continue to crop up. Reporters will be required for all of these.

EARNINGS

Earnings for full-time reporters in print media can vary from approximately $14,000 to $100,000 plus. Variables include the type of publication, its location, circulation, and prestige, as well as the reporter's experience, responsibilities, and education.

Individuals working on small-town weeklies with little experience can earn from $14,000 to $19,000. With more experience, reporters working at large dailies, weeklies, trade journals, or magazines earn between $18,000 and $35,000. Individuals with a great deal of experience can earn up to $50,000. Reporters working on major metropolitan newspapers or well-known magazines can earn up to $75,000. Some well-known journalists earn $100,000 plus.

ADVANCEMENT OPPORTUNITIES

Reporters in print media can advance their careers in a number of ways. Individuals with experience may get more interesting or important assignments. Others locate similar positions in larger or more prestigious newspapers, magazines, or journals.

Some reporters become either section editors or publication editors. There are also a great many print reporters and journalists who move into the broadcast field.

EDUCATION AND TRAINING

Educational requirements vary for print reporters. There are still a number of small-town weeklies that require no more than a high school diploma. There are two-year associate degree programs with majors in journalism available in community colleges and junior colleges throughout the country.

However, a four-year degree in journalism, communications, or even liberal arts is recommended. Courses in journalism, reporting, copy editing, mass media, journalism history, press law, and ethics are valuable.

Many individuals obtain a master's degree in journalism while they are working.

EXPERIENCE AND QUALIFICATIONS

Experience requirements vary for print reporters. Positions at many small weeklies, for example, are often entry-level jobs. While they may not require work experience, most employers expect that applicants worked on their high school or college newspaper. Another good way to get experience is participating in an internship program.

Positions at larger or more prestigious publications require work experience at smaller weeklies.

FOR ADDITIONAL INFORMATION: Learn more about the field by contacting the American Newspaper Publishers Association Foundation (ANPAF), the Community College Journalism Association (CCJA), the Newspaper Guild (NG), the Accrediting Council on Education in Journalism and Mass Communications (ACEJMC), the Association for Education in Journalism and Mass Communications (AEJMC), the National Newspaper Association (NNA), and the Dow Jones Newspaper Fund.

TIPS

- If you are in school, get involved in your high school or college newspaper.
- Internships are especially valuable. They are offered through many colleges, universities, newspapers, magazines, and trade associations.
- It is often easier to land a position with a small-town or suburban newspaper. After you obtain some experience, you can apply for positions with larger newspapers or magazines.

PRINT ADVERTISING SALESPERSON

JOB DESCRIPTION: *Sell space to advertisers for newspapers, magazines, or other print periodicals.*

EARNINGS: *$18,000 to $100,000+.*

RECOMMENDED EDUCATION AND TRAINING: *Minimum requirement is a high school diploma; most positions require a bachelor's degree.*

SKILLS AND/OR PERSONALITY TRAITS: *Aggressiveness; communication skills; sales ability; facility with numbers; personableness; self-motivation.*

EXPERIENCE AND QUALIFICATIONS: *Sales experience helpful.*

Job Description and Responsibilities

Newspapers, magazines, and other periodicals earn income in a number of ways. In addition to selling the newspaper or magazine subscriptions, print media earn money by selling advertising space to businesses who want to advertise their products and services. It is the job of print advertising salespeople, also referred to as sales reps, to solicit new advertisers and maintain existing accounts.

The salesperson may be assigned specific accounts to service or may be free to sell ads to any advertiser. Depending on the size and type of the newspaper or magazine, the salesperson may be expected to service local, regional, or national accounts.

In most print media situations, there is an advertising sales manager who oversees the various salespeople. In very small newspapers or periodicals, the sales manager may also be the salesperson.

Print advertising salespeople are expected to bring in new business as well as service existing accounts. At certain times, the sales rep may be called upon by a business interested in advertising in that specific medium. At other times, the salesperson may be expected to make "cold calls" to businesses who have expressed little or no interest in advertising.

One of the functions of the salesperson is writing sales orders for advertisement insertion. Another is designating the insertion order to the appropriate people at the newspaper or periodical. The individual is usually required to keep records of when advertisements are inserted and printed, insertion rates, discounts, billing names, and addresses.

In many instances, especially in smaller publications, the advertising salesperson will be responsible for developing copy for the ad, suggesting graphics, and so forth. In larger publications, this duty will be handled by the copywriters and graphics department. The sales rep is also responsible for getting proofs to the client and making sure that ads are approved before being printed in a publication.

Print sales reps usually work normal business hours. However, individuals may set up appointments at other times that are more convenient to clients. Successful sales reps also usually do quite a bit of networking in order to make contacts with potential clients. This is often done after work or on weekends.

EMPLOYMENT OPPORTUNITIES

Salespeople who are aggressive, hardworking, and persuasive are always in demand by newspapers, magazines, and other periodicals.

Most publications have at least two salespeople. Some larger publications have twenty or more people in this position; large, well-known newspapers and magazines employ even more. Employment options include:

- Daily newspapers (large metropolitan city papers, suburban papers, small-town newspapers)
- Weekly newspapers
- Shoppers or pennysavers
- Trade journals
- Magazines (small- or large-circulation special-interest publications)
- Freelance print salesperson

Expanding Opportunities for the 21st Century

Employment opportunities should be plentiful for good salespeople in all fields of print media in the coming century.

Freelance salespeople will see expanding opportunities in the new century. These individuals often work for two or three noncompetitive publications.

EARNINGS

Earnings for sales reps depend on the experience and selling ability of an individual. Other factors affecting take-home pay include the size, location, and prestige of the publication. Salaries range from approximately $18,000 to over $100,000. Most publications also offer fringe-benefit packages to employees in order to augment their income.

Print advertising salespeople may be paid in a number of ways. Options include salary plus a commission on sales, a straight commission, or a draw against commissions.

When commission is a factor, salespeople who sell more earn more. The percentage of commission varies, but is usually between 10 percent and 20 percent.

ADVANCEMENT OPPORTUNITIES

Print advertising salespeople can advance their careers in a number of ways. One method is to locate a position in a larger or more prestigious publication. Another method is to become a sales manager for a newspaper, magazine, or other publication. Some individuals go into selling other types of products to climb the career ladder.

EDUCATION AND TRAINING

Educational requirements vary from job to job. While the minimum requirement for some jobs is a high school diploma, most publications prefer or require a bachelor's degree. Individuals in this line of work may have majors including advertising, communications, business, marketing, or liberal arts. Useful courses include advertising, sales, business, marketing, speech, math, English, sociology, psychology, writing, and communications.

Workshops and seminars offered by trade associations or other organizations are also helpful in honing skills.

EXPERIENCE AND QUALIFICATIONS

Any type of selling experience is useful for print advertising salespeople. Individuals just entering the job market might find it easier to break into this line of work in smaller weekly publications or local magazines.

FOR ADDITIONAL INFORMATION: Associations and organizations that can provide additional information include the American Advertising Federation (AAF) and the American Association of Advertising Agencies (AAAA).

TIPS

- Positions in this field are advertised in the newspaper classified sections under the headings: "Advertising," "Sales," "Salesperson," "Newspaper," "Magazines," and "Publishing."
- Selling is selling. Remember when you prepare your resume to put down every sales job you have ever held. You might even want to include any special honors achieved, such as being the highest-selling salesperson for your high school magazine subscription drive.
- Look in the yellow pages of the telephone book to obtain the names and addresses of newspapers and magazines in the area. Send your resume and a short cover letter to the personnel manager, sales manager, or publication owner. Try to address your correspondence to a specific name— not just a title.
- Join local chambers of commerce, not-for-profit groups, and the like to make important contacts and learn about new business possibilities.

PUBLIC RELATIONS COUNSELOR

JOB DESCRIPTION: *Develop public relations and publicity campaigns; create positive image for clients; write news releases, annual reports, and speeches; design brochures; develop promotions.*

EARNINGS: *$18,000 to $150,000+.*

RECOMMENDED EDUCATION AND TRAINING: *Bachelor's degree in public relations, advertising, English, journalism, communications, or liberal arts.*

SKILLS AND PERSONALITY TRAITS: *Excellent writing skills; creativity; originality; aggressiveness; communication skills.*

EXPERIENCE AND QUALIFICATIONS: *Experience in writing, journalism, publicity, and marketing.*

JOB DESCRIPTION AND RESPONSIBILITIES

Every successful company and organization incorporates public relations into its business in some way. The main function of public relations is to build a positive image for a company, organization, industry, person, or project, and then keep that image in the public eye as much as possible. People who specialize in this field are called public relations counselors or publicists.

Successful PR people should be adept at developing public relations campaigns for clients, writing press releases, fielding media questions, editing copy or supervising the layout of publications, and designing brochures and sales pieces. Other PR functions include implementing promotions, meeting with clients, and setting up press conferences.

In some instances, an individual may be hired by a corporation to handle one or all of the company's public relations responsibilities. In other situations, a counselor is retained to serve as the company spokesperson or to advise the client on how to respond to the press.

PR counselors book clients on television and radio talk shows. They also develop and maintain accurate media and mailing lists. These lists are essential in sending press releases, articles, and other written material. Public relations people should be comfortable dealing with the media in all areas whether it be talking to reporters about a story, personally appearing on television or radio, or being interviewed by the print media as a spokesperson for a client.

Hours for public relations people vary depending on the specific job. Those working in-house for corporations or organizations will work normal hours most of the time. When special projects come up or a deadline must be met, the individual will be required to work overtime.

EMPLOYMENT OPPORTUNITIES

Public relations is becoming a business necessity as more and more organizations vie not only for the attention of the public but also for a positive image. Almost every corporation and organization has a public relations department that must be staffed. Employment settings include:

- Public relations firms
- Advertising agencies
- Corporate industry
- Not-for-profit organizations
- Entertainment companies
- Tourism and hospitality
- Trade associations
- Political candidates
- Health care facilities
- Retail businesses
- Shopping centers and malls
- Public relations consulting firms
- Freelance

Expanding Opportunities for the 21st Century

The greatest need for PR counselors will be in not-for-profit organizations. Individuals will also find that freelance PR services will be required by those in smaller corporations and organizations.

EARNINGS

Earnings for public relations counselors can vary greatly depending on the specific job or client. Other factors affecting compensation include the individual's responsibilities, education, experience, and geographic location. Annual earnings can range from $18,000 to $150,000 plus.

Public relations counselors who work on a freelance or consulting basis may get paid a set fee from a client on a per-project basis. They may also be paid a monthly retainer or may charge by the hour for their services. Retainers can range from $50 to $10,000 a month. Hourly rates can run between $10 and $200 plus an hour, depending on the individual's experience and reputation in the field. Keep in mind that many individuals who freelance have more than one client.

Earnings for full-time in-house public relations workers in corporations may range from $18,000 to $150,000 or more, depending on the experience and responsibilities of the individual and the size and location of the business, company, or organization. In general, people working in larger, more metropolitan areas will earn more than their counterparts in smaller suburban locations.

Advancement Opportunities

Public relations counselors can advance in a number of ways. One path to career advancement is to become a director of a public relations department. Another is to locate a similar position in a larger, more prestigious company. This will result in increased earnings and responsibilities. Some people freelance or open their own firms.

Education and Training

A minimum of a four-year college degree is usually required for most jobs in public relations. A master's degree is often helpful in both attaining a job and advancing a career.

Good choices for majors include public relations, journalism, communications, marketing, English, or liberal arts. Seminars, workshops, and courses in public relations, publicity, marketing, and all phases of writing will also be helpful to those just entering the workforce as well as career changers.

Experience and Qualifications

While many people decide to pursue public relations while in college, others opt for this career when they realize that they have been handling public relations projects in voluntary positions throughout their lifetime. These include volunteering to work on a political campaign or acting as a publicity chairperson or running a fund-raising event for a nonprofit organization such as the PTA, scouts, or hospital auxiliary.

Writing experience is especially useful. Many public relations people have worked as journalists or copywriters prior to their current PR jobs.

FOR ADDITIONAL INFORMATION: The Public Relations Society of America (PRSA) provides educational guidance and professional support for people interested in the public relations field. It also sponsors a student organization.

Tips

- Job openings are advertised in the classified sections of newspapers under "Public Relations," "Publicity," "Communications," and "Marketing." Positions are also advertised in trade journals.
- Taking courses and seminars in public relations, marketing, and publicity will help you hone skills and make professional contacts.
- Get hands-on experience by volunteering your services to nonprofit organizations or community groups.
- There are employment agencies specifically for public relations.

- Internships are especially useful to obtain needed experience and make contacts.

MARKETING MANAGER

JOB DESCRIPTION: *Develop and implement marketing campaigns; research market statistics; write sales material.*

EARNINGS: *$20,000 to $150,000+.*

RECOMMENDED EDUCATION AND TRAINING: *BA in communications, marketing, public relations, advertising, journalism, English, or liberal arts.*

SKILLS AND PERSONALITY TRAITS: *Creativity; aggressiveness; motivation; communication and writing skills; ambition; ability to research.*

EXPERIENCE AND QUALIFICATIONS: *Experience in marketing, advertising, promotion, and public relations.*

JOB DESCRIPTION AND RESPONSIBILITIES

A marketing manager is responsible for developing concepts and campaigns designed to introduce and promote a company's products or services.

Successful marketing is a complex affair. The marketing manager works with a number of other departments in the company including sales, promotion, advertising, and public relations to accomplish the job. The marketing department, headed by the marketing manager, is responsible for determining the amount of advertising and type of media that will be used to sell a product, service, or company. The department manager is also responsible for deciding the types of promotions, public relations, and selling techniques that will be most effective.

An important function of some marketing managers is determining the viability of new products. The individual may do this in a number of ways including extensive consumer research and test marketing. Research may entail verbal interviews or written questionnaires, searching through libraries and databases, and using information provided by trade associations. After research and test marketing are completed, the marketing manager must tabulate and review the information.

There is quite a bit of writing involved in this job including developing letters, press releases, reports, proposals, sales pieces, brochures, newsletters, and memos.

Other responsibilities of a marketing manager might include supervising staff, leading sales meetings, training sales and marketing people, and attending trade shows, conventions, and fairs on behalf of the company.

This can be a high-stress job. There is a constant need to produce. A great deal of overtime is expected when projects, special events, and promotions are under way and must be completed.

EMPLOYMENT OPPORTUNITIES

Job opportunities can be located throughout the country in metropolitan and suburban areas. Examples of industries individuals might work in include:

- Pharmaceuticals
- Book publishers
- Cosmetics
- Retail stores
- Service industries
- Banks
- Not-for-profit organizations
- Health care facilities
- Geriatric facilities
- Real estate
- Insurance
- Restaurants
- Hotel-motel chains
- Automobiles
- Educational institutions
- Radio and television stations
- Import/export

Expanding Opportunities for the 21st Century

Employment prospects are excellent for marketing managers in almost any industry in the corporate world. Nearly every midsize or larger company has a marketing department and therefore needs the services of a marketing manager. In addition, there is a large turnover in the corporate marketing field. This is due, in part, to career advancement and the general mobility of people who enter this field. Opportunities will increase for those who freelance or consult in the marketing field.

EARNINGS

Marketing managers can earn between $20,000 and $150,000 or more depending on the individual's experience, reputation, and responsibilities. Other factors affecting earnings include the specific type of industry, its size, prestige, and location.

Individuals with a great deal of responsibility working in large corporations in metropolitan areas will earn salaries between $65,000 and $150,000 plus. Earnings will be considerably lower for marketing managers in smaller organizations or those with less experience and responsibility.

ADVANCEMENT OPPORTUNITIES

The most common path to career advancement for marketing managers is to locate positions in larger, more prestigious companies or organizations. This usually results in increased responsibilities and earnings.

EDUCATION AND TRAINING

Educational requirements can vary from job to job. Most positions require at least a bachelor's degree. Some prefer a graduate degree. Good choices for majors include business administration, communications, marketing, public relations, advertising, or liberal arts.

Additional courses, seminars, and workshops in promotion, PR, marketing, communications, business, writing, psychology, sociology, research, and statistics will be useful.

EXPERIENCE AND QUALIFICATIONS

The majority of jobs require marketing managers with experience in public relations, marketing, promotion, and advertising.

FOR ADDITIONAL INFORMATION: Trade associations in the marketing field offer seminars, workshops and classes, literature, and professional guidance. Organizations to contact for more information include the American Marketing Association (AMA), the Direct Mail/Marketing Association (DM/MA), the Direct Marketing Creative Guild (DMCG), the Marketing Research Association (MRA), Sales and Marketing Executives International (SMEI), the Promotion Marketing Association of America, Inc. (PMAA), and the American Business Communications Association (ABCA).

TIPS

- Join relevant trade associations. They help you locate internships, scholarships, and training programs as well as offering career guidance and support.
- Take marketing seminars and workshops that are offered through trade associations, business organizations, and trade journals.
- Send your resume and a cover letter to the personnel director of companies, corporations, and organizations. There is a big turnover in this field. If there are no current openings, request that your resume be kept on file.
- Jobs openings may be advertised in trade journals, company house organs, and newsletters, as well as newspapers.
- Look for internship porgrams while you are still in school. These are excellent sources of experience and help you cultivate important contacts.

CHAPTER 6

Sales and Service Careers

Every time people eat in a restaurant, shop in a store, buy insurance or real estate, handle a banking transaction, or have their hair styled, they are utilizing sales and services. The classification of sales and service careers is all-encompassing. Occupations in this area can span a multitude of educational levels, experience, and skills.

Opportunities in sales and service cover jobs in health care, business, education, hospitality, retail and wholesale trade, finance, insurance, law and real estate, government, transportation, communications, and public utilities, to name a few.

The areas of sales and services are often intertwined. Many service careers are, in effect, serving the customer by selling those services. Lawyers sell legal advice, physicians sell medical expertise, and accountants sell financial services.

Some occupations, such as law enforcement and firefighting, are primarily service-oriented. Others, including retail sales managers and manufacturer's representatives, are principally sales-oriented.

The new century will bring a demand for more sales and service workers in all industries. The need for people in law, medicine, accounting, and other professional licensed careers will be balanced by a growing need for those who perform services such as food service, maintenance and cleaning, clerical work, personal care, and sales and marketing.

A great number of jobs in sales and service will be found in health care and business. Personnel supply services such as temporary help agencies will also need workers. Other areas experiencing growth include computer services, research, management, consulting, education, and retail trades.

Sales and service jobs range over a broad assortment of industries. The diversity of careers as well as space restrictions limit inclusion of all possible opportunities. Included in this section are:

Accountant	Paralegal
Actuary	Salesperson
Insurance Sales Agent	Correction Officer
Real Estate Agent	Personal Shopper
Lawyer	Hairstylist

Child-Care Worker   Private Investigator
Secretary   Property Manager

Individuals interested in sales and service careers should also review entries in other sections of this book. Health care services, geriatrics, computers, education, conservation and the environment, advertising, communications and public relations, fitness and nutrition, hospitality and travel, and home-based businesses all have opportunities in sales and service.

ACCOUNTANT

JOB DESCRIPTION: *Maintain financial records; conduct audits; prepare tax returns; advise clients on tax matters; prepare financial reports.*

EARNINGS: *$25,000 to $100,000+.*

RECOMMENDED EDUCATION AND TRAINING: *Bachelor's degree in accounting; some positions require a master's degree.*

SKILLS AND PERSONALITY TRAITS: *Good math skills; interpersonal skills; honesty; computer skills; analytical thinking.*

EXPERIENCE AND QUALIFICATIONS: *Internship is helpful; Certified Public Accountants (CPAs) must be state-licensed.*

JOB DESCRIPTION AND RESPONSIBILITIES

Certified public accountants are also known as CPAs or accountants. They may work in public accounting, management accounting, internal auditing, or government accounting.

CPAs working in public accounting firms might specialize in tax-related matters, corporate financial planning, setting up business books, or advising on ways to increase profit.

CPAs are often responsible for performing audits. Depending on the type of work situation individuals are involved with, they may perform these functions for private citizens, businesses, or the government. Accountants sometimes audit financial records to prove they have been prepared and reported correctly. Other books are audited internally to determine company efficiency, effectiveness, and compliance with laws and governmental regulations.

A great deal of work handled by accountants is now being prepared on computers. Individuals must be familiar with computer usage and relevant software programs and input procedures. Accountants also use adding machines and calculators.

Individuals working for accounting firms, businesses, or the government will usually work a standard forty-hour week. Those who are self-employed, consult, own their own business, or are partners may work much longer hours. Accountants in any employment situation may be required to work overtime during tax season, if clients are being audited, or during any type of emergency.

Employment Opportunities

CPAs may work in four major fields of accounting. These are public accounting, management accounting, internal auditing, and government accounting. They may also work on a consultant basis or be self-employed. Employment settings include:

- Public accounting firms
- Corporations in any industry
- Federal government
- State government
- Local government

Expanding Opportunities for the 21st Century

As tax laws and other financial matters become more complex, the demand for accountants will grow tremendously.

With people living longer, another area with growth potential is financial planning and management.

Earnings

Accountants entering the field will have salaries ranging from $25,000 to $30,000. Those with more experience and responsibility such as junior accountants working in public accounting will have earnings ranging from approximately $25,000 to $40,000 plus. Accountants with a great deal of responsibility and experience working in large public accounting firms, internal auditing, or management accounting may earn between $35,000 and $60,000 plus. There are individuals in these positions who earn upward of $100,000, but these positions are rare.

Individuals working for government agencies usually earn less than their counterparts in other areas of accounting.

Accountants who do consulting work or are partners or owners in their own business may earn well over $100,000. These individuals often put in longer hours than accountants employed by others.

Advancement Opportunities

Advancement opportunities for accountants are determined by the area in which they work. Public accountants start out assisting with company clients and then advance with their own client roster. Some individuals advance to senior accountant positions within the company.

Other accountants open up their own accounting firms or become consultants.

Management accountants may start in entry-level positions and move up to junior accountant or internal auditor jobs. These individuals may move into administrative or supervisory positions such as budget director, chief accountant, or controller.

EDUCATION AND TRAINING

The minimum educational requirement for accountants is a bachelor's degree in accounting. Programs are offered in colleges and universities throughout the country.

Some positions require a master's degree in either accounting or business administration with a concentration in accounting.

Individuals who hold CPA and PA designations must usually take continuing education courses to renew their licenses.

EXPERIENCE AND QUALIFICATIONS

Many employers prefer individuals who have had previous accounting experience. This can be obtained by working part time or summers for accounting firms or businesses. College internships are another good option.

Accountants may be certified and licensed. The most prominent credential for accountants is the CPA designation or certified public accountant. CPAs are state licensed and regulated.

Individual states issue CPA licenses and, therefore, requirements vary from state to state. Generally, in order to obtain a CPA designation, individuals must be college graduates. Some states may, however, substitute a certain amount of public accounting experience in lieu of educational requirements.

Aspiring CPAs must take a four-part CPA exam prepared by the American Institute of Certified Public Accountants. Though the entire four parts do not have to be passed at one time, individuals must pass at least two to obtain partial credit. They can then retake the test to pass the other sections.

Accountants may also be designated as public accountants (PAs) or Registered Public Accountants (RPAs). Less stringent standards are required for either of these designations. Other certifications are the Certified Internal Auditor (CIA), Certificate of Management Accounting (CMA), Certified Information Systems Auditor (CISA), and Certificate of Accreditation in Taxation (CAT). These credentials illustrate professional competence in the specific fields.

FOR ADDITIONAL INFORMATION: Individuals interested in careers as accountants can obtain additional information by contacting a number of organizations. These include the American Institute of Certified Public Accountants (AICPA), the National Association of Accountants (NAA), the National Society of Public Accountants (NSPA), the Accreditation Council for Accountancy (ACA), the Institute of Internal Auditors (IIA), and the American Assembly of Collegiate Schools of Business (AACSB).

Tips

- Experience is important in this field. Try to find a part-time or summer job or an internship with an accounting firm while still in school.
- Job openings are often advertised in the classified section of the newspaper under "Accountant," "CPA," "Auditor," "Internal Auditor," "Finance," "Tax Preparation," etc.
- Join trade associations and professional societies. Membership will bring you together with others in the field, help you make important contacts, and keep you abreast of changes.
- The more education you have, the better prepared you will be in this field. Professional societies and trade associations offer seminars, workshops, and courses.

ACTUARY

JOB DESCRIPTION: *Measure risk; assess cost of risk; analyze statistics to calculate probability of injury, sickness, death, and property loss.*

EARNINGS: *$32,000 to $100,000+.*

RECOMMENDED EDUCATION AND TRAINING: *Bachelor's degree plus additional study.*

SKILLS AND PERSONALITY TRAITS: *Good math skills; computer skills; analytical skills; understanding of economics; communication skills.*

EXPERIENCE AND QUALIFICATIONS: *Credentialing required.*

Job Description and Responsibilities

Almost every person in the country is affected by the work of actuaries. Actuaries are the individuals responsible for measuring the risk and assessing the cost of that risk in a variety of situations. For instance, if a person wants to purchase life insurance, he or she will have to go through an underwriting process. An actuary is responsible for putting the individual in a pool of people who have similar characteristics such as age and sex. The actuary will then determine a price for assuming the insurance risk.

When doing these calculations, the actuary must be aware that down the line the company is going to have to pay a claim on the insurance policy. The actuary will be required to determine, given certain factors, general characteristics of the individual including the normal life expectancy of people in the individual's category. The actuary will then look at the risk and put a price on it.

Actuaries working in the pension area help companies develop a retirement program. They must take into account the pool of people working in the company in order to determine how much money has to be put aside for each person. In this way, when a person retires at a specific age, the company will know how much they will have to pay out. They will also have put away the correct amount of money over the years.

Businesses use the services of actuaries to keep their companies financially solvent. If actuaries are off in their assessments, they can possibly throw companies into bankruptcy. Actuaries must make sure that prices charged for insurance will be sufficient to pay off claims and expenses if and when they occur.

After gathering information, actuaries calculate premium rates for the type of insurance offered. A great deal of work that is currently done by actuaries can be accomplished using computers.

Actuaries may be responsible for not only calculating risk and assigning costs and prices but explaining them to company management and executives. They may also be responsible for preparing tables, reports, and correspondence, and handling research.

Individuals will usually work normal business hours.

EMPLOYMENT OPPORTUNITIES

Actuaries can work in a variety of employment settings including:

- Life insurance companies
- Casualty insurance companies
- Private actuarial organizations
- Rating bureaus
- Private industry
- Consulting
- Accounting firms
- Government agencies

Expanding Opportunities for the 21st Century

Trends indicate that there will be a tremendous demand for actuaries in the areas of product liability insurance and medical malpractice. Another growing area in this field is self-insurance, especially important for large corporations choosing to insure themselves instead of using traditional insurers.

Actuaries may be employed in any field where there is risk measured in financial terms. This includes banking, assumption of mortgages, federal guaranteed loans, and the manufacturing of goods and products.

Earnings

Earnings of actuaries can vary greatly depending on the experience, responsibilities, and geographic location of the individual as well as the number of examinations that have been passed.

Actuaries who have not yet passed any exams may earn between $32,000 and $35,000. Those who have passed one examination may earn between $37,000 and $40,000. Actuaries who have passed five to seven are known as *associates* and earn between $43,000 and $58,000 annually. *Fellows* have passed an entire series of examinations and earn between $55,000 and $70,000. Actuaries with extensive experience in the field can earn between $70,000 and $100,000 or more.

Advancement Opportunities

Actuaries usually enter the job as trainees. During that time they are rotated among different departments to learn various phases of the industry.

Actuaries can advance by performing well, obtaining additional experience and education, and passing additional actuarial examinations. Individuals may climb the career ladder by becoming an assistant actuary, an associate actuary, or a chief actuary in a company.

Actuaries may also be promoted to administrative, management, and executive positions.

Education and Training

It is recommended that actuaries have a minimum of a bachelor's degree. Some individuals major in math while others minor in math and major in science, statistics, chemistry, physics, economics, or liberal arts.

There are also a number of bachelor's and master's degree programs in actuarial science offered in colleges and universities throughout the country.

It is imperative that whatever the major of the aspiring actuary, the individual take a great many math courses. Classes in computer science, insurance, and communications are useful as well.

After college, individuals must continue their studies so that they can pass the examinations that are necessary to become full actuaries.

Experience and Qualifications

Actuaries may be credentialed by the Society of Actuaries if they are working in life or health insurance or pension benefits. Those working in property and casualty insurance, such as homeowner, earthquake, or flood insurance, will be credentialed by the Casualty Actuarial Society.

In order to obtain credentialing, individuals must pass a series of tests offered by the specific society. The first four examinations are general exams to test the individual's knowledge of mathematics. Many individuals take one or two of the exams while they are still in college.

After the fourth examination, actuaries must declare a major in the type of actuarial work they want to handle. They may either choose the casualty field or select life and health insurance and/or the pension field. Individuals will then be required to take and pass a series of exams in their selected field. After passing five to seven examinations, individuals are awarded associate membership in the specific society. Subsequent to passing the entire series of exams, individuals will become fellows in the society. It often takes seven or eight years after completion of college for actuaries to get to this point.

FOR ADDITIONAL INFORMATION: For additional information contact the American Academy of Actuaries (AAA), the Society of Actuaries (SOA), the Casualty Actuarial Society (CAS), the American Society of Pension Actuaries (ASPA), and the Conference of Actuaries in Public Practice (CAPP).

TIPS

- Individuals who are still in college and considering careers as actuaries should try to take at least one or two of the required examinations. After passing one or two tests, individuals will find it easier to obtain employment in this field and will be paid higher salaries.

- There are a number of major recruiting companies located throughout the country that place actuaries.

- Jobs may be advertised in the newspaper under headings such as "Actuary" or "Actuarial Careers." However, it is more likely that openings will be advertised in trade publications.

INSURANCE SALES AGENT

JOB DESCRIPTION: *Sell life, health, disability, or property-liability insurance; assist customers in choosing policies; help settle insurance claims.*

EARNINGS: *$16,000 to $70,000+.*

RECOMMENDED EDUCATION AND TRAINING: *Requirements vary from a high school diploma to college degree; on-the-job training programs are available.*

SKILLS AND PERSONALITY TRAITS: *Personableness; good sales skills; honesty; aggressiveness; communication skills; extensive knowledge of insurance industry.*

EXPERIENCE AND QUALIFICATIONS: *State licensing required; credentialing available in specific insurance fields.*

JOB DESCRIPTION AND RESPONSIBILITIES

Insurance sales agents sell insurance policies to individuals, families, or businesses. Clients may require a variety of different types of policies including automobile insurance, homeowners, life insurance, health insurance, and various types of business insurance. Within each specialty area, there are different types of policies. It is essential that the agent explain all the options to clients so that they can intelligently purchase the correct type of policy.

Part of the job is providing quotes on the rates of various policies. In order to provide prices accurately, agents are responsible for obtaining required information.

They are also responsible for doing the background paperwork and making sure all records are complete, forms are filled out, signed, and filed. Individuals answer phone calls and questions from customers about their policies. In the event that insurance claims are made, the agents are responsible for assisting the customer in settling claims.

Sales agents who have the qualifications and credentials perform financial planning services for clients. These individuals help clients put together portfolios and advise them on securities, mutual funds, and annuities.

In order to become successful, an insurance sales agent must continually obtain new accounts. New accounts may be assigned or individuals may get them through the referrals of satisfied customers. The more clients agents have, the higher their earnings will be.

Insurance sales agents may work irregular hours. Part of their day might be spent in the office while another portion might be spent on the road meeting with new clients and selling policies.

EMPLOYMENT OPPORTUNITIES

Agents may specialize in one field of insurance or may be multiline agents selling in a variety of areas. These can include:

- Life insurance
- Property/casualty
- Health insurance
- Disability
- Securities and financial management

Expanding Opportunities for the 21st Century

This is an expanding occupation for career changers. Because nearly everyone requires some or many types of insurance, individuals with proven sales ability usually do well regardless of the condition of the economy. The field of financial planning and management is a new and growing field for qualified agents.

EARNINGS

Earnings for insurance sales agents can range dramatically depending on a number of factors. These include the experience, aggressiveness, and sales ability of the individual.

Insurance sales agents may be paid a number of different ways. They may earn a straight salary, a commission or percentage of policies sold, or a combination of both. Individuals working in financial planning may receive an hourly fee for services rendered instead of a commission. Commissions are based on the type of policy sold and the amount of the policy. Individuals are also paid a different commission on new policies from those on renewals.

There are insurance sales agents who earn only $16,000 a year and others who make over $70,000 annually. As a rule, the more experience individuals have the more they will earn. Insurance sales agents working in property/casualty insurance usually earn more than their counterparts in other areas of insurance.

ADVANCEMENT OPPORTUNITIES

Insurance sales agents have a number of options for career advancement. Some build large client rosters to increase their earnings. Others move into management or administrative positions. Many insurance sales agents open up their own insurance agency or brokerage firm.

Education and Training

Educational requirements vary from job to job. Some employers require college degrees for sales agents where as others just prefer it. Some only require a high school diploma or equivalency. Many states that require licensing may stipulate specific courses and continuing education that individuals must go through to obtain and renew licenses. Continuing education may also be required for agents desiring to become credentialed.

Training for insurance sales agents is usually obtained on the job.

Experience and Qualifications

Insurance sales agents must be licensed in the state in which they are working. Qualifications vary from state to state. Most require individuals to complete a certain number of specified courses and pass a written examination.

Various credentials are also available for insurance sales agents depending on the type of insurance they are selling. Each specific area of insurance offers different credentials and has various requirements for certification. Continuing education usually is one of the requirements.

FOR ADDITIONAL INFORMATION: Individuals interested in learning more about careers in the insurance industry can contact the National Association of Professional Insurance Agents (NAPIA), the Independent Insurance Agents of America (IIAA), the Health Insurance Association of America (HIAA), the National Association of Health Underwriters (NAHU), the National Association of Life Underwriters (NALU), and the American Society of Chartered Life Underwriters and Chartered Financial Consultants.

Tips

- Successful insurance agents use every opportunity to make contacts. They join civic groups, nonprofit organizations, and clubs.
- Contact your state's department of insurance for licensing requirements.
- Jobs are often advertised in the newspaper classified section under "Insurance," "Sales," "Underwriter," or "Group Insurance Sales."

REAL ESTATE AGENT

JOB DESCRIPTION: *Represent a real estate broker in selling, buying, renting, or leasing properties.*

EARNINGS: *$0 to $1,000,000+.*

RECOMMENDED EDUCATION AND TRAINING: *Minimum educational requirement is a high school diploma; state licensing requires a classroom training program regulated and accredited by each state.*

SKILLS AND PERSONALITY TRAITS: *Sales ability; enthusiasm; communication skills; ability to work well with others.*

EXPERIENCE AND QUALIFICATIONS: *Written examination required for licensing; sales experience useful.*

JOB DESCRIPTION AND RESPONSIBILITIES

Real estate agents are professionals who help others buy, sell, lease, or rent residential homes, apartments, land, businesses or commercial properties, office space, and other properties. Real estate agents, also called salespeople or sales associates, must work under the supervision of real estate brokers.

In most cases, the real estate agent is not an employee of a real estate broker. The individual is hired as an independent contractor. This means that the agent is not paid a salary and receives no benefits, but instead receives a commission on sales made.

Most real estate agents consider their main function to be selling properties. In order to succeed, agents must find potential buyers. This is accomplished in a number of ways. Some agents distribute promotional items such as calendars, memo pads, balloons, or cards in hopes that they will be remembered. In many agencies, each agent is given a certain amount of "phone time." This means that during that specific time, all the calls and walk-in customers will be assigned to that agent.

An agent is responsible for determining what type, size, style, and price of property the potential buyer is looking for. The agent will then go through the available houses on the market and, after telling the prospective buyers about the houses, take them to view the homes. Usually buyers want to see a number of houses before they will make an offer.

The real estate agent must take the offer and give it to the seller. If the seller agrees, a deal is struck and a contract is written. In most cases, the real estate agent will be required to negotiate between the buyer and the seller until both parties agree on selling price and terms. The agent will then work with the seller, the buyer, and the attorneys until the sale of the property is completed.

Employment Opportunities

The majority of real estate agents are seller's agents. That means that the agent represents and owes allegiance to the seller. Currently there is a trend throughout the country of agents who are known as buyer's agents. These people represent the buyer. When they find a house or other property for the buyer and the transaction is completed, the buyer, not the seller, pays the commission.

Real estate agents may work in agencies that handle a variety of different types of real estate transactions. Some of these include:

- Homes
- Land
- Commercial properties
- Business properties
- Businesses
- Home or apartment rentals
- Office rentals

Expanding Opportunities for the 21st Century

As a result of the increased mobility of the population, real estate agents will be required for home sales even when the economy is slow.

Earnings

Earnings are impossible to estimate for real estate agents. As the majority of agents are paid on a commission basis, the sky can be the limit. There are people who have earned millions of dollars selling real estate; there are others who haven't made a dime.

Earnings are dependent to a great extent on the selling ability of the individual, types and prices of properties, the current market situation, the geographic location, and a little bit of luck. In order to make money, the real estate agent must list, sell, lease, or rent properties.

Individuals are usually paid a percentage of the selling price of the property. The percentage or commission varies depending on the specific broker and the type of property. Commission may be split among several agents or the agent and the broker.

Advancement Opportunities

There are a number of different paths real estate agents can take toward career advancement. Completing a great number of transactions will increase earnings. Selling more expensive properties will accomplish the same. Real estate agents may climb the career ladder by becoming brokers or opening up their own offices. Some individuals become broker managers for other real estate brokers.

EDUCATION AND TRAINING

Real estate agents in the United States must be licensed. Licensing requirements vary from state to state. Individuals must be high school graduates and go through a classroom training program ranging from thirty to fifty hours, depending on the specific state. A written examination is also required. In order to keep the real estate license valid, many states require agents to continue their education by taking real estate courses every few years.

EXPERIENCE AND QUALIFICATIONS

As noted previously, real estate agents must be licensed by the state in which they are working. This is usually done by each specific state's department of licensing.

While some real estate brokers advertise for experienced agents, there are many who are more than willing to work with newly licensed people. The reasons for this are twofold. The first is that a great number of brokers prefer to train their own agents. The other is that newly licensed agents are usually ambitious, excited, and enthusiastic about the job.

FOR ADDITIONAL INFORMATION: Individuals interested in obtaining more information regarding careers in real estate can contact their local county's board of realtors or the National Association of Realtors (NAR).

TIPS

- Many real estate brokers (especially those who are franchised) offer free career seminars to entice new agents to work in their offices. Attend the seminars of a few different agencies to learn as much as you can about careers in real estate.
- Opportunities are advertised in the newspaper classified sections under "Sales" or "Real Estate".
- Real estate agencies do not always advertise when they are looking for new agents. Feel free to call the broker or manager of any real estate office in your area to inquire about working with them on either a full-time or part-time basis.

LAWYER

JOB DESCRIPTION: *Negotiate contracts; settle disputes; advise on legal ramifications; act as in-house counsel.*

EARNINGS: *$35,000 to $750,000+.*

RECOMMENDED EDUCATION AND TRAINING: *Bachelor's degree plus three years of law school.*

SKILLS AND PERSONALITY TRAITS: *Research skills; analytical skills; negotiating skills; communication skills.*

EXPERIENCE AND QUALIFICATIONS: *Pass state bar exam; ethics committee interviews to prove good moral character.*

Job Description and Responsibilities

Some lawyers spend most of their time in court. Some are bound to the library doing intensive research while others review the fine print in contracts and agreements or develop policy and legislation in government services.

The main functions of lawyers are advising clients of their legal rights and counseling them about legal ramifications of certain actions. They are responsible for suggesting the best courses of action for clients to take.

Some of the reasons people use the services of lawyers are because they have been arrested or charged with a crime or are being sued. Attorneys may be retained to settle litigation disputes in court or out and are responsible for trying cases in front of a jury or judge.

In addition to working in law firms, lawyers may be on the staff of large corporations to act as counsel resolving the many legal problems that can crop up in business. Individuals might also work as legal aid counsel or public defenders.

In addition to regular office hours, individuals spend time preparing cases at home and interviewing witnesses or clients after work.

Employment Opportunities

Careers in law are as varied as the people who work in the field. Individuals may work in large firms, small firms, or in their own private practice. They may work in corporation legal departments or in legal aid offices. Lawyers may specialize in areas including:

- Criminal law
- Patents and trademarks
- Tax law
- Corporate law
- Aviation law
- Maritime law

- Matrimonial and family law
- Entertainment law
- Real estate property law

- General law
- Legal aid and public defense
- Government law

Expanding Opportunities for the 21st Century

While there is no way to predict which law specialty will be most sought out in future years, there is a clear trend toward specialization. Given the demographics of society, the new century will most likely see specialization in law for the elderly. Other expanding opportunities include specialization in business law, employee benefits, and consumer protection.

EARNINGS

Earnings vary for lawyers depending on their experience, reputation, responsibilities, and specialty. Other factors affecting salary include the geographical location, size, and prestige of the specific firm or company in which the individual works.

Starting salaries for lawyers average between $35,000 and $50,000 a year. There are, however, a limited number of top law firms that start associates as high as $100,000.

Individuals working in legal departments of large corporations earn between $45,000 and $60,000 or more. Salaries skyrocket for partners in prestigious and prosperous firms, as partners share in the profits. Salaries for lawyers in firms depend on the amount of work accomplished and hours billed. There are some individuals who practice law and have annual salaries of $750,000 plus.

ADVANCEMENT OPPORTUNITIES

One road to advancement is to locate a position in a large, prestigious firm, resulting in increased responsibilities and earnings.

Others aspire to become partners in a law firm. Individuals can become junior, senior, management, or limited partners. Some lawyers open up their own law practice.

Many lawyers also strive to become judges.

EDUCATION AND TRAINING

Educational requirements for lawyers include a bachelor's degree plus three years of law school. Individuals should graduate from an American Bar Association–approved college or university and will receive a Juris Doctor, or JD, degree. A few states may permit individuals to clerk for lawyers instead of attending one or more years of law school. Clerking means that the individual will be studying with lawyers to get on-the-job training. California allows individuals to take correspondence courses in law instead of classroom training.

In order to get into law school, individuals usually must take an examination called the LSAT (Law School Admission Test).

EXPERIENCE AND QUALIFICATIONS

After completing law school, individuals must usually take the bar examination for the state in which they plan to practice. They may also be required to take and pass the multi state bar examination.

FOR ADDITIONAL INFORMATION: Individuals interested in law careers can obtain additional information from the American Bar Association (ABA), the Association of American Law Schools, and the Law School Admissions Service (LSAS).

TIPS

- Try to find internships in the law field to give you related experience.
- All law schools provide placement services.
- There are professional headhunters located in large cities. These individuals help match up candidates with the right job.
- Job openings are often advertised in the help wanted section of state or local bar association journals. You might also consider placing an advertisement in the "Position Wanted" section.
- The key to getting a good start in the legal profession is attending the best, most prestigious law school you can.

PARALEGAL

JOB DESCRIPTION: *Research prior cases; investigate cases; draft legal documentation; take case histories; assist in trial preparation.*

EARNINGS: *$20,000 to $45,000.*

RECOMMENDED EDUCATION AND TRAINING: *Requirements vary from on-the-job training to a certificate program to an associate degree or bachelor's degree in Paralegal Training or Studies.*

SKILLS AND PERSONALITY TRAITS: *Research skills; analytical skills; writing skills; ability to take directions from colleagues; ability to work independently.*

EXPERIENCE AND QUALIFICATIONS: *No experience necessary for individuals who go through certificate programs; others should have law experience.*

JOB DESCRIPTION AND RESPONSIBILITIES

A paralegal career offers an individual a practical, hands-on approach to working in law without attending law school. Paralegals assist and work under the supervision of lawyers and perform many of the same jobs as lawyers.

A great deal of this job revolves around research and investigation. For example, a paralegal may be required to research previous cases that are similar to one an attorney is currently handling. After doing the research, the paralegal may be required to analyze the facts and apply them to the current case or situation.

Paralegals are also responsible for drafting a variety of legal memorandums, contracts, agreements, pleadings, and other documentation. In many situations, the individual will be asked to take case histories from clients and assist in trial preparation and support. In the majority of states in the country, however, paralegals are prohibited from appearing in court alone, but are permitted to assist an attorney.

Other specific responsibilities of the paralegal will depend on the type of law office. For example, an individual working in a matrimonial or family law firm might assist in drafting a separation agreement or a child custody agreement.

EMPLOYMENT OPPORTUNITIES

Paralegals can work in a law firm that is small and handles general law or a large, specialized one. Each specialty of the law will offer the paralegal a variety of duties. Individuals may choose to work in:

- Generalized law firms
- Legal aid and public defenders
- Other government agencies
- Banks
- Real estate developers
- Title companies
- Insurance companies
- Corporate and business law
- Matrimonial and family law
- Freelance

Expanding Opportunities for the 21st Century

The need for paralegals will increase in the new century as it becomes more apparent that paralegals can do many legal tasks for lower salaries than lawyers. Paralegals will be needed in large law firms or those with specialties such as real estate or corporate law. Additionally, there will be expanding opportunities for paralegals in the public sector, such as providing legal aid services to the poor.

EARNINGS

Annual earnings for paralegals can range from approximately $20,000 to $45,000 depending on the experience, reputation, and responsibilities of the individual. Other factors affecting salary include the specific firm the individual is working for, its size, its prestige, and the geographic location. Generally, paralegals working in larger, metropolitan cities will earn more than those doing similar jobs in smaller communities.

ADVANCEMENT OPPORTUNITIES

Paralegals can get ahead by locating positions with larger or more prestigious firms. It is also a good idea to specialize in a specific field of law.

After working in the legal system, some paralegals decide that they want to attend law school and become lawyers.

EDUCATION AND TRAINING

There are a number of ways to become a paralegal. Some employers provide on-the-job training to legal secretaries who express an interest in advancing their careers.

There are also paralegal training programs offered by many colleges, vocational-technical schools, and adult or continuing education programs. Depending on the intensity of the program, individuals may receive a certificate or an associate or bachelor's degree with an emphasis or major in paralegal studies. Each of these programs has different entrance requirements and prerequisites. Some programs require individuals to hold a high school diploma while others require a bachelor's degree.

Length of program varies depending on the intensity and depth of each.

Paralegals may be certified by the National Association of Legal Assistants (NALA). Individuals interested in becoming a Certified Legal Assistant (CLA) must complete a certain amount of education, obtain experience, and take and pass a two-day examination.

EXPERIENCE AND QUALIFICATIONS

Paralegals who go through a formal training or certificate program are usually not required to have any additional experience. Many of these programs have internships built in that offer hands-on experience.

Aspiring paralegals who do not go through formal training programs must have some type of experience in a law office, such as working as a legal secretary.

FOR ADDITIONAL INFORMATION: Individuals interested in paralegal careers can obtain more information and valuable literature by contacting the National Paralegal Association (NPA), the National Association of Legal Assistants, Inc. (NALA), the American Bar Association (ABA), the National Federation of Paralegal Associations (NFPA), and the American Association for Paralegal Education (AAPE).

TIPS

- Before you get involved in a training program, you might want to check the ratio of graduates placed in jobs.

- Often, you can get an "in" with a law firm by doing paralegal or legal secretarial work on a temporary or freelance basis.
- Many large cities have employment agencies specializing in jobs in law and the legal profession. Remember to find out whether you or the employer will pay the fee when you get a job.
- Jobs are often listed in the newspaper classified section under "Paralegal," "Legal Assistant," or "Law."

SALESPERSON

JOB DESCRIPTION: *Assist customers; sell merchandise; handle cashier duties; take inventory; arrange merchandise.*

EARNINGS: *$9,000 to $35,000+.*

RECOMMENDED EDUCATION AND TRAINING: *No formal educational requirement for many jobs; some require high school diploma; college degree helpful in advancement.*

SKILLS AND PERSONALITY TRAITS: *Pleasantness; honesty; dependability; sales ability; good communication skills.*

EXPERIENCE AND QUALIFICATIONS: *No experience necessary for many positions.*

JOB DESCRIPTION AND RESPONSIBILITIES

Salespeople working in retail make up a large portion of the workforce in this country. Every store and shop needs the services of salespeople. Sometimes, in very small shops, the salespeople are the owners or managers. More frequently, however, even the smallest stores must hire sales help.

Good salespeople try to determine exactly what a customer's needs are. To accomplish this, the individual may ask the customer leading questions. If, for example, the salesperson is selling large appliances, it would be important to ask what price range they are considering as well as the brand or options desired. In this way, the salesperson can assist the customer in making a wise purchase.

Salespeople must know where stock is located and be able to assist consumers in finding what they are looking for. It is also helpful if the salesperson is knowledgeable about the products sold in the store. This is especially important when working in a store or department selling highly specialized products.

Individuals should be aware of all sales and special promotions sponsored by the store. They must also be familiar with store policies and procedures concerning everything from returns and exchanges to layaways and rain checks.

The salesperson may be required to stock shelves, set up advertising displays, and arrange merchandise. The salesperson may be responsible for checking inventory and reporting to store management items that have sold out or are low in stock. In many retail situations, the salesperson is also responsible for counting and sorting incoming merchandise and verifying the receipt of items on invoices. Salespeople also may be required to price products by stamping, marking, or attaching tags.

Salespeople are usually directly responsible to either the store or department manager or owner. Hours for salespeople vary depending on the shift the individual works. Overtime and part-time work may be available.

Employment Opportunities

One of the important things about being a salesperson in retail sales is that jobs are available in every part of the country. Flexible hours make it convenient for mothers who have children in school and teenagers who are attending school.

Salespeople working in retail stores and shops may work in large department or discount stores or small specialty shops in almost any industry. These include but are not limited to:

- Clothing
- Furniture
- Electronics
- Hardware and building supplies
- Pets and pet supplies
- Computer and office supplies
- Shoes
- Sports and exercise equipment
- Groceries and other food
- Grooming products
- Jewelry

Expanding Opportunities for the 21st Century

Retail salespeople will be needed in every industry, especially in grocery and discount stores. Salespeople who are knowledgeable about specialty products such as computers and computer-oriented goods will also be in demand.

Earnings

Earnings for salespeople working in retail stores can start at minimum wage and go up considerably. Factors affecting earnings include the type, size, and geographical location of a store as well as the products being sold. Other factors include the salesperson's responsibilities and experience. Some individuals work on a salary-plus-commission basis. Full-time salespeople working in this type of setting can earn between $9,000 and $35,000 or more. Most people earning salaries at the higher end of the scale either work on a commission basis or are working in retail stores selling highly specialized, high-ticket items.

ADVANCEMENT OPPORTUNITIES

Salespeople working in retail stores can advance in a number of different ways. One way is to locate positions in prestigious stores that offer the best responsibilities and earnings. After obtaining retail selling experience, many individuals move up to retail management positions.

EDUCATION AND TRAINING

While some employers prefer that salespeople hold a high school diploma or equivalency, many have no educational requirements at all. Training in using cash registers and credit card terminals will usually be provided on the job. Specialty stores may also offer in-store training for product usage and selling points.

Individuals who are interested in advancement may need a college background or degree.

EXPERIENCE AND QUALIFICATIONS

In many instances, this type of job is entry-level and no experience is necessary. This is true for most grocery, discount, and department stores.

Specialty shops selling high-ticket items may require either a complete knowledge of the product being sold or previous selling experience.

FOR ADDITIONAL INFORMATION: The best way to obtain additional information about a specific type of sales job in a retail store is to talk to the manager, owner, or personnel director. For further information and literature, contact the National Retail Merchants Association (NRMA).

TIPS

- Job openings are advertised in newspaper classified sections under "Salesperson," "Sales Help," "Retail Sales," or the name of a specific retail store or industry.
- Many stores advertise for salespeople in the window of their store.
- Even if a store does not have a sign in the window, feel free to go inside and ask the manager if there are any openings. In most cases you will be asked to fill out an application. As there is such a great turnover in retail sales, you will probably be called for an interview before you know it.
- Try to find a sales job in an industry you both enjoy and know something about. If, for example, you are an expert seamstress, consider work at a fabric shop, sewing machine store, or craft store.

CORRECTION OFFICER

JOB DESCRIPTION: *Maintain secure environment within prison; supervise inmates; enforce rules and regulations; prevent escape.*

EARNINGS: *$15,000 to $55,000.*

RECOMMENDED EDUCATION AND TRAINING: *High school diploma or equivalency.*

SKILLS AND PERSONALITY TRAITS: *Dependability; supervisory skills; interpersonal skills; communication skills; emotional stability; good judgment.*

EXPERIENCE AND QUALIFICATIONS: *No arrest record; driver's license; state age requirement.*

JOB DESCRIPTION AND RESPONSIBILITIES

Correction officers work in prisons, reformatories, and jails. Their main functions are maintaining a secure and safe environment within the prison population and making sure inmates stay incarcerated.

Within the scope of their job, correction officers are responsible for making sure that rules and regulations are followed and enforced. For example, correction officers must see that there are no guns, knives, or other instruments that can be used as weapons by the inmate population. They conduct searches of cells, prison recreation areas, cafeterias, etc. Officers also check for other contraband including drugs and alcohol.

Correction officers count inmates and lock them in cells at intervals during the day. They must constantly take measures to be sure that inmates do not try to escape.

Correction officers are required to stop fights between inmates, should they occur. Depending on the situation, there may be paperwork involved including documentation of any disturbances, violations, and unusual occurrences. In some facilities, officers must produce daily reports of activities during their shifts.

Others functions include escorting inmates to court or to doctors or hospitals outside the facility. Officers may also be responsible for investigating crimes committed within the facility.

In some situations, correction officers are stationed in cellblocks. Others are positioned in towers to monitor the prison population and to prevent escapes. Other correction officers monitor inmates via closed circuit television cameras. Depending on the work assignment, the correction officer may be required to carry a gun.

There can be a great deal of stress and pressure involved in this job. The individual must worry about riots, being taken hostage, or being injured in the line of duty.

Correction officers work eight-hour shifts. They work days, evenings, or over-night on a constant basis or may have rotating shifts. They may also be required to work on weekends. Overtime hours may often be available.

EMPLOYMENT OPPORTUNITIES

Facilities in all areas of the country are in need of correction officers. Individuals may work in facilities housing men, women, juveniles, or a combination. Correctional facilities may be maximum, medium, or minimum security. Settings include:

- Federal prisons, prison camps, and reformatories
- State prisons, prison camps, and reformatories
- County jails
- City or town jails

Expanding Opportunities for the 21st Century

Today's crowded jails and prisons mean that there will be a need to build additional institutions. There will be a great demand in the future for additional correction officers in state institutions.

EARNINGS

Annual earnings for correction officers range from approximately $15,000 to $55,000 with an average income of $25,000 to $35,000. Factors affecting earnings include the type of facility the individual is working in, its geographic location, and size. Other factors include the experience level and responsibilities of the individual.

Correction officers working in federal facilities who have a number of years experience and perform supervisory duties will earn salaries near the high end of the pay scale. Benefits and pension plans augment most correction officers' salaries.

ADVANCEMENT OPPORTUNITIES

Advancement may be obtained by promotion into supervisory or administrative positions such as a sergeant in a correctional facility. In order to achieve this, correction officers must either acquire experience or additional education or training.

EDUCATION AND TRAINING

The minimum educational requirement for most positions is a high school diploma or equivalency. Individuals who prefer to obtain a college education should consider courses in police science and law enforcement and rehabilitation.

Correction officers go through training in an academy setting, a home study course, or informal on-the-job training. Programs may last from two weeks to several months. During this period, individuals will learn rules, regulations, policies, procedures, and responsibilities. Training also includes self-defense, use of firearms, and written communication skills.

EXPERIENCE AND QUALIFICATIONS

Correction officers working in the majority of institutions must be at least 18 years old. There are a few, however, which require employees to be at least 21. Individuals must have no criminal record and are required to have a driver's license.

There is currently a trend toward certification of correction officers. At this time, however, only a few states are requiring it.

FOR ADDITIONAL INFORMATION: Additional information on careers as correction officers can be obtained by contacting the American Correctional Association (ACA), Contact, Inc., or the International Association of Correctional Officers (IACO).

TIPS

- Many jobs are obtained through the civil service system. If you are required to take a civil service test, go to the bookstore or the library and get some review books on the subject. ARCO is a major civil service test preparation publisher. These books offer sample questions and review material to help you get a better score on the test.

- Visit federal, county, and state personnel offices to find out about job openings and test dates.

- When you are completing your application or resume, make sure that you add any special training you have had in counseling or rehabilitation. If you are bilingual it should also be noted.

- Openings are advertised in newspaper classified sections under "Civil Service," "Corrections," "Peace Officers," or "Rehabilitation."

PERSONAL SHOPPER

JOB DESCRIPTION: *Select merchandise for customers; work on a one-to-one basis with buyers; coordinate colors, styles, and fabrics for customers; offer advice about merchandise.*

EARNINGS: *$24,000 to $65,000+.*

RECOMMENDED EDUCATION AND TRAINING: *Requirements vary from high school education and on-the-job training to degree in fashion.*

SKILLS AND PERSONALITY TRAITS: *Flair; good taste; honesty; enthusiasm.*

EXPERIENCE AND QUALIFICATIONS: *Experience in retail sales.*

JOB DESCRIPTION AND RESPONSIBILITIES

This is an interesting and enjoyable career for individuals who enjoy shopping. While some savor the joys of shopping, others find the experience is nothing but a headache. Even if they enjoy it, many people do not have the time. This is when the personal shopper comes into focus.

The services of personal shoppers working for retail stores are usually free to customers. Stores employ personal shoppers because the service helps build good customer relations. People tend to buy what they need and like when they are in a relaxed atmosphere. When customers use a personal shopper they get individualized attention and service.

The main function of a personal shopper is to save customers time and offer them expert advice on purchases. As most personal shoppers are not paid on a commission basis, they are not pushy and they give honest opinions about items.

The personal shopper must determine what the customer is looking for as well as obtain some personal background. For example, if the customer is looking for a winter coat, the personal shopper may ask what type of styles, color, and fabrics the individual likes. Since the personal shopper is totally familiar with the store layout and merchandise, the individual will know exactly where to find a selection of coats that fit the customer's needs. The personal shopper will then show the selection to the customer. Personal shoppers advise customers on how the garment looks. If the customer doesn't find anything suitable, the personal shopper may go back to look for new garments or may order a special size, color, or style. Personal shoppers should never make the customer feel obligated.

Selecting clothing is not the only function of personal shoppers. Many individuals in this line of work help their customers choose gifts for business associates, friends, and family. Customers often give personal shoppers lists of people for whom they need gifts, providing a description of likes, hobbies, and a price range. Personal shoppers will then scour the store for the perfect gifts. If the customer approves of the selection, the personal shopper can save the customer even more time by having the gifts wrapped and cards attached, and may even have them delivered or mailed.

Personal shoppers may work a variety of shifts depending on the store's operating hours. They set their schedules to accommodate customers.

EMPLOYMENT OPPORTUNITIES

Personal shoppers work in a variety of retail establishments. Until recently, stores that employed people in this position were usually in large metropolitan areas. Now personal shoppers can be found in all geographic locations. Personal shoppers may work in a variety of settings including:

- Department stores
- Boutiques
- Clothing stores
- Specialty shops
- Gift shops

Expanding Opportunities for the 21st Century

As more people begin to learn about the services of personal shoppers, department stores vying for the attention of customers will be in need of individuals to fill these positions. Those most in demand will have a background in retailing, merchandising, or fashion.

EARNINGS

Personal shoppers will have annual earnings ranging from $24,000 to $65,000 or more. Variables affecting earnings include the size, type, prestige, and geographic location of the store in which the individual works. Other variables include the individual's experience, duties, and reputation in the field.

Personal shoppers working in prestigious, upscale department stores in large, metropolitan areas will earn salaries at the high end of the scale. Those who are just starting out in smaller cities will earn considerably less.

ADVANCEMENT OPPORTUNITIES

There are a number of paths to career advancement for personal shoppers depending on the direction that interests them. The most common way to climb the career ladder is by locating a job in a large or prestigious store. This results in increased earnings and responsibilities. Another method of advancement is moving into a supervisory position. This can include landing a job as either the director or head of a personal shopper department or store manager.

Personal shoppers who have the training may become buyers for either specific departments or entire stores.

EDUCATION AND TRAINING

As this is a relatively new position in the mass market, it will be a while until there are unified training requirements. At this time, education and training requirements vary from job to job. Most positions expect a minimum of a high school diploma. Some jobs want a college background or degree in retailing, merchandising, or fashion.

Courses, seminars, or workshops in psychology, communications, fashion, color, merchandising, and retailing are useful.

EXPERIENCE AND QUALIFICATIONS

Most stores require their personal shoppers to have experience selling in either their store or a similar facility. Depending on the type of store or department in which an individual is working, the personal shopper should have some background in retailing, merchandising, or fashion.

Individuals must be well groomed with a coordinated, put-together look.

FOR ADDITIONAL INFORMATION: Additional information on careers as personal shoppers may be obtained by talking to individuals working in this field or personnel directors in stores. Literature and information may be acquired by contacting the National Retail Merchants Association (NRMA).

TIPS

- When you interview for this type of position, make sure that you dress the part. For example, if you are applying for a job in a prestigious boutique, you should go to the interview in a well-coordinated outfit.

- You might have to create your own job in this field. If you are already working in a store that does not have a personal shopper service, suggest it to store management and request that you be given first priority for an interview.

- Send your resume with a cover letter to the personnel director of department stores and boutiques.

- Jobs may be advertised in the newspaper classifieds under "Personal Shopper," "Fashion," "Retail Sales," "Clothing," "Gift Ideas," "Department Stores," or "Boutiques."

HAIRSTYLIST

JOB DESCRIPTION: *Cut, wash, style, and color hair; give permanents; style wigs.*

EARNINGS: *$18,000 to $40,000+.*

RECOMMENDED EDUCATION AND TRAINING: *Cosmetology/hairstyling courses.*

SKILLS AND PERSONALITY TRAITS: *Hairstyling skills; flair for working with hair; personableness; communication skills.*

EXPERIENCE AND QUALIFICATIONS: *State licensing required.*

JOB DESCRIPTION AND RESPONSIBILITIES

The major function of hairstylists is to style people's hair in a complimentary and attractive fashion. They may style women's, men's, or children's hair, or a combination of these.

The stylist is responsible for discussing exactly what the patron wants done. He or she must determine if the patron wants a trim or an entire new style, a permanent, coloring, frosting, etc.

The hairstylist washes and conditions a patron's hair. In many salons, this task is performed by someone who may not have as much experience in a salon setting or by an individual who has not completed the necessary training to be a hairstylist.

The stylist is then responsible for cutting the patron's hair in a flattering style. Depending on the desires of the patron, the stylist might set the hair in rollers or blow it dry. Sometimes, hot rollers, curling irons and brushes, or other styling tools are also used. The hairstylist must know a variety of styling techniques including teasing, blow-drying, roller sets, and comb-outs. Stylists straighten hair, give permanents, and color, rinse, lighten, tint, or frost hair.

Some hairstylists are also responsible for styling wigs and hairpieces and administering manicures or pedicures. In other instances, a manicurist or other specialist will handle these tasks. Stylists give facials, apply makeup, and offer cosmetic, nail care, and hair care advice.

Individuals working in salons owned by others are responsible to the owner or manager. Hairstylists may work full or part time. Hours can range from early morning to evening, depending on the schedule of the shop and patrons. Weekend hours may be required.

EMPLOYMENT OPPORTUNITIES

Hairstylists can be self-employed, may own their own shop, or may work in someone else's salon. They may work full or part time depending on the specific job. Individuals can work in a variety of settings, including:

- Commercial beauty shops or styling salons
- Spas
- Department stores
- Hotels
- Cruise ships
- Hospitals, nursing homes, and extended-care facilities
- Home salons
- Television stations
- Movie studios
- Theatrical productions

Expanding Opportunities for the 21st Century

As a result of the increased population of older Americans and the philosophy that people who look better usually feel better, there will be a demand for hairstylists to perform their services in nursing homes, extended-care facilities, and hospitals.

With more and more women working outside the home and in management positions, there will also be a need for hairstylists who will serve these customers in their offices.

EARNINGS

Hairstylists are compensated by base salary and tips, or a percentage of monies brought in to the salon plus tips. Earnings depend on the reputation, skills, experience, and duties of the individual as well as whether the stylist is working full or part time, owns the salon, or is working as an employee. Other factors include the geographic location of the shop, its size, clientele, and prestige.

Hairstylists working full time can earn between $18,000 to $40,000 or more. Those at the higher end of the scale work in large salons in metropolitan areas.

ADVANCEMENT OPPORTUNITIES

Hairstylists can advance their careers by locating positions in prestigious facilities. Stylists may also get ahead by opening up their own shop.

A limited number of stylists advance by performing duties for people working in television, movies, or theater.

EDUCATION AND TRAINING

Hairstylists must attend licensed, accredited schools of cosmetology/hairstyling. The course of study may be offered in high school, continuing education programs, or public or private vocational and trade schools. Courses take from six months to two years to complete depending on the specific school.

EXPERIENCE AND QUALIFICATIONS

Hairstylists must be licensed in the state in which they are working although some states do offer reciprocity. Usually licensing requirements include completion of an accredited cosmetology/hairstyling course as well as written and practical exams.

FOR ADDITIONAL INFORMATION: Individuals aspiring to a career in hairstyling can contact a number of organizations, unions, and associations for additional information. These include the National Cosmetology Association, Inc. (NCA), Hair International, the National Association of Accredited Cosmetology Schools, Inc. (NAACS), the National Accrediting Commission of Cosmetology Arts and Sciences (NACCAS), the Associated Master Barbers and Beauticians of America (AMBBA), and the United Food and Commercial Workers International Union (UFCWIU).

Licensing requirements for individual states can be obtained by contacting the department of licensing for the specific state.

TIPS

- A new trend in salons is renting out styling chairs. The salon offers the equipment needed to do your job and you bring your clientele.
- A good way to develop a clientele is to volunteer to style hair at community fund-raisers, nursing homes, and hospitals.
- You can gain clientele by going to people's homes and places of business to style their hair.
- Many high schools offer vocational programs in cosmetology/hairdressing for individuals who are still in school. If you are out of school and want to change careers, you can take an accredited cosmetology/hairstyling course on a part-time basis while you keep your job.

CHILD-CARE WORKER

JOB DESCRIPTION: *Take care of children, infants, and toddlers; organize and lead activities; prepare and serve meals and snacks.*

EARNINGS: *$9,500 to $24,000.*

RECOMMENDED EDUCATION AND TRAINING: *High school diploma preferred; formal training in child care useful.*

SKILLS AND PERSONALITY TRAITS: *Pleasure working with children; good judgment; maturity; energy; creativity; first aid skills; knowledge of child care.*

EXPERIENCE AND QUALIFICATIONS: *Experience caring for children helpful; certification and/or licensing may be required.*

Job Description and Responsibilities

People who work in child-care facilities, taking care of infants and children, are called child-care workers or day care workers. Responsibilities vary depending on the age of the children being cared for. Those caring for babies must attend to their basic needs. Babies have to be fed, diapered, held, put to sleep, comforted, and played with.

Child-care workers attending to the needs of older children have other responsibilities. Individuals must greet children, make them feel at home, and keep them occupied and happy.

In some centers, the child-care worker is responsible for planning the day's activities. In others, this responsibility falls onto the shoulders of the director, manager, or supervisor of the center. Activities can include teaching, playing games, creating arts and crafts, outdoor activities, performing skits, and reading stories. Child-care workers may also be required to prepare meals and snacks.

Child-care workers administer minor first aid and are responsible for reporting any accidents or illnesses to the supervisor as well as to the child's parents.

Hours will vary depending on the specific facility.

Employment Opportunities

One of the reasons many people become involved in child-care careers is so that they, themselves, can stay home with their children.

Child-care workers can choose to work in small, intimate day care centers located in other peoples homes or in a variety of other settings. Some of these settings include:

- Colleges and universities
- Hospitals and health care facilities
- Commercial day care centers
- Churches, temples, and synagogues
- Corporations in every industry

Expanding Opportunities for the 21st Century

Child-care workers will be in demand in corporate-run day care centers as more companies begin accommodating women who have young children and choose to work.

EARNINGS

Salaries for child-care workers vary, often starting at the minimum wage. Annual earnings can range from approximately $9,500 to $24,000. Variables include the specific center as well as its size, prestige, and geographic location. Other factors affecting earnings include the child-care workers' experience, training, and responsibilities.

Child-care workers who run their own center are paid on the basis of the number of children they care for and their ages as well as the length of time the children are cared for. Rates vary depending on the geographic location.

ADVANCEMENT OPPORTUNITIES

Child-care workers can take a number of paths to career advancement. Individuals may find positions in large facilities where they will receive increased responsibilities and earnings. They may also locate supervisory or management positions or open up their own day care centers. After obtaining some experience, some choose to go back to school and become certified teachers.

EDUCATION AND TRAINING

Education and training requirements vary from job to job. There are positions that have no minimum education, training, or experience requirements. Other jobs prefer or require an applicant to hold a high school diploma or to be a certified Child Development Associate (CDA). Individuals can receive this certification through a program offered by many high schools and colleges throughout the country. The program stresses the improvement of child-care skills and offers training and assessment of applicants.

Any courses, workshops, or seminars in child care, child development, home economics, and childhood nutrition will be helpful to child-care workers. Many larger day care centers offer on-the-job training programs or pay tuition for their employees to obtain training.

Individuals who run their own center should obtain as much training as possible and be CDA certified.

EXPERIENCE AND QUALIFICATIONS

While there are a great many positions that do not require experience, training, or certification, child-care workers who have these qualifications will have an advantage in obtaining the position as well as career advancement.

FOR ADDITIONAL INFORMATION: A number of associations and organizations offer additional information about child-care careers. Literature can be obtained from the National Child-Care Association (NCCA), the Child-Care Employee Project, and the Child Development Associate Credentialing Program.

TIPS

- If you are interested in this type of career, try to obtain training and certification. Contact your local high school or community college to see if they offer a program in this field or write to the National Credentialing Program.
- When developing your resume or filling out applications for this type of job, remember to include all child-care experience, both formal and informal.
- Jobs are often located in the newspaper classified section under "Child-Care," "Pre-School," or "Day Care."

SECRETARY

JOB DESCRIPTION: *Answer phones; type; take dictations; greet clients; file; route mail.*

EARNINGS: *$16,000 to $38,000+.*

RECOMMENDED EDUCATION AND TRAINING: *High school diploma; secretarial school or business classes helpful.*

SKILLS AND PERSONALITY TRAITS: *Good typing skills; computer skills; dependability; ability to take and transcribe dictation; good spelling; communication skills.*

EXPERIENCE AND QUALIFICATIONS: *No experience necessary for many positions.*

JOB DESCRIPTION AND RESPONSIBILITIES

Secretaries are an important part of every business. They are expected to handle a wide scope of clerical duties. One duty almost every secretary performs is typing. This includes correspondence, envelopes, reports, bills, speeches, meeting minutes, and lists. Secretaries are expected to be quick and accurate typists and should have experience with typewriters, word processors, and computers. Individuals may also be responsible for taking dictation and transcribing it.

Secretaries file photocopy documents, collate reports, sort mail, answer phones, and send faxes. They may also be expected to answer letters or other correspondence. Writing responsibilities include preparing reports, bulletins, or calendars of events. In some situations, secretaries may be required to conduct research.

In offices where there is no receptionist, the secretary is expected to greet clients, make them comfortable, and announce them to the proper people.

Depending on the specific job, secretaries may also handle payroll, bookkeeping, and social schedules. Secretaries working in specialized fields will have more technical duties. For example, an individual working as a legal secretary must often prepare contracts, summonses, motions, etc.

Full-time secretaries usually work normal business hours. They may be required to work overtime when projects are due or during office emergencies.

EMPLOYMENT OPPORTUNITIES

One notable fact about being a qualified secretary is that jobs are available throughout the country. Good secretaries are always in demand. Individuals may work full or part time or for a temporary agency in almost every industry, including:

- Public relations offices
- Banks
- Schools
- Law offices
- Medical offices
- Advertising agencies
- Manufacturers
- Wholesalers
- Retailers
- Construction companies
- Book publishers
- Record companies
- Government agencies
- Insurance companies
- Real estate companies
- Investment firms
- Shopping centers

Expanding Opportunities for the 21st Century

With the increase of electronic offices and new developments in office technology, there will be a great demand for secretaries who are proficient using computers and computer programs, modems, and fax machines. There will also be a demand for secretaries trained in specialized fields including legal, medical, and technical areas.

EARNINGS

Earnings for secretaries vary greatly depending on their specific jobs, responsibilities, experience, skills, training, and location. Those just starting out with no experience can earn from $16,000 to $20,000. Experienced secretaries handling a great deal of responsibility can expect $38,000 or more. Average salaries for secretaries range between $22,000 and $27,000.

Individuals working in specialized areas such as the legal field will usually earn more than their counterparts handling general office work. Secretaries in large, metropolitan areas will also have higher salaries.

Individuals may receive benefit packages to augment their earnings.

ADVANCEMENT OPPORTUNITIES

There are a number of paths for secretaries to take to advance. Individuals may locate positions in larger, more prestigious or more interesting offices. This will result in increased earnings and responsibilities.

Secretaries can advance into positions such as administrative assistant, office manager, or secretarial supervisor. Some individuals may even move into management or executive positions.

Other secretaries obtain additional education to become legal secretaries, paralegals, or trainers. Some open up their own temporary secretarial service.

EDUCATION AND TRAINING

A high school diploma or equivalency is usually the minimum educational requirement for secretarial jobs. Some individuals who know how to type pick up other skills on the job. Others take secretarial courses in high school or attend vocational-technical institutes, community colleges, or secretarial schools. Many employment agencies offer free refresher courses and training to job applicants as a way of enticing qualified individuals to their agency.

Training is especially important today with offices depending on computers and word processors. Secretaries, therefore, must continue their training in office technology.

EXPERIENCE AND QUALIFICATIONS

Many secretarial positions are entry level and do not require any experience. Individuals must, of course, have the necessary skills to perform the job.

There are a number of voluntary credentials secretaries can qualify for that illustrate excellence and competence in the profession. The designation of Certified Professional Secretary (CPS) is offered by Professional Secretaries International. In order to obtain this credential, individuals must take and pass a number of examinations given by the Institute for Certifying Secretaries.

Legal secretaries may also qualify for the designation of Professional Legal Secretary (PLS). In order to obtain the PLS, individuals must have at least five years of experience as a legal secretary as well as taking and passing an examination administered by the Certifying Board of National Association of Legal Secretaries.

FOR ADDITIONAL INFORMATION: Individuals interested in secretarial careers can obtain additional information by contacting Professional Secretaries

International (PSI), the Association of Independent Colleges and Schools (AICS), and the National Association of Legal Secretaries International (NALSI).

TIPS

- Get as much training as you can. The more you know about all aspects of office work, management, and technology, the more marketable you will be. Computer skills are especially important.

- Many temporary agencies offer free training and refresher courses covering computers and computer programs.

- Before you sign any contracts with an employment agency, check to see who pays the fee when you get the job, you or the employer. Fees can be high in these agencies.

- Jobs are often advertised in the newspaper under "Secretary," "Secretarial," "Office Work," "Administrative Secretary," or "Electronic Office." You might also look under specialized situations such as "Legal Secretary" or "Medical Secretary."

- Look into advancement possibilities before you accept a job. Some positions offer better advancement options than others.

PRIVATE INVESTIGATOR

JOB DESCRIPTION: *Perform background checks; do surveillance; check and verify facts; monitor activities; search for missing people; write reports detailing investigations.*

EARNINGS: *$15,000 to $85,000+.*

RECOMMENDED EDUCATION AND TRAINING: *Minimum requirement is a high school diploma; training requirements vary.*

SKILLS AND PERSONALITY TRAITS: *Good judgment; responsibility; logic; interpersonal skills; communication skills; objectivity; perseverance; observant.*

EXPERIENCE AND QUALIFICATIONS: *State licensing may be required.*

JOB DESCRIPTION AND RESPONSIBILITIES

The job description of private investigators or detectives can vary greatly depending on the type of job or client an individual is handling. One of the main responsibilities of private investigators is checking and verifying facts.

Private investigators working for private individuals or law offices may, for example, be expected to check into and monitor the activities of a client's spouse for an impending divorce or child custody action. Private investigators, or PIs, may also look for missing persons.

Individuals working for corporate clients may perform such activities as background checks on potential employees. They may be responsible for handling similar background checks for insurance reports, credit reports, or similar situations. Another duty of the PI might be to look into and solve possible corporate or industrial espionage. There is a wide range of services that PIs are called on to perform.

Private investigators may use a number of methods to do their jobs. These might include doing personal or phone interviews or using contacts to obtain information. PIs may also go through computer records or use the Freedom of Information Act to gain needed information.

Private investigators may also be expected to "tail," or follow, people without their knowledge. They may use surveillance equipment such as cameras and videos or involve themselves in watching-and-waiting stakeouts. Depending on the project, the PI may be expected to go undercover to gather information. In order to do this, successful PIs must be able to blend easily into a situation.

Part of the job of private investigators entails writing reports. Individuals are responsible for providing details of the investigation to their supervisor or client.

Hours for private investigators differ depending on the job. Individuals conducting stakeouts or tailing people may work at odd hours and for long periods of time. PIs doing background checks may work straight eight-hour shifts.

EMPLOYMENT OPPORTUNITIES

Private investigators may work for a detective agency or be self-employed. They may work for a variety of different clients, including:

- Law firms
- Insurance agencies
- Government agencies
- Gaming casinos
- Corporations
- Private individuals

Expanding Opportunities for the 21st Century

There is a growing demand for private investigators working in the field of corporate and industrial espionage. Other expanding opportunities for PIs include handling background checks on people embarking on new relationships, as well as domestic situations such as divorce and child custody.

EARNINGS

Annual earnings for private investigators can vary dramatically depending on the type of work the individual is handling, the specific employment situation, and the PIs reputation and experience. Earnings can range from approximately $15,000 to $85,000 or more.

Private investigators working for a detective company will usually be paid a salary. Those who are self-employed work on a fee basis. This may include a daily, weekly, or monthly rate plus expenses.

ADVANCEMENT OPPORTUNITIES

Advancement opportunities for private investigators depend to a great extent on the reputation and experience of the individual. The more extensive the reputation of the PI, the more clients he or she will be able to add to the roster.

Individuals who are employed by detective agencies may advance by obtaining more interesting and financially rewarding cases. They may also climb the career ladder by going out on their own.

EDUCATION AND TRAINING

Educational and training requirements vary. Generally, individuals must have at least a high school diploma. Courses or a degree in criminology, law enforcement, and criminal law are useful. Individuals may also work with experienced PIs to obtain on-the-job training.

EXPERIENCE AND QUALIFICATIONS

While prior experience in law enforcement is not mandatory, many private investigators began as police officers or have worked in other law enforcement positions. Others start their career working with more experienced investigators or in security offices. Many states require licensing for private investigators.

FOR ADDITIONAL INFORMATION: Individuals interested in becoming private investigators can contact the National Association of Legal Investigators, the Society of Professional Investigators (SPI), and their state licensing department for more information.

TIPS

- Obtain experience working for private security firms.
- If you decide to work on your own, contact law offices, insurance agencies, and corporations to find potential clients.
- Jobs may also be available as legal aid investigators or at social service agencies.
- You will be more marketable if you have second language skills.
- Cultivate as many contacts as you can in as many different fields as possible. You never can tell when you might need a favor or when some information might prove useful.

PROPERTY MANAGER

JOB DESCRIPTION: *Oversee the day-to-day management of income-producing commercial and residential properties; negotiate leases and rental agreements; handle tenant relations; negotiate contracts; collect rents.*

EARNINGS: *$30,000 to $125,000.*

RECOMMENDED EDUCATION AND TRAINING: *Educational requirements vary; formal training programs offered by trade and professional associations; college degree may be preferred.*

SKILLS AND PERSONALITY TRAITS: *Communication skills; negotiation skills; ability to deal well with people; organization.*

EXPERIENCE AND QUALIFICATIONS: *Voluntary certification is available.*

JOB DESCRIPTION AND RESPONSIBILITIES

Property managers represent owners, landlords, and/or investors of income-producing commercial and residential properties. Their main functions are to act as the owner's agent and handle the day-to-day management of properties. Individuals may manage one or more properties.

Functions are varied. Individuals will be expected to rent vacant space. The property manager may be solely responsible for handling this or may work with leasing agents. The property manager will also be responsible for negotiating leases and other rental agreements. This is done under the direction of the owners.

An important responsibility of the property manager is collecting rents and other fees. The individual will also be expected to ensure that bills, mortgages, taxes, insurance premiums, payroll, etc., are paid in a timely fashion. The property manager is responsible for developing and sticking to budgets for properties.

Another function of the property manager is to bid and negotiate contracts for security, groundskeeping, trash removal, janitorial, and maintenance services. The individual must also bid and negotiate contracts for needed supplies and equipment. Depending on the specific situation, the property manager may be expected to hire and supervise other on-site personnel, including an on-site manager, secretary, and bookkeeper.

Tenant relations are a very important responsibility of the property manager. This is especially true when managing apartment or office buildings, shopping centers, or condominium or homeowner associations. It is essential that the individual be able to deal well with people.

There is a great deal of bookkeeping in this job. All expenditures and rents must be accounted for. This may be handled by the property manager directly or may be taken care of by a bookkeeper, secretary, or on-site manager.

Other responsibilities of property managers may include dealing with government officials, community and public interest groups, and public utilities. If individuals are responsible for more than one property, they must make frequent visits. Individuals must report to landlords, owners, and investors regarding the status of properties.

EMPLOYMENT OPPORTUNITIES

Property managers may work in a variety of settings and for varied employers. These include:

- Real estate operators
- Property management companies
- Government agencies
- Shopping center developers
- Office building owners
- Apartment complex owners
- Condominium and homeowner associations

Expanding Opportunities for the 21st Century

Expanding opportunities for property managers will be found in managing office buildings, shopping centers, and other retail establishments. Other opportunities will be in handling commercial and multi-unit residential properties.

EARNINGS

Earning for property managers can range from $30,000 to $125,000 or more, depending on a number of factors. These include the education, certification, and responsibilities of the individual, as well as the specific job and geographic location.

Generally, those who are college graduates and are certified earn more than those who are not. Average earnings for those handling apartment complexes range from $30,000 to $45,000. Individuals working with shopping center developers and office buildings can earn between $40,000 and $95,000. Property managers responsible for a great number of properties can earn up to $125,000 annually.

ADVANCEMENT OPPORTUNITIES

There are a number of paths to advancement for property managers. Individuals may obtain additional training and/or certification, leading to better and higher-paying jobs. Property managers may also locate positions with more responsibility at larger and more prestigious companies.

EDUCATION AND TRAINING

Educational requirements vary. Most developers and landlords prefer to hire college graduates. Good degrees include real estate, public administration, business administration, finance, and liberal arts.

There are also many short-term training programs offered by professional and trade associations. A great deal of the training many property managers receive is on the job.

EXPERIENCE AND QUALIFICATIONS

Experience is helpful in this field. Many property managers start out as assistants, while others begin as on-site managers. There are also people who move into this type of position after getting experience as real estate brokers or salespeople.

Voluntary certification is available from a number of different organizations, depending on the area of specialization the individual is interested in. To be certified, individuals are usually expected to obtain training, get experience, and pass an examination.

FOR ADDITIONAL INFORMATION: Individuals interested in obtaining more information regarding careers in property management should contact the Apartment Owners and Managers Association of America (AOMAA), Building Owners and Managers Institute International (BOMII), Community Associations Institute (CAI), Institute of Real Estate Management (IREM), International Association of Corporate Real Estate Executives (IACREE), the National Apartment Association (NAA), or the National Association of Home Building (NAHB).

TIPS

- If you are working as a real estate agent, check with your broker to see if he or she knows of any positions in this field.
- Opportunities are often advertised in the newspaper classified section under "Real Estate," "Real Estate Developers," "Property Management," "Property Manager," "On-Site Manager," "Apartment Complex Manager," and "Office Building Management."
- Attend seminars and classes offered by trade associations. This is a good way to network as well as to learn new skills.
- Send your résumé and a short cover letter to real estate development companies, shopping center management firms, apartment complexes, etc. Ask that your resume be kept on file if there are no current openings.

CHAPTER 7

Fitness and Nutrition Careers

The proportional relationship between fat consumption and disease risk is becoming as well known as the correlation between regular exercise and better health.

This and the American ideal of thinness as beauty is responsible for our growing interest in exercise and nutrition. The increase of working women with expendable cash and career role models is another reason for the fitness boom. Gyms, spas, and health and fitness clubs have become particularly popular for single women as well as men.

Today's population is so fascinated by the fitness business that it has turned it into a multibillion-dollar enterprise. Every time an individual gets on a bicycle or puts on a pair of running shoes, he or she is making an impact on the growing number of jobs in this area.

Careers in this field are all-encompassing. There are jobs in schools, hospitals, health spas, health and fitness clubs, retail stores, wholesale markets, manufacturing, and other settings.

Careers featured in this section include:

Aerobics Exercise Instructor
Sports and Fitness Nutritionist
Personal Trainer

Individuals interested in this area might also read over career entries of Dietitian, Physical Therapist, and Physical Therapy Assistant in Chapter 1 and Salesperson in Chapter 6.

AEROBICS EXERCISE INSTRUCTOR

JOB DESCRIPTION: *Lead exercise, dance, and aerobics classes; instruct individuals in exercise equipment use.*

EARNINGS: *$12,000 to $35,000+.*

RECOMMENDED EDUCATION OR TRAINING: *Training in exercise, aerobics, and dance preferred.*

SKILLS AND PERSONALITY TRAITS: *Physical fitness; energy; personableness; communication skills; knowledge of exercise, aerobics, and dance.*

EXPERIENCE AND QUALIFICATIONS: *Some jobs require certification.*

JOB DESCRIPTION AND RESPONSIBILITIES

Current trends indicate that the physical fitness fad is becoming stronger than ever. The number of gyms, fitness centers, spas, and health clubs is increasing. In addition, many senior citizen centers, adult education programs, schools, corporations, and retirement homes are instituting health and fitness programs.

Individuals responsible for leading exercise classes are called aerobics exercise instructors, leaders, or fitness instructors. Instructors may have classes for groups or individuals in a variety of forms of exercise including aerobics, jazzercize, and calisthenics. They are frequently responsible for teaching classes to people who are at different levels of fitness.

Responsibilities and functions differ with the specific job. The instructor may perform an initial assessment of patrons to determine each individual's level of fitness in order to recommend class level. Placing someone who has not exercised in ten years in an advanced class can result in strain or injury.

After assessing levels of fitness, the instructor will instruct the class on how to perform each exercise. The instructor may then exercise with the class, or may offer inspiration and instruction.

The instructor must not only lead classes, but also make them productive and fun. To make classes more enjoyable, some instructors utilize dance routines in the exercise program. They develop routines, choose music, and put the production together much as a choreographer does.

Depending on the size and type of facility, the instructor may also be required to teach class members how to use the different types of exercise equipment and explain the physical benefits of each.

Instructors may work irregular hours in this type of job depending on the specific facility. In most circumstances, the individual will work five- to eight-hour shifts. However, there are also a great number of part-time positions.

EMPLOYMENT OPPORTUNITIES

Exercise instructors may work with men or women in any age bracket. They may, for example, teach classes to children or to senior citizens. Some instructors lead classes for pregnant women, handicapped individuals, and various other special need groups. Jobs can be located on a full- or part-time basis throughout the country. Settings include:

- Health and fitness clubs
- Gyms
- Spas
- Nursing homes
- Schools, colleges, and universities
- Adult education programs
- Church and synagogue programs
- Sports clubs
- Corporate fitness programs
- Senior citizen centers
- Community programs
- Retirement villages and developments
- Private instruction
- Camps
- Hotels and resorts
- Cruise ships

Expanding Opportunities for the 21st Century

While there will be a need for qualified aerobic and exercise instructors at health clubs and gyms, there will also be a great demand for individuals who can provide special types of exercise workouts. These include exercise classes for senior citizens, handicapped individuals, pregnant women, and young children. Corporate exercise instructors will also be in demand.

EARNINGS

Earnings for aerobics exercise instructors depend on the specific type of facility and its geographic location, size, and prestige. Other factors affecting salary include the individual's experience and duties.

Annual earnings for full-time instructors can range from $12,000 to $35,000 or more. Instructors working in large, prestigious spas and gyms in major cities will have earnings on the higher end of the scale. Those working in smaller facilities will earn considerably less.

Aerobics exercise instructors who provide stimulating, fun, and exciting workouts will build a following and command a higher salary.

ADVANCEMENT OPPORTUNITIES

There are a number of different paths for aerobics instructors to take for career advancement. The most common is to locate a position in a large or prestigious club, gym, or spa.

Depending on the facility, promotions might include exercise director, specialist, or club manager.

EDUCATION AND TRAINING

There are no specific educational requirements for aerobics exercise instructors. However, it is recommended that the individual have as much exercise training as possible.

A number of colleges offer degree programs in exercise and fitness. There are also a wide choice of useful courses, seminars, and workshops offered throughout the country in aerobic techniques, exercise physiology, exercise biochemistry, exercise science, etc.

On-the-job training is offered at some spas and gyms. Health club franchises and chains often provide extensive training. In some work situations, an aerobics exercise instructor must go through the gym's instructor training program prior to beginning work.

An effective way to obtain training in the use of exercise equipment is directly through the manufacturer. Manufacturers often send representatives to teach instructors the correct use of their equipment.

Other options for obtaining training include trade associations and organizations. These groups provide members with training in aerobics, dance, and exercise. Many of them are also beginning to offer certification.

EXPERIENCE AND QUALIFICATIONS

Some instructor positions will require experience, while others will not. The same holds true for certification requirements. While certification is not always necessary, it will provide an edge over applicants who do not hold this credential. One of the main certifying agencies for aerobics exercise instructors is the Aerobics and Fitness Association of America.

FOR ADDITIONAL INFORMATION: A number of organizations and associations offer vocational and educational guidance, training, and professional support to individuals interested in becoming aerobics exercise instructors. These include the Aerobics Center, the International Dance-Exercise Association (IDEA), and the Aerobics and Fitness Association of America (AFAA).

TIPS

- Contact corporate headquarters of health and fitness clubs and gyms that are franchise operations. These groups offer training programs and job placement.
- Send your resume and a cover letter to spas, health clubs, and gyms as well as community centers, retirement villages, and adult education programs. Inquire about openings and request that your resume be kept on file if no current jobs are available.

- Openings for aerobics exercise instructors are advertised in the newspaper classified section under headings such as "Aerobics," "Exercise," "Fitness," "Spas," "Health Club," "Gym," and "Fitness Recreation Programs."

SPORTS AND FITNESS NUTRITIONIST

JOB DESCRIPTION: *Analyze the nutritional needs of professional, amateur, or scholastic athletes; plan meals; counsel athletes regarding nutrition.*

EARNINGS: *$18,000 to $85,000+.*

RECOMMENDED EDUCATION AND TRAINING: *Educational requirements vary from one-year programs to a master's degree in nutritional science.*

SKILLS AND PERSONALITY TRAITS: *Interpersonal skills; communication skills; knowledge of nutrition, athletics, and fitness; personableness; understanding.*

EXPERIENCE AND QUALIFICATIONS: *Experience in nutrition and fitness helpful.*

JOB DESCRIPTION AND RESPONSIBILITIES

Sports and fitness nutritionists have been used by professional athletes and sports teams for a number of years. The job is becoming more prevalent, though, as scholastic and amateur athletes as well as the general population are requiring the services of these nutritionists.

Responsibilities vary depending on the specific job and the individual's level of education. Clients for sports and fitness nutritionists include professional athletes and athletic teams, scholastic athletic teams, and individuals interested in increasing their level of fitness.

Before doing anything else, the nutritionist will usually talk to the athlete to determine what type of diet is currently followed, and what physical activities the individual performs regularly. The nutritionist will then analyze the nutritional requirements of the athlete and plan meals with this information.

It is essential that the nutritionist understand the food likes and dislikes as well as the eating routines and schedules of the individual. Planning a nutritious food program is useless unless someone can and will follow it. Athletes, especially younger ones who are prone to eating "junk food," may need explanations of the parallel between nutrition and performance.

The individual may work on a one-on-one basis with athletes or may be required to develop a nutritional analysis for a team or group of people. This might be the case, for example, when a nutritionist is working with a college team. Within the scope of the job, the nutritionist may also be responsible for developing and maintaining food budgets.

The nutritionist is expected to keep records of the client's needs, prescribed programs, and progress. In some cases, athletes have to either take off or put on weight. The sports and fitness nutritionist will work with individuals to attain these goals.

It is extremely important that individuals understand how foods can affect their athletic performance. Some nutritionists lecture groups of athletes on nutrition and healthy eating patterns. Individuals may also offer cooking instruction to the athletes themselves or to the chefs that prepare their meals.

EMPLOYMENT OPPORTUNITIES

Employment opportunities for sports and fitness nutritionists are increasing steadily as more people begin to realize the importance of nutrition in relation to health and fitness. Jobs can be located throughout the country.

Health and fitness nutritionists may work in a variety of settings including:

- Health and fitness clubs
- Gyms
- Sports teams
- Individual athletes
- Consulting
- Sports medicine clinics

Expanding Opportunities for the 21st Century

As more people continue to take part in the exercise and fitness trend, there will be an increased need for sports and fitness nutritionists in health clubs and gyms throughout the country.

EARNINGS

Earnings for sports and fitness nutritionists range from $18,000 to $85,000 plus. Factors affecting salaries include experience, education, responsibilities, and duties of the individual as well as the specific job.

Most sports and fitness nutritionists earn between $18,000 and $35,000. Sports and fitness nutritionists for major sports teams or athletes will have earnings at the higher end of the scale.

ADVANCEMENT OPPORTUNITIES

Sports and fitness nutritionists can advance in a number of ways. Individuals may locate a position with a large or prestigious health club or clinic or become the nutritionist for a well-known team or athlete. Sports and fitness nutritionists might also be promoted to the director of sports nutrition for a team or a clinic.

EDUCATION AND TRAINING

Educational requirements vary for sports and fitness nutritionists from a one-year program in nutrition to a bachelor's degree with a major in foods and nutrition or a master's degree in nutrition. The higher the individual's education level, the more career options he or she will have. Those seeking to work for professional sports teams, athletes, and sports medicine clinics should have a graduate degree.

Classes, seminars, and symposiums on athletics, fitness, exercise, nutrition, and food will also be useful.

EXPERIENCE AND QUALIFICATIONS

Many jobs require an individual to be a registered member of the American Dietetic Association (ADA). In order to become a registered dietitian (RD), nutritionists must fulfill certain requirements, including completion of a bachelor's degree in foods and nutrition or institution management from an accredited college. Individuals seeking an RD credential must also obtain clinical experience through an accredited college, an accredited internship program, or an approved preprofessional practice program.

FOR ADDITIONAL INFORMATION: Contact the American Dietetic Association (ADA) for additional information on careers in this field.

TIPS

- You can often create your own job, even if one isn't available. Contact health clubs, spas, and gyms. Send your resume with a short cover letter explaining the benefits of a nutritionist. You may have to work part time at a couple of clubs in order to get your career started, but it is worth the effort.
- Job openings may be advertised in the newspaper's classified display section under "Nutritionist," "Sports Nutritionist," "Fitness," or "Dietary," "Health Club," "Health Spa," "Spas," or "Gyms".

PERSONAL TRAINER

JOB DESCRIPTION: *Plan and supervise fitness regime for clients on a one-on-one basis.*

EARNINGS: *$35 to $750+ a session.*

RECOMMENDED EDUCATION AND TRAINING: *Training in exercise, fitness, nutrition, and health.*

SKILLS AND PERSONALITY TRAITS: *Physical fitness; energy; health consciousness; personableness; enthusiasm; familiarity with first aid procedures.*

EXPERIENCE AND QUALIFICATIONS: *Experience working in gyms, fitness centers, health clubs.*

JOB DESCRIPTION AND RESPONSIBILITIES

Personal trainers are responsible for assisting people on a one-on-one basis to attain their optimum level of fitness. Though usually self-employed, they often work with gyms, health spas, or clubs on a consulting basis.

The most common method for a personal trainer to obtain clients is by working first as an exercise instructor in a gym. Patrons, in turn, may request private classes. If people are happy with their trainer, they will usually tell their friends and business associates. This can build a large roster of clients and a successful business for the personal trainer.

Personal trainers are responsible for a total assessment of the physical fitness level of a new client. The individual must determine what the client wants to accomplish in a training program. In some cases the client needs to lose weight, tone up, or increase physical fitness or stamina.

Trainers design fitness programs specifically for their clients. They instruct the client about proper exercise techniques, exercise with the individual, or offer inspiration. Trainers are also responsible for developing healthy diet plans for clients to help them lose or maintain weight or to improve eating habits.

Hours are usually irregular in this line of work. Workouts must be scheduled for the convenience of clients. Sessions may range from one hour per client to three or four hours for those training for a specific reason, such as an athletic event or a movie role. Sessions may be scheduled in a variety of locations ranging from the client's house or place of business to private or public gyms or the trainer's own studio.

Personal trainers must answer to their clients. If clients are not happy with the workouts or results, they will usually find another trainer.

EMPLOYMENT OPPORTUNITIES

Personal trainers must usually develop their own list of clients. This can be accomplished by working at a gym, health club or spa, through word of mouth, or by advertising in newspapers, in magazines, or on television and radio. The personal trainer who is aggressive, knowledgeable, and good at the job should have no problem getting started. Clients may include:

- Athletes
- Actors, actresses
- Corporate clients
- The general population interested in total physical fitness

Expanding Opportunities for the 21st Century

The demand for personal trainers in corporate fitness programs will increase as management begins to realize the correlation between fitness, health, and productivity. Better health means lower insurance and medical costs.

EARNINGS

Earnings for personal trainers are dependent on a number of factors. These include the number of clients the individual has as well as the type of clients. Personal trainers working with major celebrities charge more than those working in corporate fitness programs. Earnings are also dependent on the trainer's experience, responsibilities, and reputation as well as the geographic location.

Personal trainers earn from $35 to $750 or more a session. Those earning the latter will usually be working for celebrities or major athletes. An average fee for a session in a large city could range from $50 to $200.

ADVANCEMENT OPPORTUNITIES

In order to advance their careers, personal trainers must either develop a larger roster of clients or charge more for services.

There are also personal trainers who open up their own gyms or health clubs.

EDUCATION AND TRAINING

There are no specific educational requirements for personal trainers. However, it is essential that the individual know as much as possible about fitness, exercise, and nutrition. Some personal trainers have degrees in physical education, exercise physiology, exercise biochemistry, or exercise science. Others were trained as aerobics exercise instructors or fitness leaders in spas, private gyms, or health clubs.

A great many trainers receive training in the usage of exercise equipment from company manufacturers.

EXPERIENCE AND QUALIFICATIONS

Personal trainers should have experience working in the exercise, fitness, health, and nutrition fields. Working as an exercise instructor or fitness leader at gyms, spas, and health clubs can be helpful.

FOR ADDITIONAL INFORMATION: For more information on careers in fitness as personal trainers, contact the Aerobics and Fitness Association of America (AFAA), the Association for Fitness in Business (AFB), or the Aerobics Center (AC).

TIPS

- Many exercise and fitness equipment manufacturers look for representatives throughout the country. This is an excellent opportunity to learn how to use exercise equipment and make contacts in the fitness world.
- A job as an exercise instructor in a local gym will help you make important contacts and provide valuable training and experience.
- If you are considering college, find one with a program geared toward fitness or nutrition. If you are currently in college, volunteer to work with sports teams to learn how they train for a season.

CHAPTER 8

Education Careers

Much of our individual success is based on education, training, and continued learning experiences. Our society is currently taking a greater interest in education as we begin to realize that without at least basic academic skills, good jobs are difficult to locate.

Many occupations require a college education. Other fields rely on trade, vocational-technical schools, or on-the-job training programs. Educators are required to assist people who want to learn new skills as well as upgrade their old ones.

Rising enrollments are projected for both elementary and secondary schools during the 21st century. As a result, there will be a demand for teachers in both public and private schools. In addition, many current teachers will be reaching retirement age by the new century. The demand for educators in all grade levels and interest areas will be especially high in large cities and in small rural vicinities.

Employment opportunities will not be limited to elementary and secondary schools. Instructors will also be required for adult and continuing education at vocational-technical and trade schools and at the college level. While the enrollment of younger college students is declining, the number of older students seeking additional education and new skills has increased. College educators will be needed to teach classes for occupations that are experiencing growth such as health care, medical technology, geriatrics, business, computers, and engineering.

Careers for school counselors, too, will be plentiful throughout the 21st century as a result of increased secondary school enrollment and state laws requiring counselors in elementary schools. Another major reason for the increased need of school counselors is the multiplicity of problems that students must now deal with. These include suicide, drug and alcohol abuse, and dysfunctional families.

More careers in education that are projected to increase include teachers' aides and administrators. Opportunities exist and will continue to exist in a variety of public and private institutions.

The careers discussed in this section include:

Teacher (Elementary and Secondary School)
School Counselor
Adult Education Teacher

TEACHER—ELEMENTARY AND SECONDARY SCHOOL

JOB DESCRIPTION: *Teach students; develop ideas for classes; prepare tests; grade papers; meet with parents; supervise extracurricular activities.*

EARNINGS: *$26,000 to $55,000+.*

RECOMMENDED EDUCATION AND TRAINING: *Bachelor's degree in education; many schools require a master's or permanent certification.*

SKILLS AND PERSONALITY TRAITS: *Teaching ability; communication skills; patience; creativity; organization.*

EXPERIENCE AND QUALIFICATIONS: *Student teaching and certification usually required.*

JOB DESCRIPTION AND RESPONSIBILITIES

Teachers work at the elementary or secondary level in public, private, or parochial institutions. Their duties vary depending on the type of job they are hired for and the grade level they teach.

Elementary teachers lead kindergarten or first through sixth grades. They teach general classes or specialties such as music, art, or physical education.

Secondary school teachers work with junior or senior high school students. In these situations, teachers are generally responsible for a specialty such as art, music, languages, physical education, social studies, history, geography, the various sciences, health, English, or math.

While teachers usually follow a mandated curriculum, they are required to develop activities for each class and decide how to teach each subject. It is essential that they plan interesting, inspiring lessons to make learning a positive experience.

Teachers handle paperwork and record attendance, grades, report cards, and student progress. They prepare and review homework, develop tests, and grade papers. Other responsibilities include attending conferences, workshops, and meetings, including parent-teacher meetings, faculty meetings, educational workshops, and conferences with administrators.

Some teachers act as advisers for school organizations such as the debate club, Spanish club, or drama club. They may also be required to attend and chaperon school-sponsored extracurricular activities.

Individuals usually work normal school hours. They put in extra time, though, to plan classes, write reports, go to meetings, and attend school-sponsored events.

Many people enjoy the flexibility of teaching because schools are usually closed during holidays and summer months. They also enjoy knowing that they have selected a career that plays an important role in the development of young people.

EMPLOYMENT OPPORTUNITIES

Teachers can work in public, parochial, or private schools. Some individuals tutor students who are at home. Teachers can specialize in a vast array of subjects depending on their interests. Some of these include:

- Music
- Math
- Art
- Sciences
- Health
- Social studies
- Physical education
- English
- Foreign languages
- Special education

Expanding Opportunities for the 21st Century

One of the greatest demands for teachers will be in secondary schools where trends indicate there will be a rise in enrollment. As a result of the retirement of many current elementary teachers, there will also be an increased need at this level as the new century approaches.

Demand for teachers in all grade levels and interest areas will be high in large cities and in small rural locations.

Opportunities in special education are also expected to expand in the 21st century as a result of legislation emphasizing training and employment for students with disabilities.

EARNINGS

Earnings for teachers can range from $26,000 to $55,000 or more depending on the specific type of employment setting (private, parochial, or public school), its size, prestige, and location. Other factors affecting earnings include the individual's education, experience, seniority, and responsibilities. Teachers often receive extra compensation for handling extracurricular activities such as coaching.

Teachers just entering the profession can earn between $26,000 and $32,000.

Those with more experience can earn up to $55,000 or more. Compensation is usually augmented by liberal fringe-benefit packages.

ADVANCEMENT OPPORTUNITIES

Teachers can advance after obtaining additional experience and education. Some individuals become department heads. Others become administrators, specialists, or supervisors. Many teachers locate similar positions in larger school districts where the pay is higher.

Individuals who stay at the same school for a number of years have the opportunity to be tenured. Salaries usually increase with seniority.

EDUCATION AND TRAINING

The minimum educational requirement for teachers is a bachelor's degree in education. Many school districts require their teachers to have or obtain a master's degree.

EXPERIENCE AND QUALIFICATIONS

Teachers working in public schools are required to be certified. Certification requirements vary from state to state. Generally, however, in order to be certified, individuals must complete an approved teacher training program at a four-year college; go through a supervised student teaching program; and pass an examination to prove competency in basic skills, teaching skills, and subject matter proficiency.

FOR ADDITIONAL INFORMATION: Individuals interested in becoming teachers can obtain additional information by contacting the American Federation of Teachers (AFT), the National Education Association (NEA), or the National Council for Accreditation of Teacher Education (NCATE).

TIPS

- College placement offices receive notices of teacher openings at schools.
- Major cities often have employment agencies that specialize in locating positions for teachers. Before you get involved, remember to find out who pays the fee when you get the job: you or the employer.
- Remember to get letters of recommendation from several of your professors at school as well as your student teaching supervisor.
- Positions in summer school are often easier to obtain. They can help get your foot in the door.

SCHOOL COUNSELOR

JOB DESCRIPTION: *Counsel students on higher education and career possibilities.*

EARNINGS: *$26,000 to $55,000.*

RECOMMENDED EDUCATION AND TRAINING: *Master's degree in counseling.*

SKILLS AND PERSONALITY TRAITS: *Enjoy working with young adults; counseling and communication skills; attention to detail; computer skills.*

EXPERIENCE AND QUALIFICATIONS: *Teaching and counseling certification.*

Job Description and Responsibilities

Now, more than ever, there are vast arrays of opportunities for students to consider. They can choose to go to trade or vocational school, a junior or community college, or a state or private four-year college or university, or go right into the workplace. School counselors are responsible for helping students make these decisions.

In order to accomplish this, counselors talk to students about their interests, goals, and aspirations. They might also administer tests to help students determine their talents, ambitions, hopes, and desires.

Once the counselor has determined the direction the student wishes to go, the two will work on accomplishing this objective. If, for example, the student hopes to go to college, the counselor is responsible for helping the individual look into possibilities. Counselors must be aware of college admission requirements, entrance exams, and available financial aid in order to help students make their choices.

A main responsibility for counselors is helping students find realistic career options. To do this, individuals may offer career education and information programs. Counselor's may, for example, have career fairs or invite successful people in a variety of businesses to lecture at the school.

School counselors are often called in when students are having difficulties. They work with the student, parents, teachers, and school administrators to solve problems and put students back on track.

In recent years, counselors have had a difficult job trying to help students deal with a range of social problems including dysfunctional family situations, drug and alcohol use and abuse, suicide, death, and disease.

School counselors usually work the same hours as teachers. Individuals are responsible to either the department head, principal, or superintendent, depending on the structure of the school.

Most counselors find that helping young people achieve their goals is a fulfilling and rewarding experience.

EMPLOYMENT OPPORTUNITIES

Almost all schools throughout the country employ counselors. Some districts employ only one or two, while larger districts may have a great number of people working in this department. Individuals have the option of working in either:

- Public school systems
- Private schools

Expanding Opportunities for the 21st Century

Trends indicate that due to rising enrollment in secondary schools throughout the country, there will be a growing demand for counselors in the public school system. Additionally, there will be a need for individuals qualified to counsel not only in the fields of career and vocational guidance but social issues as well, including drug and alcohol abuse and suicide.

EARNINGS

School counselors have earnings ranging from $26,000 to $55,000. Variables affecting salaries include the specific school as well as its size, student population, prestige, and geographic location. Other considerations are the counselor's education, experience, and seniority.

School counselors usually receive a liberal benefit package to augment their salaries. Individuals working in state systems usually receive pension plans.

Because they work during the school year, much the same as teachers do, counselors can obtain summer jobs if they wish.

ADVANCEMENT OPPORTUNITIES

School counselors can advance their careers by locating positions in large, prestigious school districts. This can result in higher-than-average responsibilities and earnings. Counselors may also be promoted into supervisory or administrative positions such as department head. Obtaining additional education is a good way for a teacher to further his or her career.

School counselors who stay at the same job for a number of years may be granted tenure. This means that the job is secure and the individual cannot be fired unless there is a major problem.

EDUCATION AND TRAINING

School counselors working in public schools are usually required to hold counseling and teaching certification. Requirements necessary for certification vary from state to state. Generally, to obtain certification individuals must teach for a number of years and hold a master's degree in counseling.

Experience and Qualifications

School counselors working in public schools are usually required to hold counseling and teaching certifications. Requirements necessary for certification vary from state to state. Generally, to obtain certification individuals must teach for a number of years and hold a master's degree in counseling.

FOR ADDITIONAL INFORMATION: Interested individuals can obtain additional information by contacting their state department of education, the American Counseling Association (ACA), the American School Counselor Association (ASCA), and the American Association for Counseling and Development (AACD).

Tips

- College placement offices usually list job openings.
- Opportunities may be advertised in school newsletters, personnel offices, or on job boards.
- Check the classified section of newspapers under "Education," "Counseling," "Guidance," "High School Counselor," or "Schools."

ADULT EDUCATION TEACHER

JOB DESCRIPTION: *Instruct adult students; assist adults in updating skills; teach basic education courses; prepare students for GED exams; train people for occupations not requiring college.*

EARNINGS: *$20,000 to $55,000.*

RECOMMENDED EDUCATION AND TRAINING: *Educational requirements vary depending on specific state and subject matter.*

SKILLS AND PERSONALITY TRAITS: *Enjoy working with people; teaching ability; communication skills; patience; creativity; organization; understanding.*

EXPERIENCE AND QUALIFICATIONS: *Qualifications vary; states may require teacher certification.*

Job Description and Responsibilities

Adult education teachers may work in a number of areas in the educational field, including teaching adult basic education programs. Adult education teachers working in this area are responsible for teaching basic classes such as reading, writing, and math to adults. They may be expected to instruct students who do not speak English. They may also help those without a high school diploma prepare for the General Educational Development Examination, or GED. Often adult education teachers working in this area do so part time. Many individuals work full time as schoolteachers for children or may work as instructors or professors in colleges.

Adult education teachers may also instruct in the vocational-technical area, where they teach students skills for occupations that do not require a college degree. These might include jobs such as hairdressers, dental hygienists, technicians, travel agents, cooks, truck drivers, auto mechanics, and welders.

In the area of continuing education, adult education teachers help individuals update their skills to make them more marketable and enable them to do better with their jobs. For example, the adult education teacher may offer training in bookkeeping or computer skills.

Many adults take continuing education classes to enrich their lives, relax, learn new skills, and meet people. Almost every community offers continuing education classes in a variety of subjects from cooking and yoga to photography and foreign languages. All of these courses need adult education teachers.

Adult education teachers may use a variety of methods to teach their students. These include lecturing, demonstrating, and providing hands-on-experience. Individuals are expected to help students attain their maximum potential. It is often easier working with adults who are in school because they choose to be, as they are usually highly motivated to do well.

Depending on the specific area the individual is working in, he or she may be expected to prepare lessons, assignments, and homework, as well as to develop tests and grade papers. Adult education teachers may handle paperwork and record attendance, grades, and student progress.

EMPLOYMENT OPPORTUNITIES

Adult education teachers can work full or part time. Individuals may work in a variety of settings, including:

- Public school systems
- Community and junior colleges
- Universities
- Job training centers
- Private industry and business providing job training for employees
- Vocational trade schools
- Community centers

Expanding Opportunities for the 21st Century

The demand for adult education programs has been rising and is expected to continue into the 21st century. Expanding opportunities for adult education teachers will surface for those working in adult basic education for a number of reasons. These include the changes in certain legislative and immigration policies requiring basic competency in English and civics. People are also finding that, without basic education, it is difficult to locate a good job.

Other opportunities will develop for those working in vocational technical education as people switch jobs or seek new ones as a result of changing technology.

EARNINGS

Earnings for adult education teachers can vary greatly depending on a number of factors, including the specific type of employment settings as well as whether the individual is working full or part time. Those working full time can expect earnings ranging from $20,000 to $55,000. Other factors affecting earnings include the individual's education, experience, and responsibilities.

ADVANCEMENT OPPORTUNITIES

Adult education teachers can advance their careers by obtaining additional experience, education, and skills. Some individuals climb the career ladder by moving into administrative positions in education departments or corporate training departments. Other individuals find similar positions in larger school districts, vocational schools, or corporations where the pay is higher.

EDUCATION AND TRAINING

Educational requirements vary depending on the type of teaching the individual is involved with. Those teaching basic adult education must usually hold a minimum of a bachelor's degree in education. Many positions require their teachers to have or obtain a master's degree. Most states also require teacher certification.

Individuals teaching at vocational-technical schools may or may not require a formal college education. Professional experience may often be acceptable for those teaching continuing education classes.

EXPERIENCE AND QUALIFICATIONS

Individuals who teach basic adult education must usually go through a student teaching experience while still in college. This helps prepare them for the job when they graduate.

Teachers working in public schools in all states are required to be certified. Certification requirements vary from state to state. Generally, however, in order to be certified, individuals must complete an approved teacher training program at a four-year college; go through a supervised student teaching program; and pass an examination to prove competency in basic skills, teaching skills, and subject matter proficiency.

Adult education teachers working at vocational-technical schools or institutes may be required to hold certification in their specific field in order to teach.

FOR ADDITIONAL INFORMATION: Individuals interested in becoming adult eduction teachers can obtain additional information by contacting the American Association for Adult and Continuing Education (AAACE), the American Vocational Association (AVA), and the ERIC Clearing House on Adult, Career and Vocational Education.

TIPS

- Jobs in teaching adult continuing education classes may often be located by contacting local government agencies.
- Other positions may be located by contacting school systems, colleges and vocational-technical schools, community organizations, etc.
- If you are in college, remember to get letters of recommendation from several of your professors at school as well as from your student teaching supervisor.
- Positions may be advertised in the classified section of newspapers under headings such as "Education," "Adult Education," "Continuing Education," "Teaching," "Vocational Trade School," and "Instructors."

CHAPTER 9
•••••••••••••

Hospitality and Travel Careers

The hospitality and travel industry includes transportation, food, lodging, entertainment, and the attraction businesses.

The lodging industry ranges from bed-and-breakfast inns, independent resorts, hotels, and motels to major hotel/motel chains.

The transportation industry, a vital link to all parts of our economy, is composed of limousines, auto rentals, private cars, bus lines, railroads, airlines, ships, and boats.

The food service industry consists of coffee shops, small cafés, diners and fast-food operations, bars, lounges, restaurants, specialty food establishments, and catering companies. The food service division of hotels and motels, corporate dietary services, and institutional food service is also part of this industry.

Our society is entertainment-oriented. To some, entertainment is an evening at a nightclub or theater and to others it is a day at the ballpark. Attractions include theme parks, amusement parks, historic sites, and museums.

More people utilize the services of the hospitality and travel industries today than ever before, and this interest is expected to continue into the 21st century. Traveling is now easier and faster. New automobiles, highways, quickways, and freeways have been built to make ground transportation more comfortable. In some areas and industries, the workweek has been either shortened or compressed leaving more leisuretime opportunties.

People can get to almost any destination within the country in a few hours by getting on an airplane. Even those who want to travel around the world can do so more quickly than was ever possible. While air transportation may be expensive, airlines run discounts and specials making this mode of transportation affordable. Hotels and motels also conduct special rate reductions, making lodging less expensive during certain time periods.

Another factor affecting the expansion of these industries is business travel in this country and abroad. Though business travel does decrease during an economic slump, there are still many businesses that require travel arrangements and lodging.

The hospitality and travel industries encompass a vast number of careers in a variety of areas. Skill levels, education, training, and experience requirements can vary depending on the specific career. Opportunities exist for pilots, bus drivers, air traffic controllers, flight attendants, engineers, mechanics, reservations agents, travel agents, and tour packagers.

Administrative and management positions in hotels, motels, restaurants, and clubs must also be filled. Just as necessary will be chefs, cooks, hostesses, waitresses, waiters, and ticket clerks.

The diversity of careers in this field as well as space restrictions limit inclusion of all possible opportunities. Careers included in this section are:

Hotel/Motel Manager
Restaurant Manager
Travel Agent
Pilot
Flight Attendant

HOTEL/MOTEL MANAGER

JOB DESCRIPTION: *Oversee all operations of a hotel or motel; supervise staff; handle guest problems.*

EARNINGS: *$25,000 to $90,000+.*

RECOMMENDED EDUCATION AND TRAINING: *Educational requirements vary. Programs leading to certificates or associate's and bachelor's degrees are preferred.*

SKILLS AND PERSONALITY TRAITS: *Administrative skills; supervisory skills; management skills; personableness; communication skills.*

EXPERIENCE AND QUALIFICATIONS: *Experience working in hospitality industry.*

JOB DESCRIPTION AND RESPONSIBILITIES

Hotel and motel managers are responsible for overseeing the operation of the hotel or motel. Their specific duties vary depending on the job and the size of the facility. Individuals may be employed as general manager, resident manager, or shift manager. No matter the title, the individual's main function is to make sure that the establishment runs smoothly.

The larger the facility, the more specialized the manager's duties will be. In very large facilities, the manager will oversee all the assistant managers in making sure that the operation of the hotel/motel is efficient and profitable. In smaller facilities, managers will have more general duties. All administrative personnel and assistant managers report to the general manager of the hotel/motel.

General managers are responsible for hiring staff as well as training and supervision. In large facilities this may be handled by an assistant manager or a personnel director. However, even in large hotels the general manager will usually be part of the interview and hiring process for management and administrative employees.

The general manager is responsible for setting room rates, developing services for guests, and standards for housekeeping and food service. Once standards are set, the general manager is responsible for making sure that everything is kept up to par.

Managers deal with guest complaints and problems in a variety of ways. The individual may, for example, offer a guest an upgraded room if the promised room is not available. If guests complain about treatment or problems with their room, the manager may decide to waive their room charge. Maintaining good customer relations is important.

A large portion of the facility's profits often come from food and beverages. The manager oversees food and beverage services such as room service, restaurants, coffee shops, and lounges. The individual may develop promotions for food service establishments in the facility as well as the hotel/motel itself.

Managers also authorize expenses, allocate funds to various departments, approve expenditures, and audit income that comes into the facility.

Individuals in this position work long, hard hours. All problems that occur in the hotel as well as unexpected events become the responsibility of the manager. The manager is responsible to the owner of the facility or the CEO.

EMPLOYMENT OPPORTUNITIES

Hotel/motel managers can be employed by very large facilities or small roadside inns. Some managers work directly for the hotel or motel, while others are employed by companies contracted to run the facilities.

Individuals work in a variety of employment settings. Some of these include:

- Luxury hotels
- Inns
- Conference centers
- Convention hotels
- Chain and franchise hotels and motels
- Privately owned hotels
- Privately owned motels
- Health spas
- Resorts
- Dude ranches
- Suite hotels

Expanding Opportunities for the 21st Century

Even when the country is experiencing poor economic growth, business travel must continue. As a result, more and more hotels and motels will be catering to the business traveler.

Another growing trend that is expected to continue is domestic vacationing. As a result of various problems in other parts of the world, many people are choosing domestic vacation spots in lieu of foreign holidays. This, too, will create a continuing demand for hotels and motels within the country.

EARNINGS

Earnings of hotel and motel managers can range dramatically, depending on the education, training, experience, and responsibilities of the individual. Other factors affecting salary include the type, size, location, and prestige of the hotel or motel.

Hotel and motel managers can earn annual salaries ranging from $25,000 to $90,000 or more. Individuals with a great deal of experience and responsibilities, working in very large facilities, can earn between $55,000 and $90,000 plus. Some managers may also receive bonuses and liberal benefits.

ADVANCEMENT OPPORTUNITIES

Hotel and motel managers can advance in a number of ways. Resident managers can advance to general manager. Those who are shift managers become either a resident or a general manager. Some individuals are promoted to manage several hotels or motels in a specific area.

Hotel and motel managers can also advance their careers by locating positions in larger or more prestigious facilities.

EDUCATION AND TRAINING

The minimum educational requirement for hotel or motel managers is a high school diploma or equivalency. While a college education or degree is not always required, it is preferred. Some managers have degrees in liberal arts, communications, public relations, or business management. Individuals who are interested in careers in hotel/motel management should also consider a degree program in hotel and restaurant administration.

Courses include hotel and motel administration, marketing, public relations, accounting, economics, housekeeping, food service management and catering, hotel maintenance engineering, marketing, computer usage, and data processing.

Individuals without a formal education in hotel/motel management can move up from other jobs such as reservations manager, desk clerk, convention service manager, front service manager, or assistant manager. These people usually go through either on-the-job training or a formal training program sponsored by the hotel.

EXPERIENCE AND QUALIFICATIONS

Hotel and motel managers must have experience working in the hospitality industry. Some obtain this by working in other positions such as desk clerk, reservations manager, convention sales, convention manager, food and beverage service worker, or assistant manager. Others have had prior experience working in restaurants, lounges, and other food service facilities.

FOR ADDITIONAL INFORMATION: Individuals interested in pursuing careers in hotel or motel management can obtain addition information from the American Hotel and Motel Association (AH & MA), the Educational Institute of the American Hotel and Motel Association (EIAHMA), and the Council on Hotel, Restaurant, and Institutional Education (CHRIE).

Tips

- Larger hotel and motel chains usually offer more opportunities for training, advancement, and earnings than smaller, independent facilities.
- Large cities have employment agencies specializing in jobs in the hospitality industry.
- Contact large hotel and motel chains to learn more about their management training programs.
- Schools, colleges, and universities offering programs in hotel or restaurant management usually have placement services.
- Jobs may be advertised in the newspaper classified section under headings such as "Hotel," "Motel," "Inns," "Resorts," "Conference Centers," "Convention Centers," "Hospitality," "General Manager," "Resident Manager," etc.

RESTAURANT MANAGER

JOB DESCRIPTION: *Oversee restaurant operation; hire and train employees; deal with customer service problems.*

EARNINGS: *$16,000 to $50,000.*

RECOMMENDED EDUCATION AND TRAINING: *Some positions require an associate or bachelor's degree in restaurant management; others require a high school diploma.*

SKILLS AND PERSONALITY TRAITS: *Supervisory skills; interpersonal skills; business aptitude; communication skills.*

EXPERIENCE AND QUALIFICATIONS: *Experience in food service.*

JOB DESCRIPTION AND RESPONSIBILITIES

Restaurant managers are responsible for overseeing the operation of the establishment in which they work.

Responsibilities most restaurant managers must handle include recruiting, interviewing, hiring, and training restaurant employees. Personnel may include assistant managers, hosts, hostesses, waiters, waitresses, bus people, and cleaning staff. Hiring cooks and chefs may be the responsibility of the manager or may be handled by the owner of the establishment.

When recruiting personnel, the manager is responsible for writing and placing advertisements, putting up signs, and developing applications. During the interview process, the manager checks references and makes determinations regarding which people to hire. The individual must explain restaurant procedures, rules, and regulations to prospective employees and oversee training while supervising all employees.

Managers in some establishments are responsible for scheduling and keeping track of hours worked by employees and handling payroll duties, taxes, and unemployment compensation. They pay bills to suppliers for food, equipment, and services. In other establishments, these tasks will be handled by the owner or bookkeeper. Managers must make sure that their restaurant and its employees comply with health and safety rules and local liquor laws.

When dealing with customer complaints, managers always try to solve problems quickly and with the least amount of fuss. Sometimes the manager will not charge patrons for their meal or a portion of it to resolve a problem.

Managers are usually responsible for counting cash and charge receipts at the end of the shift. They must then balance the cash receipts against the day's sales.

Hours vary depending on the type of establishment. Individuals may be required to work overtime, nights, and/or weekends. Restaurant managers are responsible to the owner of the establishment.

EMPLOYMENT OPPORTUNITIES

Almost every restaurant and food service has a manager. Small or family-owned restaurants may find the owner, hostess, or host performing the duties of the manager. Larger establishments may have a day manager and a night manager. Individuals may work in a variety of settings including:

- Fast-food restaurants
- Chain or franchise restaurants
- Coffee shops
- Diners
- Hotel restaurants
- Motel coffee shops
- Department store restaurants
- Full-service restaurants
- Specialty restaurants

Expanding Opportunities for the 21st Century

Dining out is becoming a necessity rather than a luxury. With the increase in single parents and two-parent families where both adults work, more families are eating out.

Because of the great turnover of personnel working in franchise and chain restaurants and fast-food establishments, there is always a need for managers.

EARNINGS

Annual earnings of restaurant managers can range considerably depending on the size, type, location, and prestige of the establishment. Other important factors include the experience, responsibilities, and education of the individual.

Restaurant managers working in fast-food restaurants, coffee shops, and diners earn annual salaries ranging from $16,000 to $30,000 or more. Those in full-service restaurants can earn from approximately $19,000 to $50,000 plus. Managers with a great deal of experience in large, metropolitan areas will be paid at the high end of the scale.

Individuals in many establishments receive benefit packages.

ADVANCEMENT OPPORTUNITIES

With experience, restaurant managers can find positions in large or prestigious establishments. Some individuals become regional managers for a group of restaurants. Others open up their own restaurants.

EDUCATION AND TRAINING

Educational requirements for restaurant managers vary from job to job. Most require applicants to have at least a high school diploma or equivalency. Some positions require either a two- or four-year degree in restaurant and food service management. In addition to classroom study and laboratory work, many of these programs offer supervised internships.

Many restaurants, especially chains and franchises, offer extensive training programs where individuals learn every aspect of the operation of the restaurant. Restaurants with no formal programs usually offer informal on-the-job training.

EXPERIENCE AND QUALIFICATIONS

In order to qualify for most positions in restaurant management, individuals must have experience in the food service industry. Some restaurant managers start out as waitresses, waiters, hosts, hostesses, or fast-food workers. Others participate in training programs or work as apprentices or assistant restaurant managers.

Voluntary certification is available for individuals working in this field. Managers can earn the designation Foodservice Management Professional (FMP) for the Educational Foundation of the National Restaurant Association by completing classes, passing a written exam, and meeting standards of work experience in the field.

FOR ADDITIONAL INFORMATION: Interested individuals can obtain additional information by contacting the Educational Foundation of the National Restaurant Association (EFNRA), the Council on Hotel, Restaurant and Institutional Education, and the National Association of Trade and Technical Schools (NATTS).

TIPS

- If you are still in school, obtain a part-time or summer job in a restaurant as a waiter, waitress, host, hostess, or fast-food worker.
- Job openings are advertised in the newspaper's classified section. Look under headings such as "Restaurant Manager," "Management—Food Service," "Food Service," "Fast-food," "Full-Service Restaurants," etc.
- Both two- and four-year programs in restaurant and food service management usually have placement services.
- Send your resume and a short cover letter to restaurants and food service establishments in your area.

TRAVEL AGENT

JOB DESCRIPTION: *Assist people with travel plans; make transportation and lodging reservations; book tours.*

EARNINGS: *$13,000 to $55,000+.*

RECOMMENDED EDUCATION AND TRAINING: *On-the-job or formal training program.*

SKILLS AND PERSONALITY TRAITS: *Communication skills; computer skills; understanding of travel industry; interpersonal skills.*

EXPERIENCE AND QUALIFICATIONS: *Requirements vary; travel experience is helpful.*

JOB DESCRIPTION AND RESPONSIBILITIES

Travel agents assist people with travel plans for business or pleasure. It does not cost the traveler any more to make a reservation through a travel agent than it does to make it personally. Instead, the agencies are paid a commission by companies that are providing the services. These include airlines, car rental companies, motels, hotels, railroads, and cruise lines.

The main function of a travel agent is to book travel arrangements. Customers may call or visit an agency when they are planning a trip. The travel agent is responsible for determining the customer's destination, departure date, and mode of transportation. The individual must also find out if the traveler wants to travel the most economical way or first class.

Travel agents use computers to access information about airline flights, prices, and schedules. They provide similar information if the traveler needs car rentals and hotel or motel accommodations.

It is important to remember that the best travel arrangements are not always the cheapest. An inexpensive flight that forces the traveler to change planes three times before arrival may not be the best fare for a business executive. The same fare, however, may be perfect for a student traveling on a limited income. The travel agent must determine the preferences of the traveler.

Other duties of a travel agent include answering travel inquiries, filing correspondence, writing tickets, and putting tours together.

One of the perks many travel agents enjoy is traveling on "fam," or familiarization, trips. These trips help the agent learn about various destinations and are sponsored by the airlines, cruise lines, regional organizations, and hotels.

EMPLOYMENT OPPORTUNITIES

Individuals may work for commercial travel agents or in the corporate travel department of a large company. Full- and part-time opportunities are available in many agencies throughout the country. Individuals may be salaried, act as independent agents, or own their own agency. Travel agents can specialize in specific types of travel arrangements, including travel for:

- Pleasure
- Groups
- Tours and packages
- Business
- Singles

Expanding Opportunities for the 21st Century

Travel agents specializing in business travel arrangements or working in corporate travel departments will be in demand in the new century. As the costs of necessary business travel skyrocket, management will seek ways to keep prices down.

EARNINGS

Earnings for full-time travel agents can range from $13,000 to $50,000 or more. Variables include the individual's responsibilities, experience, and sales ability. Sales ability is especially important when travel agents are being paid on a salary plus commission basis. Commissions vary, depending on the type of travel, from about 5 percent to 12 percent.

Other factors affecting earnings include the size and geographical location of the agency.

ADVANCEMENT OPPORTUNITIES

Travel agents may advance their careers in a number of ways. One method is by booking more travel arrangements and receiving increased earnings through commission. Agents may also be promoted to office manager.

Individuals may acquire additional training to become a certified travel counselor or pass a written examination and be awarded a certificate of proficiency from the American Society of Travel Agents.

Another path many agents choose is to open up their own travel agencies.

EDUCATION AND TRAINING

Most agencies prefer candidates who have either a high school diploma or an equivalency. There are some agents who have formal training and others who receive on-the-job training.

Formal training courses are often offered through community colleges, four-year colleges and universities, vocational schools, and adult education programs.

The American Society of Travel Agents and the Institute of Certified Travel Agents offer home study courses in travel agency skills.

Hotel/motel chains, major airlines, and cruise companies provide specialized workshops, courses, and seminars on selling a variety of different types of travel, including accommodations, airline travel, and cruise travel.

EXPERIENCE AND QUALIFICATIONS

While travel agency experience is always preferred, many positions do not require it. Those who have worked as receptionists, secretaries, or clerks will, however, have an edge over other workers. Other prior jobs that might prove useful in a career as a travel agent include working in an airline, rental car agency, or hotel as a reservation agent.

FOR ADDITIONAL INFORMATION: Individuals interested in obtaining additional information on careers as travel agents should contact the American Society of Travel Agents (ASTA) or the Institute of Certified Travel Agents (ICTA).

TIPS

- If you are still in school or considering a career change, consider a part-time job in a travel agency as a receptionist or clerk. This will give you an edge over other applicants when applying for a job as an agent.
- Job openings are advertised in the classified section of the newspaper under "Travel," "Travel Agent," "Hospitality," or "Tourism."
- Some agencies seek out agents to work independently. In this type of setup, the agency provides the equipment needed to book travel, such as phones and computers. Independent travel agents receive commissions rather than salary.

PILOT

JOB DESCRIPTION: *Fly aircraft; plan flights; choose routes; determine altitude and speed; maintain equipment.*

EARNINGS: *$35,000 to $175,000+.*

RECOMMENDED EDUCATION AND TRAINING: *Some airlines require two years of college, others prefer a college degree.*

SKILLS AND PERSONALITY TRAITS: *Ability to make quick decisions under pressure; good judgment.*

EXPERIENCE AND QUALIFICATIONS: *Commercial pilot's license issued by the FAA.*

JOB DESCRIPTION AND RESPONSIBILITIES

Pilots fly airplanes, helicopters, and other aircraft. The pilots most people are familiar with are those working for commercial airlines. Other pilots fly cargo planes or crop dusters. Helicopter pilots work for rescue teams or fly for television or radio stations providing road condition reports.

Before they take off, pilots must plan their flight. This includes talking to flight dispatchers and weather forecasters to learn about weather conditions that may affect flight. This is important in determining the route, altitude, and speed required to get the plane safely to its final destination. Pilots may also be required to file instrument flight plans with air traffic controllers so that flights can be coordinated with other traffic.

Pilots are responsible for checking their aircraft to make sure everything is working correctly. They may check engines, instruments, controls, etc.

On most commercial flights there are at least two pilots and sometimes three. The senior pilot is called the *captain*. This individual is responsible for supervising the other pilots, the flight attendants, and other crew members.

The *copilot* is responsible for assisting the pilot with a variety of tasks. The copilot may, for example, communicate with the air traffic controller, monitor the instruments, and fly the aircraft.

On some aircraft there may be a third pilot called the *flight engineer*. This job is being phased out because of new technology. When there is a flight engineer, the individual will assist both the pilot and copilot. The flight engineer may monitor instruments and systems, operate instruments, make in-flight repairs on instruments or equipment, and watch for other aircraft.

Additional duties of pilots include steering the aircraft, checking instrument panels, keeping in contact with air traffic control, and monitoring warning devices. Those working for small airlines or flying smaller aircraft may load the plane personally or make sure it is loaded correctly, supervise refueling, and perform minor maintenance.

Pilots in all fields are required to write and file records of flights for the FAA as well as their company.

Hours vary depending on their employment situation. Individuals working for airlines usually have scheduled routes. Most flying days, pilots will be required to layover away from their home base. Individuals may fly during the morning, afternoon, evening, or night.

Airline pilots are only allowed, by law, to fly 100 hours a month or 1,000 a year. In addition to flying, pilots usually work a similar number of hours each month handling nonflying responsibilities.

EMPLOYMENT OPPORTUNITIES

Pilots may work in a variety of employment situations. Most civilian pilots work for commercial airlines. Other employment possibilities include:

- Private flights
- Air taxi companies
- Private industry (flying executives or company cargo)
- Crop dusting
- Sightseeing planes and helicopters
- Traffic helicopters for radio or television stations
- Government opportunities
- Military flying

Expanding Opportunities for the 21st Century

Due to mandatory retirement requirements in this field, and the growth of the travel industry, there is a steady demand for pilots in the commercial airline industry.

EARNINGS

Pilots earn approximately $40,000 to $175,000 annually. Earnings are dependent on a number of factors including the specific employment situation and the individual's experience and responsibilities. Other factors include the type, size, and maximum speed of an aircraft and the number of hours and miles flown by the pilot. Individuals might also receive extra pay for flying night or international flights.

Pilots working for commercial airlines usually earn more than their counterparts in other industries. Commercial pilots earn between $40,000 and $50,000 if they are flight engineers. Those who have copilot responsibilities earn between $55,000 and $68,000. Captains working for commercial airlines earn $100,000 to $125,000 or more. There are some senior captains who earn up to $175,000.

Pilots working in other industries may have annual earnings ranging between $35,000 and $65,000. Copilots may earn between $35,000 and $40,000.

Most pilots usually have liberal benefit packages to augment their earnings.

ADVANCEMENT OPPORTUNITIES

A great deal of the advancement for pilots is earned through experience and seniority. Individuals start out as flight engineers, then become copilots, and then captains. The best flying assignments go to those with the most seniority.

Pilots working in other industries may start out working as flight instructors to build up their flying hours. They may then move into positions flying with smaller airlines or charter companies. Some advance to positions with major airlines.

EDUCATION AND TRAINING

Educational requirements vary with the job. Some airlines may have a minimum requirement of two years of college. Most major airlines prefer to hire college graduates.

Education and training for pilots can be obtained through either military or civilian flying schools. There are close to 600 civilian flying schools certified by the FAA. Some of these are affiliated with colleges and universities that offer degree credit for pilot training.

In addition to other education, pilots working for commercial airlines go through several weeks of comprehensive training both in classrooms and in simulators. Individuals are required to continue training to keep up with technological advances and new equipment.

EXPERIENCE AND QUALIFICATIONS

All pilots must have a commercial pilot's license issued by the FAA. There are a variety of ratings for the license. Pilots paid to transport passengers or cargo need a commercial pilot's license with an instrument rating. Helicopter pilots must have a commercial pilot's certificate with a helicopter rating. Qualifications for both of these licenses include 250 hours or more of flight experience. Individuals must also be at least 18 years of age, pass a comprehensive physical examination, have 20/20 vision with or without corrective lenses, good hearing, pass a drug screening test, and have no physical handicaps that might impair performance. Individuals must also take and pass a written examination on FAA regulations, navigation techniques, and principles of flight. There is also a practical examination where applicants must demonstrate flying ability to FAA examiners.

In order to fly in bad weather, pilots must have their license rated to fly by instruments. To get this rating individuals must have 105 hours of flight experience that includes at least 40 hours flying by instruments. Individuals must also pass a written examination and demonstrate the ability to fly by instruments.

Pilots who work for airlines have more stringent requirements. They must also take and pass an FAA written examination as well as a flight examination. Those who do will be awarded flight engineer's licenses. Captains must obtain an airline transport pilot's license. These individuals must be at least 23 years of age and have a minimum of 1,500 hours of flying experience. This must include night flying and instrument flying.

Pilots must go through routine physical examinations and tests to illustrate flying skills. These may be required by both the government and the company for which the individual works.

FOR ADDITIONAL INFORMATION: Individuals interested in learning more about careers as pilots can obtain additional information by contacting the Future Aviation Professionals of America (FAPA), the Air Line Pilots Association (ALPA), the Air Transport Association of America (ATAA), the Allied Pilots Association (APA), and the Flight Engineers' International Association (AFL-CIO).

Tips

- Job openings are often advertised in aviation trade magazines.
- Jobs may also be located in companies operating aircraft at local airports.
- Individuals can obtain valuable experience and flight training in the military.
- After you have your commercial FAA pilot's license send your resume with a short cover letter to the personnel director of all the major airlines.

FLIGHT ATTENDANT

JOB DESCRIPTION: *Assist passengers during flight; prepare passenger cabins; instruct passengers in use of emergency equipment; serve refreshments.*

EARNINGS: *$15,000 to $50,000+.*

RECOMMENDED EDUCATION AND TRAINING: *High school diploma plus airline-sponsored training program.*

SKILLS AND PERSONALITY TRAITS: *Interpersonal skills; communication skills; good grooming; poise; articulateness; dependability; level-headedness.*

EXPERIENCE AND QUALIFICATIONS: *Minimum age requirements range from 19 to 21 years old.*

JOB DESCRIPTION AND RESPONSIBILITIES

Flight attendants are responsible for providing comfort and safety to airplane passengers. Attendants are usually assigned a base to work from. The base is one of the cities that the airline flies in or out of. Individuals working full time will be required to fly approximately 80 hours a month. They spend a similar amount of time handling other duties on the ground.

Attendants must usually be at the airport an hour before flight time to receive a briefing by the flight captain or other personnel. During this time, they are instructed about weather conditions that may affect the flight and passengers who have special needs.

Flight attendants are expected to prepare passenger cabins before flight, greet passengers as they board the plane, point out or show them to their seats, and check tickets. They may also help passengers store overhead baggage and hang up coats.

An important duty of flight attendants is to show passengers where emergency equipment is located and how to use it. They must also point out emergency exits. These precautions are necessary in case of an emergency. Before the plane takes off, the attendant must make sure that all seats are in the proper position and seat belts are fastened.

Flight attendants pass out pillows, blankets, and other items to make passengers more comfortable. They answer questions, distribute newspapers and magazines, serve meals, and take away finished trays.

In some situations, attendants are required to help calm crying babies or find quiet activities for bored children. Attendants may start movies and hand out headphones for the movie or music.

Other important duties of flight attendants are administering first aid, keeping passengers calm during emergencies, instructing them on procedures, and, if necessary, helping them evacuate the plane.

When airplanes are landing, attendants make sure seats are in the correct positions, trays are up, and seat belts are fastened. Once the plane lands, individuals help people gather up their belongings and assist them off the aircraft.

Flight attendants work varying hours depending on flight schedules. This includes morning, afternoon, evening, or night travel. They may also work weekends and holidays. Flight attendants are responsible to the first or lead flight attendant of the aircraft.

When flight attendants are away from their home base, the airline pays for hotel accommodations and meals. This job offers individuals the opportunity to travel extensively and meet new people.

One of the perks in this job is substantial flight discounts to anywhere the airline goes. Families of the attendant may also be able to enjoy similar savings.

Employment Opportunities

Flight attendants may work part or full time for commercial airlines, companies that rent airplanes, or for individuals who own private planes.

Attendants may work on either domestic or international flights or a combination. There are large commercial airlines, commuter airlines, and small regional airlines. Some of the major airline companies include:

- Continental Airlines
- American Airlines
- Trans World Airlines
- USAir
- United
- Northwest

Expanding Opportunities for the 21st Century

Most airlines charge similar prices for trips going to the same destination. One of the most important things airlines can do to attract customers is to provide better services than competitive airlines. Flight attendants are the individuals whom the public associates with the service of each airline. As a result, airlines are interested in hiring flight attendants who have the experience and personality to deal with the public. Many prefer to hire those who also have a college background. In particular demand are employees whose degrees emphasize public and customer relations.

Earnings

Annual salaries of flight attendants range from approximately $15,000 to $50,000 or more. Earnings are determined, to a great extent, on their experience. Those just entering the field may earn salaries at the lower end of the scale. Attendants with more experience earn between $20,000 and $25,000. Senior flight attendants with a great deal of experience and responsibility earn up to $50,000. Individuals may receive additional compensation for flying at night or to international locations. They are also paid extra for overtime.

Minimum earnings are set by bargaining unions.

ADVANCEMENT OPPORTUNITIES

Flight attendants start out as reserve attendants. This means that they must be available on short notice. They are assigned to one of the airline's bases and are called to fill in for individuals who are out due to illness or on vacation. They might also be called in to work on extra or new flights that have been added to routes.

It may take one to six years to move off reserve status, depending on the number of flight attendants who retire, leave the job, or are promoted. Once off reserve status, flight attendants may bid on assignments for airline bases or flights. Assignments are granted on the basis of seniority. Senior flight attendants, therefore, usually receive the choice assignments.

Flight attendants can advance to lead or first flight attendant on the aircraft. They may also choose administrative or managerial positions including flight service instructor, recruiting representative, and customer service director.

EDUCATION AND TRAINING

Flight attendants must be high school graduates. Some employers, however, prefer to hire individuals who have a college degree.

Once flight attendants are hired by an airline, they must go through a comprehensive training program. Each large airline has its own program. Smaller airlines may send their employees to schools owned by other airlines.

Training programs for flight attendants last between four and six weeks and consist of classroom study and practice flights. Programs cover passenger relations, first aid, emergency procedures for operating oxygen systems, evacuating planes, flight regulations, duties and responsibilities, company operations and policies, and dealing with terrorism.

Flight attendants must take from twelve to fourteen hours of continuing training every year on passenger relations and emergency procedures.

EXPERIENCE AND QUALIFICATIONS

Minimum age requirements vary with the airline. Some require attendants to be at least 19 years old, while others set minimum ages at 20 or 21.

Flight attendants are also required to be high school graduates.

FOR ADDITIONAL INFORMATION: Individuals interested in flight attendant careers can obtain additional information by contacting the Future Aviation Professionals of America (FAPA), the Association of Flight Attendants (AFA), and the Transport Workers Union of America (TWUA).

Tips

- Fluency in a second language makes you more marketable in this occupation.
- Send your resume with a short cover letter to every airline.
- Prior jobs dealing with the public are helpful in obtaining a position. If you are still in school, consider a part-time or summer job in customer service, customer relations, guest relations, or public relations.

CHAPTER 10

Science and Engineering Careers

As a result of relentless international competition for technology in the world, an increasing demand exists for engineers, technicians, technologists, and scientists. Without these professionals, American technology will be seriously disadvantaged in the future.

In the records of history from the papyrus scrolls and stone tablets of ancient times to the newspapers of recent years, one can recognize the demands placed on scientists and engineers to resolve the problems of the day—from the design of the pyramids and the stone arches to the telegraph, the telephone, and the Brooklyn Bridge.

The future promises to be more complex. The need for scientists and engineers in the year 2000 will reflect the complexities of today's living and the need to tackle newer tasks in a more efficient or automated manner. The demand for technicians, technologists, and professionals who can meet the challenges of the new century will far exceed that of the past.

Chemists, physicists, agricultural scientists, environmentalists, and medical technologists will all be in sharp demand.

Other chapters of this book discuss careers in medical technology, environment, conservation, and computer sciences. People interested in science and engineering careers should also review these sections. The diversity of careers in this field as well as space restrictions limit inclusion of all possible opportunities. The careers in this chapter include:

Meteorologist
Biochemist
Civil Engineer
Mechanical Engineer

METEOROLOGIST

JOB DESCRIPTION: *Forecast weather; collect data on atmospheric characteristics; analyze past weather factors.*

EARNINGS: *$19,000 to $100,000+.*

RECOMMENDED EDUCATION AND TRAINING: *Bachelor's degree with major in meteorology; some positions require master's or Ph.D.*

SKILLS AND PERSONALITY TRAITS: *Analytical skills; manual dexterity; aptitude for the sciences; communication skills; computer skills.*

EXPERIENCE AND QUALIFICATIONS: *Many entry-level jobs do not require experience.*

JOB DESCRIPTION AND RESPONSIBILITIES

Every time a weather forecast is made, the services of a meteorologist are used.

Meteorologists are called on to perform their job for a variety of reasons. One of their main functions is forecasting weather. These forecasts are important for both long- and short-term issues and preparation. Meteorology is also used to learn more about environmental matters such as ozone depletion, air pollution, or trends in global warming.

Weather forecasts are used by many industries. Every television station and radio station, for example, uses either its own meteorologist or the services of a weather forecaster.

Airlines, cruise ships, boats, and freighters all must have an indication of weather predictions before making final plans for travel. Agricultural industries such as farmers rely on weather forecasts to plant and harvest food.

The main function of meteorologists is to study the atmosphere and its elements. The word *atmosphere* refers to the air that surrounds the earth. Those who specialize in forecasting the weather are known as *synoptic* or *operational* meteorologists. These individuals accumulate data on air pressure, humidity, temperature, and wind velocity. After study and analysis, this information is used to make long- and short-term weather predictions.

Data collection is more sophisticated today than ever before. Weather satellites, radar, and computer models of the atmosphere are used extensively. Individuals must know how to input information and retrieve it, but a great deal of the analysis can now be achieved with computer technology.

Physical meteorologists specialize in research. They study weather phenomena, the chemical and physical properties of the atmosphere, the transfer of atmospheric energy, and the transmission of light, radio, and sound waves.

A third specialty in the meteorological field is that of climatology. *Climatologists* analyze past records of wind, sunshine, rainfall, and temperatures in specific areas. This specialization is used to help plan sizes of heating and cooling systems and aid in effective land utilization and the design of better buildings.

Meteorologists may work varied hours depending on their employment situation. Some individuals work nights and weekends.

EMPLOYMENT OPPORTUNITIES

The largest employer of meteorologists is the National Oceanic and Atmospheric Administration. A good portion of these employees work for the National Weather Service throughout the United States. Other employment settings include:

- College or university faculties
- Radio or television stations
- Research departments
- Department of Defense
- Private weather consultants
- Engineering service firms
- Nonprofit organizations
- Ski resorts

Expanding Opportunities for the 21st Century

Increased use of private weather forecasting and meteorological services by radio and television stations, farmers, commodity investors, and construction firms will create new positions in the private sector.

There will also be an increase in employment by the National Weather Service to improve short-term and local area weather forecasts.

EARNINGS

Meteorologists earn from $19,000 to $100,000 plus. Salaries vary depending on the specific employment situation and geographic location as well as the responsibilities, duties, experience, and education of the individual.

Meteorologists with bachelor's degrees that are just entering the field will earn from $19,000 to $25,000. Those with master's degrees have salaries ranging from $21,000 to $33,000 plus. Individuals with Ph.D. degrees will usually earn starting salaries ranging from $38,000 to $40,000 plus. As individuals obtain more experience their earnings can go up to $45,000 or more.

There are meteorologists who report the weather on television or radio who earn up to $100,000 or more.

ADVANCEMENT OPPORTUNITIES

Meteorologists can advance by locating jobs in large or prestigious markets. More experience and education can result in more complex jobs and higher pay. Some meteorologists also move into supervisory or administrative positions.

Another option is opening a weather consulting service. Some meteorologists may become on-air radio or television personalities. However, it should be noted that not all weather reporters are meteorologists.

EDUCATION AND TRAINING

Meteorologists must have a minimum of a bachelor's degree. Some jobs require a major in meteorology while others just require a specific number of course hours in the area. Other possible majors include physics, earth science, geophysics, and atmospheric sciences.

There are some employers that prefer or require individuals to hold a master's or Ph.D. in meteorology. These may include teaching and research jobs.

EXPERIENCE AND QUALIFICATIONS

A bachelor's degree is necessary to become a meteorologist. Individuals can obtain entry-level jobs with no experience. They must, however, have training in weather analysis and forecasting.

FOR ADDITIONAL INFORMATION: Individuals interested in learning more about careers in meteorology can contact the American Meteorological Society (AMS) or the National Oceanic and Atmospheric Administration Personnel Office.

TIPS

- Internships or apprenticeships provide valuable on-the-job training.
- Many positions in this field are civil service jobs. Contact the Interagency Board of the United States Civil Service Examiners of Washington, D.C., to learn more about opportunities.
- Colleges and universities offering programs in meteorology usually have placement services for their graduates.

BIOCHEMIST

JOB DESCRIPTION: *Conduct basic research; collect data; perform and analyze experiments.*

EARNINGS: *$25,000 to $75,000+.*

RECOMMENDED EDUCATION AND TRAINING: *Minimum of a bachelor's degree in biochemistry or chemistry; master's or Ph.D. required for certain positions.*

SKILLS AND PERSONALITY TRAITS: *Aptitude for sciences; good math skills; communication skills; manual dexterity; curiosity.*

EXPERIENCE AND QUALIFICATIONS: *Experience requirements vary.*

JOB DESCRIPTION AND RESPONSIBILITIES

The work of biochemists is part biology and part chemistry. Biochemists study the chemical composition of living systems including animals, plants, insects, viruses, and microorganisms. They attempt to understand the complex chemical combinations and reactions involved in a variety of life forces such as metabolism, reproduction, growth, and heredity.

Changes are occurring in scientific objectives. Scientists have been chiefly interested in determining causes and effects, that is, what series of reactions occurred for certain things to happen. Now biochemists are beginning to look more at how to control the things that happen.

Biochemists have a variety of duties, depending on their specific job and the industry in which they work. Biochemists in health-related fields or pharmacology may search for ways to diagnose, treat, and cure illnesses or for new and better pharmaceuticals.

Biochemists in agricultural chemical companies may be responsible for researching the effect of new pesticides and herbicides on the growth of plant life. Those working in the food industry research nutrients, supplements, preservation, and other factors in the development of foods.

Biochemists use various equipment in the course of their jobs. Technology has increased the efficiency and speed of many tests as new equipment is more sophisticated than ever and can identify compounds more accurately.

Other responsibilities of biochemists include preparing reports on experiments and tests and supervising laboratory personnel. An interesting potential of biochemical genetic research is the possibility that more genetic diseases may be predicted and treated through an understanding of how genes operate and enzymes function. For example, future research may find a way to treat the cells in an individual with diabetes so that the cells have the ability to produce insulin.

Biochemists will usually work fairly normal hours. They will be expected to work overtime when a project must be completed or a deadline is near.

EMPLOYMENT OPPORTUNITIES

Biochemists may work in a variety of employment settings. These include:

- Government agencies
- Pharmaceutical companies
- Agricultural chemical companies
- Colleges and universities
- Food manufacturers
- Feed manufacturers
- Consumer product manufacturers

Expanding Opportunities for the 21st Century

Biochemists will be in demand in the pharmaceutical, biotechnology, and environmental protection fields. One of the largest growth areas for biochemists will be in research for the prevention and cure of AIDS.

EARNINGS

Earnings for biochemists vary depending on experience, education, responsibilities, and the specific industry in which they work. Salaries can range from $25,000 to $75,000 or more.

Generally, the more education and experience individuals have, the higher their salaries. Individuals working for federal government agencies will usually earn less than their counterparts in the private sector.

ADVANCEMENT OPPORTUNITIES

Biochemists can advance in a number of ways. They may obtain experience and additional education and locate positions in large or prestigious companies. Advancement potential includes promotions to project director or head biochemist.

Many biochemists decide to go into research. Others become professors at colleges and universities.

EDUCATION AND TRAINING

Biochemists are required to hold a minimum of a four-year bachelor's degree in biochemistry or chemistry. Positions in teaching will usually require a graduate degree.

The American Chemical Society approves college and university programs in the chemistry field. In addition to basic biochemistry and chemistry courses, individuals should take classes in cell biology, biochemical methods, genetics, and research.

EXPERIENCE AND QUALIFICATIONS

Experience requirements vary for biochemists depending on the specific position. There are many entry-level jobs for biochemists. These positions are often filled by recent college graduates and offer on-the-job training programs in lieu of experience.

FOR ADDITIONAL INFORMATION: Individuals interested in learning more about a career as a biochemist can contact the American Chemical Society (ACS), the American Institute of Chemists (AIC), the American Association for Clinical Chemistry (AACC), and the American Society of Biological Chemists (ASBC).

TIPS

- The American Chemical Society has a career service offering career information and guidance.
- Colleges and universities with biochemistry programs usually have placement offices that list openings.
- Jobs are advertised in the classified section of newspapers and trade journals.

CIVIL ENGINEER

JOB DESCRIPTION: *Plan the construction of bridges, roads, tunnels, buildings, etc.; supervise the construction of structures; determine costs.*

EARNINGS: *$26,000 to $75,000+.*

RECOMMENDED EDUCATION AND TRAINING: *Bachelor's degree in engineering.*

SKILLS AND PERSONALITY TRAITS: *Scientific aptitude; math skills; analytical skills; communication skills; computer skills.*

EXPERIENCE AND QUALIFICATIONS: *State licensing or registration required for work that affects property, health, and life.*

JOB DESCRIPTION AND RESPONSIBILITIES

Without the design skills of a civil engineer, bridges could conceivably collapse under the weight of cars and trucks, roads could crumble, and buildings could topple.

Civil engineers plan and supervise construction of roads, bridges, tunnels, sewage systems, subways, airports, and water supply systems. These professionals are also responsible for planning shopping centers, housing projects, and large office buildings.

Specialization options within the field of civil engineering include environmental, structural, water resources, construction, transportation, or geotechnical engineering.

Whatever the speciality, a civil engineer's major functions include the design of the project and, in some cases, overseeing its construction. Buildings, roads, bridges, and all other structures must be designed so that they are structurally sound.

Within the scope of their job, civil engineers must determine costs of materials, labor, and equipment. They must also have a complete knowledge of zoning regulations, ordinances, fire codes, and health and safety regulations.

Civil engineers may be responsible for testing and maintaining structures that they have designed. This is especially true for bridges, which must be tested and checked regularly to make sure that there are no major cracks or weaknesses. If any develop, the bridges must be repaired.

Deadlines are common in the construction industry. Civil engineers will often be required to work under stressful conditions including time constraints and monetary limitations.

Civil engineers use calculators and adding machines to help them with their work. More recently, many civil engineers are also using computers to assist in designing structures. Computer aided design (CAD) programs are becoming especially useful because plans can be completed quicker and more accurately than by other methods.

Civil engineers may travel around the country or the world depending on their employer. There are a great many individuals working in this area for American firms in foreign countries. Some stay in one place only long enough to complete a project and then move on to another location.

EMPLOYMENT OPPORTUNITIES

Civil engineers may work full or part time in a variety of employment situations. These include:

- Government agencies
- Private engineering firms
- Architectural firms
- Self-employment
- Public utilities
- Railroads
- Manufacturing industries
- Construction companies

Expanding Opportunities for the 21st Century

Civil engineers will be in demand as a result of population growth and the resulting demands placed on the infrastructure. Individuals will be needed to design large buildings, waste disposal systems, and water resources and transportation systems.

EARNINGS

Civil engineers earn from $26,000 to $75,000 or more. This varies with the education, experience, responsibilities, and geographic area of the individual as well as the specific industry.

Civil engineers holding bachelor's degrees, just entering private industry, earn from $26,000 to $32,000. With additional education and experience, annual earnings range from $29,000 to $75,000. Civil engineers working for the federal government will earn lower salaries than their counterparts in private industry.

ADVANCEMENT OPPORTUNITIES

Civil engineers can advance their career by obtaining additional education and experience. Some climb the career ladder as a result of assignment to more complex projects. Others locate positions in prestigious firms. Civil engineers may also be promoted to jobs as technical specialists.

Individuals who have advanced education may move into supervisory, management, or administrative positions, or may choose to go into teaching.

EDUCATION AND TRAINING

The minimum education needed to become a civil engineer is a bachelor's degree in engineering. Many individuals go on to get a master's degree or a Ph.D.

Courses in the first two years of the bachelor's program consist of math and basic sciences such as physics and chemistry. Other courses include social sciences, humanities, English, and introductory engineering. During the final two years, students are expected to take all engineering courses with a major emphasis in civil engineering.

Many employers offer on-the-job training as well as seminars, classes, and workshops. Civil engineers often continue their education to keep up with trends in technology.

EXPERIENCE AND QUALIFICATIONS

Civil engineers must be state-registered or -licensed if their work affects property, health, and/or life. Registration or licensing is also required for civil engineers who offer their services to the public.

In order to obtain registration, individuals must have a college degree from an engineering program accredited by the Accreditation Board for Engineering and Technology. They must also have at least four years of relevant work experience and pass a state examination.

FOR ADDITIONAL INFORMATION: Individuals interested in careers as civil engineers can obtain additional information by contacting JETS-Guidance, Accreditation Board for Engineering and Technology (ABET), the National Society of Professional Engineers (NSPE), the American Society for Engineering Education (ASEE), the Society of Women Engineers (SWE), or the American Society of Civil Engineers (ASCE).

TIPS

- Civil engineers who specialize in structures often earn extra income by performing structural exams on houses for home buyers.
- Job openings are advertised in the classified section of the newspaper. Look under headings such as "Engineer," "Civil Engineer," "Structural Engineer," "Environmental Engineer," "Sanitary Engineer," "Construction," etc.
- If you are still in school, look for an internship with a civil engineer who specializes in a field in which you are interested.

MECHANICAL ENGINEER

JOB DESCRIPTION: *Design and develop power-producing machines; analyze plans for machinery.*

EARNINGS: *$29,000 to $80,000+.*

RECOMMENDED EDUCATION AND TRAINING: *Bachelor's degree in mechanical engineering; some positions require a master's or Ph.D.*

SKILLS AND PERSONALITY TRAITS: *Scientific aptitude; math skills; manual dexterity; analytical skills; communication skills; computer skills.*

EXPERIENCE AND QUALIFICATIONS: *State licensing or registration required for work that affects property, health, and/or life.*

JOB DESCRIPTION AND RESPONSIBILITIES

Mechanical engineers design and develop different types of machinery. They may be responsible for almost any type of engine or moving equipment.

Mechanical engineers often specialize within an industry. Some specialties include energy conversion systems; motor vehicles; heating, ventilating, and air-conditioning; special machinery for industries; and instrumentation.

Mechanical engineers may be responsible for the actual design of machinery or may perform other duties such as analyzing or drawing plans. Some mechanical engineers are responsible for conducting research.

Other duties include the maintenance of machinery or the supervision of equipment production. In some positions individuals might also be involved in technical sales.

Whether mechanical engineers are designing an internal combustion engine for an automobile or preparing the design for an air-conditioning system, their job is to make sure that the machinery is as efficient as possible. This is especially important now as energy conservation and environmental protection have become timely issues.

Mechanical engineers, as all others in the engineering field, must deal with deadlines. Individuals must be able to deal with the stressful conditions of finishing a project and meeting a deadline.

Mechanical engineers use calculators and adding machines to assist them with their work. The engineering field is also beginning to rely on computers and computer aided design (CAD) programs to assist in design and development of machinery systems.

Individuals usually work fairly normal hours. They may be required to work overtime when a project is due or near deadline.

EMPLOYMENT OPPORTUNITIES

Mechanical engineers may work full or part time in a variety of employment situations. The majority of individuals in this field work in the manufacturing industry. Some employment settings include:

- Machinery manufacturers
- Transportation equipment manufacturing firms
- Electrical equipment manufacturing firms
- Fabricated metal products manufacturing firms
- Business consulting services
- Engineering consulting services
- Federal government agencies

Expanding Opportunities for the 21st Century

Mechanical engineers will be needed to answer the demand for more efficient industrial machinery and machine tools. They will also be called on to develop new designs to meet the technological demands of the 21st century.

EARNINGS

Mechanical engineers earn approximately $29,000 to $80,000 or more. Salaries depend on the education, experience, responsibilities, and geographic area of the individual as well as the specific industry he or she is employed in. Generally, mechanical engineers working for the federal government earn lower salaries than their counterparts in private industry.

Individuals holding bachelor's degrees and just entering private industry may earn $29,000 to $36,000. With additional education and experience, annual earnings range from $35,000 to $80,000 or more.

ADVANCEMENT OPPORTUNITIES

It is essential for the advancement of mechanical engineers to continue their training and education in order to keep current on technological advances.

Mechanical engineers may be promoted by being assigned more complex projects. Some individuals may climb the career ladder by locating similar positions in more prestigious firms. Engineers with advanced degrees may choose to go into teaching.

Many mechanical engineers can be promoted to jobs such as technical specialists, or supervisory, management, or administrative positions.

EDUCATION AND TRAINING

Mechanical engineers should have at least a bachelor's degree in engineering with an emphasis in mechanical engineering. A master's or Ph.D. degree may be required for some administrative, supervisory, or teaching positions.

Courses in the first two years of the bachelor's program consist of math and basic sciences such as physics and chemistry, social sciences, humanities, and introductory engineering. During the final two years, students are expected to take all engineering courses, with a major emphasis in mechanical engineering.

It is recommended that mechanical engineers continue their education to keep up with trends in technology. Many employers also offer on-the-job training as well as seminars, classes, and workshops.

EXPERIENCE AND QUALIFICATIONS

Mechanical engineers must be state-registered or -licensed if their work affects property, health, and/or life.

In order to obtain registration, individuals must have a college degree from an engineering program that is accredited by the Accreditation Board for Engineering and Technology. They must also have at least four years of relevant work experience and take and pass a state examination.

FOR ADDITIONAL INFORMATION: Individuals interested in careers as mechanical engineers can obtain additional information by contacting JETS-Guidance, Accreditation Board for Engineering and Technology (ABET), the National Society of Professional Engineers (NSPE), the American Society for Engineering

Education (ASEE), the Society of Women Engineers (SWE), the American Society of Heating, Refrigeration and Air-Conditioning Engineers, Inc. (ASHRAE), and the American Society of Mechanical Engineers (ASME).

TIPS

- Join trade associations. These groups often offer continuing education in the form of seminars, workshops, classes, and symposiums.
- Job openings are often advertised in the classified section of the newspaper under "Engineer," "Mechanical Engineer," "Manufacturing," or specific industries.
- If you are still in school, look for an internship in mechanical engineering. This will give you good on-the-job training as well as an opportunity to make important professional contacts.

CHAPTER 11

Home-Based Business Careers

The exact number of home-based businesses in America today is difficult to estimate. What we do know for certain, though, is that every year more people are trying their hand at either a full-time home-based business or one that will generate supplemental income.

There are a number of reasons for the expansion of home-based businesses. A great motivating factor is the natural desire of many individuals to be their own boss. Home-based businesses offer greater freedom both personally and professionally. Individuals involved in this type of venture can reap the rewards of their own hard work.

One of the most persuasive advantages of the home-based business, for many, is the opportunity to handle personal responsibilities, such as raising children, while running the business.

The tremendous expansion of new technology has made it easier than ever to run a business from one's home. The prices of personal computers, printers, modems, and fax and photocopy machines have gone down dramatically, making this equipment affordable for today's consumers.

Using a computer, modem, and telephone, an individual can work in the home and, within seconds, send completed work anywhere in the world. This is helpful in business ventures such as telecommunications, home-based word processing, accounting, the financial industry, and desktop publishing services, to name just a few.

Home-based businesses encompass a large variety of opportunities in which the primary activity is in the home. In many instances, businesses start in the home and grow so dramatically that the entire activity must be moved into larger quarters.

Generally, home-based businesses can be started with a relatively low overhead. Some people create home offices in their den, spare bedroom, living room, basement, or garage. Others actually have temporary offices on the kitchen table.

Owners may find that certain business operating equipment may be less expensive to rent at the beginning. Almost every business requires a phone and an answering machine. Computers, printers, fax machines, and modems are also helpful in all businesses for preparing promotional material, price quotes, and packaging.

The key to success in a home operation is to remember that it is a business and must be treated as such. Customers and clients must feel confident that the owner is capable and competent.

Every home-based business requires its own specific skills, personality traits, education level, training, and experience. In order to be successful, individuals who get involved in any type of home-based business must have good business skills, be dependable, and have the desire to be successful. They must be self-starters. Often, being self-employed is more difficult than working for a boss. People tend to drive themselves harder and assume greater responsibilities.

Before starting a home business, prospective owners should check into local zoning regulations, department of health regulations, and other applicable rules and regulations.

The diversity of careers in this field as well as space restrictions limit inclusion of all possible opportunities. The home-based businesses discussed in this chapter include:

Catering Service	Home Instruction Service
Bed-and-Breakfast Inn Owner	Cleaning Service
Word Processing Service	Event Planning Service
Desktop Publishing Business	Pet-Sitting Service
Gift Basket Service	Bookkeeping and Accounting Service
Image Consulting Service	Adult Day Care Service
Child-Care Service	Information Broker Service
Publicity Consulting Service	

CATERING SERVICE

BUSINESS DESCRIPTION: *Prepare food for parties, home meals, meetings, and events; deliver and/or serve food; develop themes.*

POSSIBLE CLIENTS: *Charities and other not-for-profit groups; organizations; trade associations; corporations; individuals having parties, weddings, showers, and bar mitzvahs; families in which both spouses work.*

EDUCATION AND TRAINING: *Courses in cooking, baking, garnishing, and food decoration.*

SKILLS AND PERSONALITY TRAITS: *Cooking and baking skills; decorating and garnishing skills; communication skills; business skills.*

REQUIRED EQUIPMENT OR SUPPLIES: *Food; oven, range, refrigerator, freezer, pots, pans, dishes, china, glassware, silverware; car or van to deliver food.*

OPTIONAL EQUIPMENT OR SUPPLIES: *Industrial equipment and cookware.*

ADVANTAGES: *Very low overhead. Caterers can either prepare food in their customers' kitchens or rent kitchens or kitchen equipment.*

DETAILS TO CONSIDER: *Local department of health rules and regulations; liability insurance.*

Home catering businesses are springing up around the country. This is an opportunity for people who truly enjoy cooking and are good at it to turn their hobby into a money-making venture.

Home catering is becoming popular for a number of reasons. Many people who need or like to entertain do not have the time to prepare food, do not like to cook, or are not skilled in the craft of food preparation. Catering services are also finding a market in households where both spouses work.

Because of local health codes, individuals usually cannot use their own primary kitchen for catering purposes. Home caterers can, however, turn a room, basement or garage in their house into a separate kitchen that will adhere to local department of health rules and regulations. In order to save money, many people buy second-hand equipment when starting out.

To keep start-up costs and expenses low, many caterers either prepare food in their client's kitchen or rent facilities. Churches, synagogues, not-for-profit organizations, and schools have kitchens that are seldom used and often rent available space at a very low fee.

Caterers can specialize in specific types of food or prepare a variety. For example, some caterers specialize in the preparation of ethnic food while others handle natural foods and vegetarian meals. There are also caterers who prepare only appetizers or desserts. Some caterers may handle only cocktail parties while others prefer to cater children's parties. A new trend in home catering is preparing and delivering meals to families where both spouses work. Another trend that is becoming increasingly popular is making and delivering nutritious meals to the elderly. This service is usually purchased by adult children who live at a distance from their aging parents.

Most caterers start out on a small scale and increase their services as their list of clients grows.

The best way to build a clientele in this business is through word of mouth. Advertising in local papers, sending out press releases, and having parties for potential clients are also effective ideas.

Functions and responsibilities of caterers include:

- Developing menus
- Talking to potential clients about menus
- Creating themes for events
- Shopping for food
- Preparing food
- Transporting food
- Serving food
- Cleaning up

BED-AND-BREAKFAST INN OWNER

BUSINESS DESCRIPTION: *Rent out rooms in home or separate building to travelers and vacationers; clean rooms; cook and serve breakfast.*

EDUCATION AND TRAINING: *Courses in cooking, baking, garnishing, and decorating food. Hospitality industry workshops or classes.*

SKILLS AND PERSONALITY TRAITS: *Personableness; enthusiasm; cooking and baking skills; communication skills; good business skills.*

REQUIRED EQUIPMENT OR SUPPLIES: *House with one or more extra bedrooms and bath; pretty, unique, or antique comforters, sheets, towels, room accessories, etc.; dining tables large enough to accommodate guests; cleaning equipment and kitchen equipment.*

OPTIONAL EQUIPMENT OR SUPPLIES: *Industrial equipment and cookware.*

ADVANTAGES: *Bed-and-breakfast owners have the opportunity to meet a variety of people while earning extra income in their own home.*

DETAILS TO CONSIDER: *Zoning regulations; health department regulations; liability insurance.*

Bed-and-breakfast inns are usually quaint, romantic, and/or charming homes. Sometimes the owners live in the home and rent out one or more bedrooms to guests. In other situations, the inn is a separate building near the house. Bed-and-breakfasts in cities may be part of a brownstone. As a rule, rates charged to guests are lower than in hotels.

In addition to providing the room, these establishments offer breakfast. While some inns just offer a Continental type of breakfast of toast, juice, and tea or coffee, the B & Bs that are most successful offer a vast array of goodies. Homemade muffins, jams and jellies, pancakes, waffles, homemade bread, and/or biscuits are served with fresh-brewed coffee or gourmet and herbal tea.

Some bed-and-breakfasts may host teatime complete with tea, biscuits, cookies, and dainty finger sandwiches. Others offer hors d'oeuvres. A few of the larger bed-and-breakfasts also serve dinner for an additional fee.

Bed-and-breakfasts are located throughout the country. They are most popular in vacation or resort settings or in large cities where traditional hotels and motels are extremely expensive.

Bed-and-breakfast rooms may have their own bathrooms or may share facilities. Bedrooms in the most successful bed-and-breakfasts are cheerful, interesting, romantic, and/or decorated in a special way. Some have old quilts, rocking chairs, and oak dressers. Others are more modern in their decor. Most B & Bs also have a central public room where guests can sit, talk, read, and play quiet games.

There are a number of organizations throughout the country that screen people who want to stay at bed-and-breakfasts. Others have no screening restrictions. As guests do stay in the same house with the B & B owners and their families, they are often asked not to smoke or drink.

Bed-and-breakfast owners must have excellent interpersonal skills. Part of the job is making guests feel at home. A great number of guests at bed-and-breakfasts throughout the country are repeat customers.

Some of the functions and responsibilities of bed-and-breakfast owners include:

- Greeting guests
- Explaining house rules and regulations
- Showing guests to their room
- Discussing points of interest in the area
- Making guests comfortable so they feel at home
- Decorating rooms
- Cleaning bedrooms, dining area, and public rooms (some owners hire housekeepers)
- Making and serving breakfast

WORD PROCESSING SERVICE

BUSINESS DESCRIPTION: *Type documents, correspondence, term papers, etc., on word processor or computer; check for spelling, grammar, and content.*

POSSIBLE CLIENTS: *Writers; students; small businesses, researchers, not-for-profit organizations; lawyers; physicians; trade associations; corporations; temp agencies.*

EDUCATION AND TRAINING: *Courses in typing, computer usage, and word processing.*

SKILLS AND PERSONALITY TRAITS: *Quick, accurate typing; good grammar, spelling, and punctuation; communication and business skills.*

REQUIRED EQUIPMENT OR SUPPLIES: *Computer, word processor, and printer; computer programs; floppy disks; stationery.*

OPTIONAL EQUIPMENT OR SUPPLIES: *Photocopy machine, fax machine; modem; collator.*

ADVANTAGES: *For people who already have a computer and printer, this business can be started with very low overhead.*

DETAILS TO CONSIDER: *Local zoning rules and regulations; liability insurance.*

To start a word processing service, individuals need a computer with a word processing program and a quality printer.

While the best type of printer to have is laser quality, a good second choice is the less expensive ink jet printer. Individuals who do not own the equipment can often rent it from office supply houses or computer stores.

In order to be successful in a home word processing business, individuals must be quick, accurate typists. They must know how to correctly format a variety of letters and documents.

Some people who start word processing businesses utilize other skills and specialize in a specific area of business. For example, individuals who have a knowledge of legal terminology may seek out business from attorneys; those who are familiar with medical jargon may perform word processing services for physicians.

One of the mainstays for many in the word processing service is creating and preparing resumes. Another is handling term papers for students.

The services of an independent word processor fit the bill for many small businesses that cannot afford the time or the money for a full-time secretary. Large corporations, in an attempt to keep employee benefit rates down, are also contracting with independent word processing businesses.

Independent word processors may charge by the finished page, the hour, or the project. Additional fees are often charged for extra services such as developing a resume or other documents, copying, folding, collating, and putting correspondence into envelopes.

In order to build a clientele, individuals may have to advertise in local papers, put up flyers in schools, stores, and shopping centers and send out promotional mailings to potential clients.

Functions of independent word processors include:

- Typing documents such as reports, correspondence, and term papers with a word processing program on computers
- Typing envelopes
- Preparing and developing resumes
- Formatting copy
- Proofreading copy for errors in spelling, grammar, and content
- Making copies of documents
- Preparing mailings for clients
- Delivering finished work to clients

DESKTOP PUBLISHING BUSINESS

BUSINESS DESCRIPTION: *Handle layout and design of brochures, flyers, letters, posters, reports, booklets, pamphlets, newsletters.*

POSSIBLE CLIENTS: *Small businesses; not-for-profit organizations; corporations; newsletter publishers; restaurants; theaters; trade associations; public relations firms.*

EDUCATION AND TRAINING: *Courses in computer use, word processing, computer graphics, page layout, and writing.*

SKILLS AND PERSONALITY TRAITS: *Creativity; graphic sense; accurate typing; good grammar, spelling, and punctuation; eye for style; communication skills; business skills.*

REQUIRED EQUIPMENT OR SUPPLIES: *Computer; laser or ink jet printer; word processing programs, layout programs, graphics, and stationery.*

OPTIONAL EQUIPMENT OR SUPPLIES: *Photocopy machine, fax machine, and modem.*

ADVANTAGES: *Flexible hours.*

DETAILS TO CONSIDER: *Local zoning rules and regulations; liability insurance.*

Desktop publishers put together designs and produce mechanicals for a variety of items such as brochures, flyers, letters, posters, and newsletters. To accomplish this they use a computer page layout program, computer graphics, and a word processing program.

Individuals design the layout of a document using different sizes and varieties of type fonts. They may also add pictures or graphics that have been computer-generated, scanned, or are from a computer graphic or art software program.

Some desktop publishers just design and lay out a document. Other individuals also prepare the text. Individuals may charge on an hourly basis or a per-project rate.

Any business that uses printed material is a potential client. This includes small businesses in any industry, not-for-profit organizations, large corporations in any industry, newsletter publishers, restaurants, theaters, trade associations, public relations firms, or advertising agencies. Private individuals are also a source of business. For example, a family holding a garage sale may need posters or flyers.

The best ways to find clients for this type of business is by advertising in local papers, leaving cards and brochures in quick print shops, putting flyers on store bulletin boards, and sending promotional mailings to potential clients.

Functions and responsibilities of desktop publishers may include:

- Designing layout of documents, reports, posters, brochures, etc.
- Typing copy into computer
- Determining best font size and type
- Adding graphics
- Preparing or developing copy
- Making copies of documents
- Delivering finished projects to clients

GIFT BASKET SERVICE

BUSINESS DESCRIPTION: *Plan, design, and arrange creative, visually aesthetic gift baskets; develop themes for baskets; deliver and send baskets.*

POSSIBLE CLIENTS: *Corporations; small businesses; offices; individuals, for occasions such as birthdays, holidays, graduations, and showers.*

EDUCATION AND TRAINING: *Classes are often offered in adult or continuing education in the creative development and arrangement of gift baskets.*

SKILLS AND PERSONALITY TRAITS: *Creativity; eye for style and balance; good taste; communication skills; good business skills.*

REQUIRED EQUIPMENT OR SUPPLIES: *Assortment of baskets, selection of gifts and goodies; selection of filling materials, cellophane, decorations; telephone to take orders.*

OPTIONAL EQUIPMENT OR SUPPLIES: *Shrink-wrap machine to wrap baskets; 800 telephone number for ordering baskets.*

ADVANTAGES: *People who are creative will enjoy this business; flexible hours.*

DETAILS TO CONSIDER: *Liability insurance; local department of health rules and regulations if food is being included in baskets.*

Creators of gift baskets must choose unique assortments of gifts and goodies and arrange them creatively. Successful gift basket creators make the basket an exciting gift alternative that is unique and creative. A custom-made gift basket can make a big splash or a simple statement. It can easily be designed to match the special likes and interests of the recipient and to fit each personality perfectly.

Once a theme has been determined, a gift and accessory assortment can be selected and artfully arranged in a decorated or trimmed basket.

People send gift baskets for anniversaries, holidays, birthdays, housewarmings, births of babies, baptisms, bereavements, bridal party gifts, college student care packages, employee awards or honors, etc.

There are a number of ways to build up a clientele for this type of business. Advertising in the local newspaper, putting up flyers, and sending out promotional mailings are all useful strategies. Individuals may also create sample baskets and deliver them to potential clients announcing the opening of their business, or attract clients at craft shows and fairs.

Functions and responsibilities include:

- Choosing correct size, shape, and color of baskets or other containers
- Decorating and trimming baskets and their contents
- Shopping for baskets, containers, and contents

- Developing basket themes
- Filling, arranging, and creating gift baskets
- Wrapping baskets
- Delivering and/or sending baskets

IMAGE CONSULTING SERVICE

BUSINESS DESCRIPTION: *Perform color and image analysis; assist clients in choosing clothing, accessories, and makeup; offer advice about clothing and accessories.*

POSSIBLE CLIENTS: *Corporate executives; bankers; secretaries; lawyers; physicians; celebrities; salespeople; newscasters; executives; people reentering the job market; students.*

EDUCATION AND TRAINING: *Courses in color analysis, image analysis, cosmetology, and fashion.*

SKILLS AND PERSONALITY TRAITS: *Ability to coordinate clothing and accessories; tact; pleasant demeanor; good taste; honesty; enthusiasm; interpersonal skills; confidence; business skills.*

REQUIRED EQUIPMENT OR SUPPLIES: *Color swatches for color analysis; mirror for figure analysis; room with natural, incandescent, and fluorescent lighting.*

OPTIONAL EQUIPMENT OR SUPPLIES: *Video recorder to tape before and after pictures; computer enhancement equipment.*

ADVANTAGES: *Individuals who enjoy shopping and have a knack for coordinating outfits can have a lucrative business; hours are flexible.*

DETAILS TO CONSIDER: *Individuals holding group consultations in their home should check into zoning regulations.*

Image consultants assist people in obtaining a more pulled-together look. Clients often want to appear more polished, confident, warm, or authoritative.

While the majority of clients now are women, the new trend points to men as a potentially large client base. Most image consultants work on a one-on-one basis with clients. Some consultants are also starting to do image workshops and clinics for groups. These can be run in the client's home or may be done in a rented church, synagogue, or school meeting room.

People use image consultants when they are looking for new jobs; in response to promotions; when they have lost or gained a great deal of weight; if there are changes in lifestyle; or when they are tired of their current look.

Image consultants may develop a clientele by advertising in the local newspaper, sending out promotional brochures or letters to potential clients, or by word of mouth. Individuals may also obtain clients by tailoring speeches or presentations to the needs of not-for-profit groups and charity organizations.

Image consultants perform a vast array of duties. Some individuals specialize in just one function, such as color analysis. Others work on the client's total image. Some of the functions of an image consultant can include:

- Meeting with client to determine lifestyle, desired look, clothing requirements, etc.
- Going shopping with client
- Choosing new clothing
- Going through client's existing wardrobe
- Determining the best colors, fabrics, and styles for client
- Determining client's body type
- Assisting client in types, colors, and application of makeup
- Running group image workshops and clinics (optional)
- Private consultations

CHILD-CARE SERVICE

BUSINESS DESCRIPTION: *Care for children, toddlers, or infants; provide a stimulating environment; organize and lead activities; prepare and serve meals and snacks.*

POSSIBLE CLIENTS: *Working parents; students who have children.*

EDUCATION AND TRAINING: *Courses in CPR and childhood development.*

SKILLS AND PERSONALITY TRAITS: *Knowledge of child care; knowledge of CPR; responsibility; patience; good judgment; business skills.*

REQUIRED EQUIPMENT OR SUPPLIES: *Toys; games; blankets; cribs (if caring for infants); nonbreakable dishes and glasses; telephone.*

OPTIONAL EQUIPMENT OR SUPPLIES: *Swing set.*

ADVANTAGES: *Individuals performing child-care services in their home can stay with their own children while earning an extra income.*

DETAILS TO CONSIDER: *Insurance; state licensing; zoning.*

Child-care services are becoming a necessity for many working families. Individuals performing child-care functions may look after children of any age, including infants, toddlers, or older children. Many times child-care services are run directly from people's homes. Most people limit the number of children they care for at one time. If they have more than four or five children in their care, they usually hire extra help. In many states, child-care workers and/or services are regulated and must be licensed.

Before taking charge of children, individuals running child-care services should meet with the parents and the child at the caregiver's home. This allows the child to become familiar with the surroundings.

It is important to determine the habits of the child and foods he or she likes and dislikes. The individual must also obtain phone numbers where parents can be reached in an emergency. Caregivers must have the ability to perform cardiopulmonary resuscitation (CPR).

Good child-care services do not just let children sit in the house all day and watch television. Instead, they have a number of planned activities. For example, the child-care worker may read to the children, play and interact with them, teach them things, etc. Sometimes, the caregiver will bake cookies or prepare a meal and the children will help. At other times, the caregiver may go to the supermarket or perform other errands and take the children along.

Many of the proprietors of home-based child-care services choose this type of business because it affords them the opportunity to stay home with their children and still earn an income. Parents must be very comfortable with the caregiver and have a great deal of confidence in his or her abilities.

Clientele is developed through word of mouth, advertisements in local newspapers, or posters on grocery and/or store bulletin boards.

Individuals who perform child care have a number of responsibilities and functions. These include:

- Childproofing house or rooms where children will be
- Meeting with child and parent(s) before first care day
- Learning about child's allergies, likes, dislikes, and habits
- Caring for child until parent returns
- Playing and interacting with children
- Providing stimulating activities
- Making sure children are safe at all times
- Giving children snacks, meals, etc.
- Providing nap time
- Assisting children with personal hygiene
- Changing babies' diapers
- Giving bottles
- Cuddling, hugging, and carrying babies

PUBLICITY CONSULTING SERVICE

BUSINESS DESCRIPTION: *Obtain publicity; write press releases; take photographs; talk with media.*

POSSIBLE CLIENTS: *Corporations; not-for-profit organizations; small businesses; self-employed individuals; entertainers; special events.*

EDUCATION AND TRAINING: *Degree in English, communications, public relations, or journalism; or courses, seminars, or workshops in writing, English, publicity, public relations, and marketing.*

SKILLS AND PERSONALITY TRAITS: *Communication skills; good writing skills; persuasiveness; enthusiasm; creativity; aggressiveness; computer skills; business skills.*

REQUIRED EQUIPMENT OR SUPPLIES: *Telephone; computer or word processor; printer.*

OPTIONAL EQUIPMENT OR SUPPLIES: *Photocopy machine; fax machine; modem.*

ADVANTAGES: *Most businesses and not-for-profit organizations need publicity; smaller businesses cannot hire someone full time.*

DETAILS TO CONSIDER: *Zoning; insurance.*

Publicity consulting services are hired to obtain publicity for clients. They may be retained on a per-project basis to handle publicity requirements for one event or project, or they may be on a monthly retainer.

With the increase of new home businesses, this service is growing. While the publicity consultant performs many of the same duties as an in-house publicist, businesses do not have to pay for employee fringe-benefit packages or create office space. Many businesses also do not need full-time publicists or feel that a consultant may bring a fresh approach to the company's publicity needs.

Publicity consulting services may easily be run by one person from his or her home. Individuals need a room to work in, a telephone, desk, chair, and computer and printer or word processor. These can be rented to defray start-up expenses.

For people who are creative and like to write, this is an ideal home-based business opportunity. The basic duty of the service is to create methods to obtain positive publicity for a client.

Publicity consultants write professional press releases, send them to the media, and follow up to make sure they get in. In some cases, the consultant arranges for photographs to be taken and sent to the media. Individuals in this line of work need to come up with unique ideas and creative angles to gain attention from the media.

The consultant may also call local media to suggest feature articles on the client, product, or service. Other responsibilities include booking the client on television or radio news, variety or talk shows, and arranging press conferences.

Publicity services may charge by the project or may be on a monthly retainer. Expenses such as long-distance phone calls and mailings are usually reimbursed by the client.

Publicity consulting services can develop a clientele in a number of ways. These include advertising in the business section of local newspapers and sending out promotional flyers, brochures, and letters. Many services handle the publicity for a not-for-profit organization at no fee or a reduced rate in order to build goodwill and obtain exposure for themselves. Word-of-mouth advertising by satisfied customers is the best way to build a client roster.

Publicity consulting services may be required to handle a variety of duties, including:

- Consulting with clients about services required
- Developing publicity campaigns for client
- Preparing and writing press releases, press kits, and feature articles
- Developing a hook or angle regarding client's story
- Taking photographs (or arranging for photos for client)
- Arranging press conferences
- Talking to media on behalf of client
- Arranging for feature stories
- Arranging for client appearances on television and radio talk, variety, and news shows

HOME INSTRUCTION SERVICE

BUSINESS DESCRIPTION: *Teach new skills to people in a home-based situation.*

POSSIBLE CLIENTS: *Any individual who wants to learn a new skill; executives; secretaries; homemakers; students; children.*

EDUCATION AND TRAINING: *Courses, seminars, and/or workshops in area to be taught.*

SKILLS AND PERSONALITY TRAITS: *Ability to speak in front of groups; articulateness; confidence; good communication skills; business skills.*

REQUIRED EQUIPMENT OR SUPPLIES: *Chairs; desks or tables; telephone; additional equipment or supplies will vary with specific courses.*

OPTIONAL EQUIPMENT OR SUPPLIES: *VCR; video camera; additional equipment or supplies will vary for specific courses.*

ADVANTAGES: *This is an excellent opportunity to earn an income by sharing skills; hours are flexible.*

DETAILS TO CONSIDER: *Zoning requirements; insurance.*

The number of home instruction services is expanding and expected to increase even more by the year 2000. People are no longer relying solely on formal education programs in colleges and universities to learn skills. Home instruction may be taught on a one-on-one basis or may include a number of students in a class. The determining factors will be the type of instruction promised as well as the size of the instructor's home "classroom."

Some of the more popular home instruction classes include exercise, dancing, cooking (especially ethnic cooking), nutrition, sewing, languages, crafts, and computer and software use. These classes are just the tip of the iceberg. There are few skills not being taught in this type of setting. It is necessary, however, that the instructor be an expert in the specific field.

Many people take classes, courses, seminars, or workshops not only to learn new skills but to enhance their quality of life. Others want to pursue a new hobby or learn more about a subject so they can start their own home business.

Start-up expenses are usually minimal for this type of service. For example, cooking lessons can be offered in the instructor's own kitchen. An individual teaching sewing may instruct one client at a time using either his or her own sewing machine or, if teaching more than one person, request that clients bring in their own machine. The same concept can be used when teaching computer courses. Individuals may also rent equipment to defray cost at the start-up of their business.

Classes can be any length. Some home instruction classes are one hour. Others continue on a weekly basis for a specified amount of time. It is up to instructors to determine how much time they want to put into the business.

Generally, rates depend on the length and subject matter of the class, the experience and reputation of the instructor, and the prices other instructors are charging in the local area.

A clientele can be developed in a number of ways. These include advertising in local magazines and newspapers, and on radio or television. Flyers and posters circulated throughout the community will also help as will sending brochures to potential clients. Satisfied students will usually spread the word. Publicity also is useful in obtaining clients. Sending press releases about the service to print and broadcast media may result in feature articles in newspapers and guest appearances on local television shows.

Some people increase clientele by branching out. For example, individuals offering adult cooking classes may expand their business by holding classes especially for children on weekends or after school.

Individuals involved in this type of service will have varied responsibilities. These include:

- Developing courses
- Preparing class curriculums and outlines
- Setting up the home "classroom"
- Teaching skills
- Answering questions
- Promoting the home instruction service

CLEANING SERVICE

BUSINESS DESCRIPTION: *Clean homes and/or offices.*

POSSIBLE CLIENTS: *Corporate executives; banks; insurance companies; advertising agencies; lawyers; physicians; dentists; families with both spouses working; single-person households.*

EDUCATION AND TRAINING: *No education or training necessary.*

SKILLS AND PERSONALITY TRAITS: *Physical fitness; positive attitude; verbal communication skills; honesty; organization; reliability; business skills.*

REQUIRED EQUIPMENT OR SUPPLIES: *Telephone; vacuum cleaner; mops; rags, cleaning supplies; transportation to and from clients' homes or businesses.*

OPTIONAL EQUIPMENT OR SUPPLIES: *Industrial cleaning equipment and supplies; carpet shampoo machine.*

ADVANTAGES: *Flexible hours.*

DETAILS TO CONSIDER: *Individuals may have to be bonded.*

Some home-based cleaning services are one-person operations. The proprietor takes on only as much work as he or she can handle alone. Other services send two or more people into the home or business to tackle cleaning jobs. There are also franchised cleaning services where all of the business details are organized when purchasing a franchise. Everything from equipment to letterheads, promotions to polish, is made available.

Cleaning services may either bring their own equipment and supplies or use the client's. Special equipment such as carpet cleaning machines may be rented to keep start-up costs low.

Cleaning services may charge in a number of different ways. Individuals may charge an hourly fee or a flat rate per project, house, or office. Services often have additional fees for major projects, including shampooing carpets, washing windows, preparing a house for sale, and spring cleaning.

It is important that the individual and the client communicate exactly what is to be accomplished. Many cleaning services have checklists to be sure that everything that is required is completed satisfactorily. Some services call clients after the job to make sure they are satisfied.

Cleaning services may be retained for a regular weekly or biweekly visit or for a one-time cleaning service. Cleaning services should be able to provide references and in some cases, individuals must also be bonded.

There is such a great demand for this type of service that people have only to put up flyers and they will usually start getting calls. Another method of building a clientele is sending promotional literature to banks, bakeries, insurance companies, offices of doctors, dentists, lawyers, chiropractors, and other local businesses.

Some of the duties and services of a cleaning service include:

- Consulting with client to determine needs and requirements
- Buying cleaning supplies and equipment
- Cleaning, vacuuming, dusting, etc.
- Handling special cleaning projects
- Finding employees or subcontractors

EVENT PLANNING SERVICE

BUSINESS DESCRIPTION: *Develop themes for events; choose sites; negotiate contracts; arrange for special permits; book entertainment.*

EDUCATION AND TRAINING: *No special education or training required.*

SKILLS AND PERSONALITY TRAITS: *Creativity; attention to detail; negotiation skills; ability to read and understand contracts; public relations skills; communication skills; business skills.*

REQUIRED EQUIPMENT OR SUPPLIES: *Telephone; computer and word processor; printer.*

OPTIONAL EQUIPMENT OR SUPPLIES: *Tents; toll-free 800 telephone number; photocopy machine; videotape equipment; van or truck.*

ADVANTAGES: *This is a good opportunity for people who enjoy planning events; start-up costs are modest.*

DETAILS TO CONSIDER: *Insurance; lawyers may be required to look over contracts.*

Event planners organize meetings, press conferences, weddings, showers, conventions, fund-raisers, fashion shows, reunions, bar mitzvahs, parties, golf tournaments, and a variety of other events.

Event planners develop a theme for the occasion, put everything together, and make the event successful. For example, if the theme of a party is a Mexican motif, the planner might have mariachi dancers and strolling guitar players as entertainment. Food and drinks would revolve around Mexican favorites. Decorations might be piñatas, Mexican straw hats, and big, bold, colorful flowers.

People use the services of an event planner for a number of reasons. The most important is that all event details are professionally and competently handled. The event planner will meet with potential clients and determine the size and type of event and the estimated budget. He or she then will develop two or three themes for the client to select from. Once a theme is decided upon, the event planner will coordinate all aspects of the event from sending out invitations to the final cleanup.

Event planners may be contracted to coordinate small events or large galas. Individuals usually charge a set fee for handling the entire project.

Word-of-mouth advertising from satisfied customers is one of the best ways of attracting clients. Other methods include advertising in local newspapers, preparing and sending press releases to local media, and mailing promotional brochures and letters to potential clients. Event planners may also offer their services to run an event for a charity or not-for-profit group in order to obtain community exposure.

Responsibilities of event planners include:

- Consulting with potential clients
- Determining size and type of event as well as budget
- Scouting for appropriate event sites
- Negotiating contracts for site rentals, caterers, equipment, and supplies
- Arranging for any special permits that may be necessary
- Hiring waiters, waitresses, bus people, clean-up people, etc.
- Finding appropriate entertainment and speakers
- Booking the entertainment
- Making sure everything goes according to schedule

PET-SITTING SERVICE

BUSINESS DESCRIPTION: *Take care of other people's pets; feed and exercise pets; play with the animals.*

POSSIBLE CLIENTS: *Anyone who has a pet: business executives who travel; people going on vacations; people who are hospitalized.*

EDUCATION AND TRAINING: *No special education or training is required.*

SKILLS AND PERSONALITY TRAITS: *Enjoy being around dogs, cats, and other pets; ability to relate to animals; reliability; dependability; maturity; communication skills.*

REQUIRED EQUIPMENT OR SUPPLIES: *Fenced-in yard; pet toys, leashes, blankets or towels; pet food (if owners are not providing food).*

OPTIONAL EQUIPMENT OR SUPPLIES: *Rug cleaner.*

ADVANTAGES: *This is an ideal business for people who love animals. No special skills or equipment are needed other than relating well to animals.*

DETAILS TO CONSIDER: *Animals are required to have proper immunizations. Local zoning rules and regulations; liability insurance.*

Pet-sitters are a relatively new alternative to boarding kennels. Pet-sitters care for people's pets when they go on vacation, travel for business, or are away from home for any reason. Pet-sitters sometimes take the pet into their own home. Many owners feel more comfortable leaving their pet in a home environment where they can roam about the house, receive personal attention, and interact with people.

While pet-sitters can care for any type of animal, cats and dogs are the usual. Other possibilities include turtles, rabbits, white mice, ferrets, hamsters, snakes, and birds.

Charges for pet-sitting vary from $10 per day to $35 per day, depending on the specific pet, the services rendered, and the geographic location.

Before pet-sitters take charge of animals they should find out about the pet's habits, food likes and dislikes, and allergies. Individuals should also find out if the pet gets along with other animals.

Pet-sitters can build up a clientele by advertising in the local paper; putting up flyers and posters in local pet stores, feed shops, and veterinarians' offices; and sending brochures to potential clients. Individuals can also send press releases to local media and discuss the possibilities of a special-interest article about the service. Word-of-mouth advertising by satisfied customers is the best method of obtaining new clients.

Responsibilities of pet-sitters include:

- Meeting with pet and pet owner prior to pet-sitting date
- Finding out about pet's habits, likes, dislikes, and allergies
- Obtaining copy of pet's immunization records
- Obtaining the out-of-town phone number of the pet owner
- Obtaining veterinarian's name and phone number
- Obtaining a letter stating that emergency medical procedures can be performed on the pet
- Feeding, taking out, playing with, and interacting with pet
- Exercising pet
- Making sure pet is safe

BOOKKEEPING AND ACCOUNTING SERVICE

BUSINESS DESCRIPTION: *Handle bookkeeping and accounting needs; keep business records; prepare tax forms.*

POSSIBLE CLIENTS: *Small businesses; corporations; lawyers; dentists; physicians; individuals.*

EDUCATION AND TRAINING: *Degree in accounting helpful; bookkeeping courses; classes in preparation of income tax.*

SKILLS AND PERSONALITY TRAITS: *Bookkeeping and accounting skills; math skills; computer skills; business skills.*

REQUIRED EQUIPMENT OR SUPPLIES: *Desk; chairs; telephone; calculator or adding machine.*

OPTIONAL EQUIPMENT OR SUPPLIES: *Computer; photocopy machine.*

ADVANTAGES: *Individuals who have accounting degrees can develop profitable home-based accounting businesses.*

DETAILS TO CONSIDER: *State licensing for CPAs; insurance.*

Individuals who have degrees in accounting and knowledge of bookkeeping and income tax preparation have the skills necessary to start their own home-based bookkeeping or accounting business.

Individuals formerly employed in accounting firms can often build their client roster from former contacts. Other methods of building a clientele include advertising in local newspapers, putting up flyers in neighborhood shops and malls, and sending out promotional letters and brochures. Friends, colleagues, and associates all are potential clients.

Many companies utilize the services of a freelance bookkeeper instead of hiring a full-time employee. This method of employment saves the company money on employee benefits, a full-time salary, and permanent office space.

Proprietors of bookkeeping services must enjoy working with figures and have excellent math skills. Accounting and bookkeeping skills and knowledge of tax forms and laws are necessary. Individuals should be dependable and accurate and have the ability to work neatly. Many people in this position do the major portion of their work with the assistance of a computer and computer programs. Therefore, computer skills are mandatory.

Fees will depend on the specific services handled as well as the amount of time the services take to accomplish. Other factors affecting fees include the geographic location as well as the individual's education, training, and experience. Those who are CPAs will be able to command higher fees than people who just have bookkeeping training.

Owners of home-based bookkeeping and/or accounting services perform a variety of duties including:

- Consulting with new clients to determine accounting or bookkeeping needs
- Preparing individual's income taxes
- Preparing corporate taxes
- Advising on tax matters (if trained in that field)
- Setting up and maintaining company books
- Handling business payroll
- Performing accounts receivable
- Handling billing
- Handling personal bookkeeping
- Taking care of small business bookkeeping needs
- Reconciling checkbook

ADULT DAY CARE SERVICE

BUSINESS DESCRIPTION: *Care for adults who are no longer capable of living alone; prepare and serve meals; provide social stimulation and interaction.*

POSSIBLE CLIENTS: *Stroke patients; Alzheimer's patients; mentally impaired adults; senior citizens who cannot stay alone.*

EDUCATION AND TRAINING: *Home nursing courses; first aid; CPR; recreational therapy or classes for home health aides.*

SKILLS AND PERSONALITY TRAITS: *Compassion; creativity; interpersonal skills; emotional stability; physical strength.*

REQUIRED EQUIPMENT OR SUPPLIES: *Comfortable furniture; television; telephone; ramps and handicapped bathroom facilities may be required.*

OPTIONAL EQUIPMENT OR SUPPLIES: *Craft supplies; board games; VCR*

ADVANTAGES: *The need for adult day care is growing.*

DETAILS TO CONSIDER: *Licensing requirements; insurance; zoning.*

Adult day care services are a relatively new venture. They are a spin-off of child day care services. Clients are elderly or disabled people who cannot be left alone all day. Many of the clients of this type of service are living with their children who are at work all day. Others may live with spouses or other family members. While the individuals do not require constant supervision, they usually need a certain amount of attention and care. The service is especially useful for Alzheimer's patients and stroke victims.

Adult day care provides a place for geriatric clients to come during the day where they will be looked after. Depending on the intensity of the service, individuals may plan an extensive slate of activities or just provide a daytime haven.

Adult day care providers may, for example, schedule outings to shopping centers, malls, special events, restaurants, etc. The adult day care provider might also offer activities such as craft making, cake and cookie baking, and game playing.

Individuals are required to prepare and serve nutritious meals and snacks for clients. Depending on the abilities of clients, day care providers may be responsible for assisting them at mealtime. The day care provider assists clients with medications and with personal hygiene, especially in situations where clients may be incontinent.

In addition to providing care for basic needs, this service often offers clients an opportunity for personal contact that might not be possible living alone. The adult day care provider may also have young children or pets that the geriatric client can interact with.

Before taking responsibility for a client, the adult day care provider should gather as much information as possible about the individual. This includes obtaining names and phone numbers of physicians and people to contact in case of emergency; lists of medications taken, with instructions and times they must be administered; and information on habits, allergies, likes, and dislikes. It is especially important that the caregiver have the ability to perform cardiopulmonary resuscitation (CPR).

Clientele can be developed by contacting local social services agencies, advertising in newspapers, and distributing posters and flyers throughout the community. The need is so great for this type of service that the problem may be too many clients instead of too few.

Services like this may often be regulated by government agencies. Depending on the state, adult day care service providers may need licensing or registration.

Individuals performing adult day care service have a number of responsibilities including:

- Caring for clients
- Making clients comfortable in their surroundings
- Providing intellectual stimulation and social contact
- Preparing and serving nutritious meals and snacks
- Helping clients eat
- Assisting clients with personal hygiene
- Developing activities to keep clients busy
- Providing a comfortable area for clients to nap
- Administering medications properly and on time

INFORMATION BROKER SERVICE

BUSINESS DESCRIPTION: *Locate specific information and data on a variety of subjects; conduct interviews and surveys; perform on-line computer searches.*

POSSIBLE CLIENTS: *Corporations; small businesses; new business owners; advertising and public relations agencies; students; writers; developers of new products; physicians; dentists.*

EDUCATION AND TRAINING: *Training in research methods; computer classes.*

SKILLS AND PERSONALITY TRAITS: *Organization; attention to detail; extensive knowledge of research methods; ability to work alone; ability to access on-line databases; computer skills.*

REQUIRED EQUIPMENT OR SUPPLIES: *Computer; modem; printer; telephone.*

OPTIONAL EQUIPMENT OR SUPPLIES: *Fax machine; photocopy machine.*

ADVANTAGES: *This is a relatively new service that is expected to expand in the future.*

DETAILS TO CONSIDER: *Costs of accessing on-line computer databases.*

Information broker services may have clients anyplace in the country or the world. With the new technological advances of the computer, modem, and fax machines, individuals can not only access information but send it directly to the client in a matter of minutes.

Information services are used by a variety of people for various reasons. Individuals opening new businesses may, for example, be interested in knowing how many similar businesses are in the same area.

Advertising and public relations agencies, as well as other corporations and businesses, often use the information brokers to obtain demographics of specific areas or potential buyers. Information broker services may also conduct interviews and surveys to research and obtain necessary data.

Fees depend on the type of services performed and the amount of time it will take to complete a project. Charges can be made either on a per-project basis, an hourly basis plus expenses, or a combination. Expenses will include the charge for accessing of on-line databases, phone calls, photocopying, faxing, and sending documents.

Methods for building a clientele include advertising in the business section of newspapers or trade journals and volunteering to speak at civic and business group meetings. Promotional mailings will also help.

Information broker services may perform a number of duties. These include:

- Consulting with clients to determine the exact information required
- Going to libraries, universities, companies, etc., to research the required information
- Using books, magazines, files, and other sources to locate information
- Conducting interviews and surveys
- Conducting on-line database searches
- Gathering information
- Copying articles and documents
- Sending, faxing, or delivering information

APPENDIX

Trade Associations, Unions and Other Organizations

The following is a listing of trade associations, unions, and organizations mentioned in the "For Additional Information" sections of each job entry. There are also a number of other associations listed that might be useful in obtaining information on the careers discussed in this book.

Names, addresses, and phone numbers are included so that contact can be made with any of the organizations for information regarding membership, career guidance, scholarships, or internships.

Many of the organizations have branch offices located throughout the country. Organization headquarters will usually provide the phone number and address of the closest local branch.

Accreditation Council for
Accountancy (ACA)
1010 North Fairfax Street
Alexandria, VA 22314
703-549-6400

Accrediting Bureau of Health
Education Schools (ABHES)
29089 U.S. 20 West
Elkhart, IN 46514
219-293-0124

Accrediting Council on Education in
Journalism and Mass
Communications (ACEJMC)
School of Journalism
University of Kansas
Lawrence, KS 66045
913-864-3973

Advertising Club of New York
155 East 55th Street
Suite 202
New York, NY 10022
212-935-8080

Advertising Research Foundation
(ARF)
641 Lexington Avenue
New York, NY 10022
212-751-5656

Advertising Women of New York,
Inc. (AWNY)
153 East 57th Street
New York, NY 10022
212-593-1950

Aerobics and Fitness Association
of America (AFAA)
1520 Ventura Boulevard
Sherman Oaks, CA 91403
818-905-0040

Aerobics Center
12200 Preston Road
Dallas, TX 75230
214-239-7223

Affiliated Advertising Agencies
International (AAAI)
2280 South Zanadu Way
Aurora, CO 80014
303-671-8551

Air Pollution Control Association
(APCA)
1 Gateway Center
Pittsburgh, PA 15230
412-232-3444

Air Transport Association of
America (ATAA)
1301 Pennsylvania Avenue
Suite 1100
Washington, DC 20004
202-626-4000

Airline Pilots Association (APA)
1625 Massachusetts Avenue N.W.
Washington, DC 20036
703-689-2270

Alcohol and Drug Problems Association (ADPA)
1555 Wilson Boulevard
Suite 300
Arlington, VA 22209
703-875-8684

Allied Pilots Association (APA)
P.O. Box 5524
Arlington, TX 76005
214-988-3188

American Academy of Actuaries
(AAA)
1100 17th Street N.W.
Washington, DC 20006
202-223-8196

American Academy of Physician
Assistants (AAPA)
950 North Washington Street
Alexandria, VA 22314
703-836-2272

American Advertising Federation
(AAF)
1101 Vermont Avenue N.W.
Suite 500
Washington, DC 20005
202-898-0089

American Assembly of Collegiate
Schools of Business (AACCB)
600 Emerson Road
Suite 300
St. Louis, MO 63141
314-872-8481

American Association for Adult and
Continuing Education (AAACE)
1200 19th Street N.W.
Suite 300
Washington, DC 20036
202-429-5131

American Association for Music
Therapy (AAMT)
P.O. Box 80012
Valley Forge, PA 19484
601-265-4006

American Association for Paralegal
Education (AAPA)
P.O. Box 40244
Overland Park, KS 66204
913-381-4458

American Association for Clinical Chemistry (AACC)
2101 L Street N.W.
Suite 202
Washington DC 20037
202-857-0717

American Association for Counseling and Development (AACD)
5999 Stevenson Avenue
Alexandria, VA 22304
703-823-9800

American Association of Advertising Agencies (4A's)
666 Third Avenue
New York, NY 10017
212-682-2500

American Association of Blood Banks (AABB)
8101 Glenbrook Road
Bethesda, MD 20814
301-907-6977

American Association of Colleges of Osteopathic Medicine (AACOM)
6110 Executive Boulevard
Suite 405
Rockville, MD 20852
301-468-0990

American Association of Colleges of Pharmacy (AACP)
1426 Prince Street
Alexandria, VA 22314
703-739-2330

American Association of Colleges of Podiatric Medicine (AACPA)
1350 Piccard Drive
Suite 322
Rockville, MD 20850
301-990-7400

American Association of Dental Examiners (AADE)
211 East Chicago Avenue
Suite 1812
Chicago, IL 60611
312-440-7464

American Association of Dental Schools (AADS)
1625 Massachusetts Avenue N.W.
Washington, DC 20036
202-667-9433

American Association of Homes for the Aging (AAHA)
901 E Street N.W.
Suite 500
Washington, DC 20004
202-783-2242

American Association of Medical Assistants (AAMA)
20 North Wacker Drive
Suite 1575
Chicago, IL 60606
312-899-1500

American Association of Nurse Anesthetists (AANA)
222 South Prospect
Park Ridge, IL 60068
708-692-7050

American Association of Respiratory Care (AARC)
11030 Ables Lane
Dallas, TX 75229
214-243-2272

American Association of Retired Persons (AARP)
601 E. Street N.W.
Washington, DC 20049
202-434-2277

American Bar Association (ABA)
750 North Lake Shore Drive
Chicago, IL 60611
312-988-5000

American Bed and Breakfast Association (ABBA)
P.O. Box 1387
Midlothian, VA 231113
804-379-2222

American Board of Registration for Electroencephalgraphic Technologists (ABRET)
P.O. Box 11434
Norfolk, VA 23517
804-627-5503

American Business Communication Association (ABCA)
University of North Texas
College of Business
Department of Management
Denton, TX 76203
817-565-4423

American Chemical Society
1155 16th Street N.W.
Washington, DC 20036
202-872-4600

American Chemical Society Career Services (ACSCS)
1155 16th Street N.W.
Washington, DC 20036
202-872-4600

American Chiropractic Association (ACA)
1701 Clarendon Boulevard
Arlington, VA 22909
202-276-8800

American College of Health Care Administrators (ACHCA)
325 South Patrick Street
Alexandria, VA 22314
703-549-5822

American College of Healthcare Executives (ACHE)
1 North Franklin
Suite 1700
Chicago, IL 60606
312-424-2800

American Correctional Association (ACA)
8025 Laurel Lakes Court
Laurel, MD 20707
301-206-5100

American Council on Pharmaceutical Education (ACPE)
311 West Superior Street
Chicago, IL 60610
312-664-3575

American Craft Council (ACC)
72 Spring Street
New York, NY 10012
212-274-0630

American Dance Therapy Association (ADTA)
2000 Century Plaza
Suite 108
Columbia, MD 21044
301-997-4040

American Dental Assistants Association (ADAA)
203 North LaSalle Street
Suite 1320
Chicago, IL 60601
312-541-1550

American Dental Association
(ADA)
211 East Chicago Avenue
Chicago, IL 60611
312-440-2500

American Dental Hygienists'
Association (ADHA)
444 North Michigan Avenue
Suite 3400
Chicago, IL 60611
312-440-8929

American Dietetic Association
(ADA)
208 South LaSalle Street
Suite 1100
Chicago, IL 60604
312-899-0040

American Federation of Government
Employees (AFGE)
80 F Street N.W.
Washington, DC 20001
202-737-8700

American Federation of State,
County and Municipal Employees
(AFSCME)
1625 L Street N.W.
Washington, DC 20036
202-429-1000

American Federation of Teachers
(AFT)
555 New Jersey Avenue N.W.
Washington, DC 20001
202-879-4400

American Forestry Association
(AFA)
1516 P. Street N.W.
P.O. Box 2000
Washington, DC 20005
202-667-3300

American Geological Institute (AGI)
4220 King Street
Alexandria, VA 22302
703-379-2480

American Geriatrics Society (AGS)
770 Lexington Avenue
New York, NY 10021
212-308-1414

American Health Care Association
(AHCA)
1201 L Street N.W.
Washington, DC 20005
202-842-4444

American Hospital Association
(AHA)
1 North Franklin
Sujite 27
Chicago, IL 60606
312-422-3000

American Hotel and Motel Association (AH & MA)
1201 New York Avenue N.W.
Suite 600
Washington, DC 20005
202-289-3100

American Institute for Design
and Drafting (AIDD)
P.O. Nox 799
Rockville, MD 20848
301-460-6875

American Institute of Biological
Sciences (AIBS)
730 11th Street N.W.
Washington, DC 200001
202-628-1500

American Institute of Certified
Public Accountants (AICPA)
1211 Avenue of the Americas
New York, NY 10036
212-575-6200

American Institute of Chemists
(AIC)
7315 Wisconsin Avenue N.W.
Bethesda, MD 20814
301-652-2447

American Institute of Graphic Arts
(AIGA)
164 Fifth Avenue
New York, NY 10010
212-807-1990

American Institute of Physics (AIP)
1 Phsics Ellipse
College Park, MD 20740
301-209-3100

American Marketing Association
250 South Wacker Drive
Suite 200
Chicago, IL 60606
312-648-0536

American Medical Association
(AMA)
515 North State Street
Chicago, IL 60610
312-464-5000

American Medical Record Association (AMRA)
John Hancock Center
Suite 1850
875 North Michigan Avenue
Chicago, IL 60611
312-787-2672

American Medical Technologists
(AMT)
710 Higgins Road
Park Ridge, IL 60068
312-823-5160

American Meteorological Society
(AMS)
45 Beacon Street
Boston, MA 02108
617-227-2425

American Newspaper Publishers
Association Foundation (ANPAF)
The Newspaper Center
11600 Sunrise Center
Reston, VA 22091
703-648-1000

American Nurses' Association
(ANA)
600 Maryland Avenue S.W.
Washington, DC 20024
202-651-7000

American Occupational Therapy
Association (AOTA)
P.O. Box 31220
Bethesda, MD 20824
301-652-2682

American Optometric Association
243 North Lindbergh Boulevard
St. Louis, MO 63141
3143-991-4100

American Osteopathic Association
(AOA)
142 East Ontario Street
Chicago, IL 60611
312-280-5800

American Physical Therapy Association (APTA)
1111 North Fairfax Street
Alexandria, VA 22314
703-684-2782

American Podiatric Medical Association (APMA)
9312 Old Georgetown Road
Bethesda, MD 20814
301-571-09200

American Registry of Diagnostic
Medical Sonographers (ARDMS)
2368 Victory Parkway
Cincinnati, OH 45206
513-281-7111

American Registry of Radiologic
Technologists (ARRT)
1255 Northland
St.Paul, MN 55120
612-687-0048

American Society for Information
Science (ASIS)
8720 Georgia Avenue Suite 501
Silver Springs, MD 20910
301-495-0900

American Society of Aging (ASA)
833 Market Street
Suite 511
San Fransisco, CA 94103
415-974-9600

American Society of Agricultural
Engineers (ASAE)
950 South Cherry
Suite 508
Denver, CO 80222
303-759-5091

American Society of Biological
Chemists (ASBC)
9650 Rockville Pike
Bethesda, MD 20814
301-530-7145

American Society of Civil Engineers
(ASCE)
C/O Kelly Cunningham
1015 15th Street N.W.
Suite 600
Washington, DC 20005
202-789-2200

American Society of Clinical
Pathologists (ASCP)
2100 West Harrison
Chicago, IL 60612
312-738-1336

American Society of Cytology (ASC)
400 West 9th Street
Suite 201
Wilmington, DE 19801
302-429-8802

American Society of
Electroneurodiagnostic Technologists
(ASET)
204 West 7th Street
Carroll, IA 51401
712-792-2978

American Society of Heating,
Refrigeration and Air-Conditioning
Engineers, Inc. (ASHRACE)
1791 Tullie Circle, N.E.
Atlanta, GA 30329
404-636-8400

American Society of Hospital
Pharmacists (ASHP)
7272 Wisconsin Avenue
Bethesda, MD 20814
301-657-3000

American Society of Magazine
Editors (ASME)
913 3rd Avenue
New York, NY 10022
212-872-3700

American Society of Mechanical
Engineers (ASME)
345 East 47th Street
New York, NY 10017
212-705-7722

American Society for Medical
Technology (ASMT)
7910 Woodmont Avenue
Bethesda, MD 29854
301-657-2768

American Society of Pension
Actuaries (ASPA)
4520 North Fairfax
Suite 820
Arlington, VA 22203
703-516-9300

American Society of Radiologic
Technologists (ASRT)
15000 Central Avenue, S.E.
Albuquerque, NM 87123
505-298-4500

American Society of Travel Agents
(ASTA)
1101 King Street
Alexandria, VA 22314

American Telemarketing Association
(ATA)
444 N. Larchmont Boulevard
Los Angles, CA 90004
213-463-2330

American Therapeutic Recreation
Association (ATRA)
P.O. Box 15215
Hattiesburg, MS 39404
601-264-3413

American Veterinary Medical
Association (AVMA)
1931 North Meacham Road
Suite 100
Schaumburg, IL 60173
708-925-8070

Art Directors Club, Inc. (ADC)
250 Park Avenue South
New York, NY 10003
212-674-0500

Associated Master Barbers and
Beauticians of America (MBBA)
124 NE Main Street
P.O. Box 273
Palmyra, PA 17078
717-838-0795

Association for Fitness In Business
(AFB)
60 Revere Drive
Suite 500
Northbrook, IL 11464
708-480-9574

Association for Computer Operations Management (ACOM)
742 East Chapman Avenue
Orange, CA 92666
717-997-7966

Association for Computing Machinery (ACM)
1515 Broadway
New York, NY 10036
212-869-7400

Association for Computing Machinery, Special Interest Group On
Programming Languages (SIGPL)
1515 Broadway
New York, NY 10036
212-869-7400

Association for Gerontology in
Higher Education (AGHE)
1001 Connecticut Avenue N.W.
Suite 410
Washington, DC 20036
202-429-9271

Association for Systems Management
(ASM)
1433 West Bagley Road
Cleveland, OH 44138
216-243-6900

Association of American Law
Schools (AALS)
1201 Connecticut Avenue S.W.
Suite 800
Washington, DC 20036
202-296-8851

Association of American Medical
Colleges (AAMC)
2450 N. Street N.W.
Washington, DC 20037
202-828-0400

Association of American Veterinary
Medicine Colleges (AAVMC)
1101 Vermont Avenue
Suite 710
Washington, DC 20005
202-371-9195

Association of Computer
Professionals (ACP)
9 Forrest Drive
Plainview, NY 111803
516-938-8223

Association of Computer Programmers and Analysts (ACPA)
5170 Meadow Wood Boulevard
Lyndhurst, OH 44124
216-461-4803

Association of Data Processing
Service Organizations (ADPSO)
1616 N. Fort Myer Drive
Suite 1300
Arlington, VA 22209
703-522-5055

Association of Environmental
Engineering Professors (AEEP)
C/O Dr. Richard J. Luthy
Department of Civil Engineering
Carnegie Mellon University
Pittsburgh, PA 15213
412-268-2949

Association of Flight Attendants (AFA)
1625 Massachusetts Avenue N.W.
Washington, DC 20011
202-328-5400

Association of Ground Water
Scientists and Engineers (AGWSE)
6375 Riverside Drive
Dublin, OH 43017
614-761-1711

Association of Physician Assistant
Programs (APAP)
950 North Washington Street
Alexandria, VA 22314
703-836-2272

Association of Schools and Colleges
of Optometry (ASCO)
6110 Executive Boulevard
Rockville, MD 20852

Association of Surgical Technologist
(AST)
7108- C S. Alton Way
Englewood, CO 80112
303-694-9130

Association of University Programs
In Health Administration (AUPHA)
1911 Fort Myers Drive
Suite 503
Arlington, VA 22209
703-524-5500

Cardiovascular Credentialing
International (CCI)
4456 Corporation Lane
Suite 120
Virginia Beach, VA 23462
804-497-3380

Casualty Actuarial Society (CAS)
1100 North Glenbe Road
Suite 600
Arlingotn, VA 22201
703-276-3100

Child Development Associate
Credentialing Program (CDACP)
1341 G Street N.W.
Suite 400
Washington, DC 20005
202-265-9090

Childcare Employee Project
733 15th Street N.W.
Suite 800
Washington, DC 20005
510-653-9889

Civil Service Employees Association
(CSEA)
P.O. Box 7125
Capitol Street
Albany, NY 12210
518-434-0191

Committee on Allied Health Education and Accreditation (CAHEA)
535 North Dearborn Street
Chicago, IL 60610
312-645-4660

Communications Workers of
America (CWA)
1925 K Street N.W.
Washington, DC 20006
202-728-2300

Computer Aided Manufacturing
International (CAMI)
1250 E. Copeland Road
Suite 500
Arlington, TX 76011
817-860-1654

Computer and Business Equipment
Manufacturers Association (CBEM)
1250 Eye Street N.W.
Suite 200
Washington, DC 20005
202-737-8888

Computer and Communications
Industry Association (CCIA)
666 11th street N.W.
Suite 600
Washington, DC 20001
201-783-0070

Computer Software and Services
Industry Association (CSSIA)
1616 North Fort Myer Drive
Suite 1300
Arlington, VA 22209
703-522-5055

Conference of Actuaries In Public
Practice (CAPP)
475 North Martingale
800
Schaumburg, IL 60173
708-706-3535

Contact, Inc.
P.O. Box 81826
Lincoln, NE 68501
402-464-0602

Council For The Advancement and
Support of Education (CASE)
11 Dupont Circle, N.W., Suite 400
Washington, DC 20036
202-328-5900

Council for Accreditation of Counseling and Related Education
Programs (ACREP)
American Association For Counseling
and Development
5999 Stevenson Avenue
Alexandria, VA 22314
703-823-9800

Council on Chiropractic Education
(CCE)
7975 North Hayden Road
No. A-210
Scottsdale, AZ 85258
602-443-8877

Council on Hotel, Restaurant and
Institutional Education (CHRIE)
1200 17th Street N.W.
Washington, DC 20036
202-331-5990

Council on Social Work Education
(CSWE)
1600 Duke Street
Suite 300
Alexandria, VA 22314
703-683-8080

Data Processing Management
Association (DPMA)
505 Busse Highway
Park Ridge, IL 60068
312-825-8124

Dental Assisting National Board,
Inc. (DANB)
216 East Ontario Street
Chicago, IL 60611
312-642-3368

Direct Mail/Marketing Association
(DM/MA)
1120 Avenue of the Americas
New York, NY 10036
212-768-7277

Direct Marketing Association
(DMA)
1120 Avenue of the Americas
New York, NY 10036
212-768-7277

Direct Marketing Creative Guild
(DMCG)
C/O Richard Sachinis
Graphic Experience
341 Madison Avenue
New York, NY 10017
212-867-0806

Division of Allied Health Education
and Accreditation of the American
Medical Association (DAHEAAMA)
535 North Dearborn Street
Chicago, IL 60610
312-645-5000

Dow Jones Newspaper Fund
P.O. Box 300
Princeton, NJ 08543
609-452-2820

Educational Foundation of the
National Restaurant Association
(EFNRA)
250 South Wacker Drive
No. 1400
Chicago, IL 60606
312-715-1010

Educational Institute of the American Hotel and Motel Association
(EIAHMA)
888 Seventh Avenue
New York, NY 10106
212-265-4506

Electronics Industries Association
(EIA)
2001 I Street N.W.
Washington, DC 20006
202-457-4900

Electronics Technicians Association
International (ETAI)
602 North Jackson Street
Greencastle, IN 46135
317-653-8262

Environmental Industry Council
(EICO)
529 14th Street N.W.
Suite 655
Washington, DC 20045
202-737-3018

Environmental Management Association (EMA)
4350 Dipaolo Center
Suite C
Glenview, IL 60025
708-699-6362

Environmental Protection Agency (EPA)
401 M Street S.W.
Washington, DC 20460
202-382-2973

Flight Engineers' International Association (AFL-CIO)
1926 Pacific Coast Highway
No. 202
Renondo Beach, CA 90277
310-316-4094

Future Aviation Professionals of America (FAPA)
4959 Massachusetts Boulevard
Atlanta, GA 30337
404-997-8097

Gerontological Society of America (GSA)
1275 K Street N.W.
Washington, DC 20005
202-842-1275

Graphic Artists Guild (GAG)
11 West 20th Street
New York, NY 10011
2120463-7730

Hair International
124-B East Main Street
P.O. Box 273
Palmyra, PA 17078
717-838-0795

Hazardous Materials Control Research Institute (HMCRI)
1 Church Street
Suite 200
Rockville, MD 20850
301-251-1900

Hazardous Waste Treatment Council (HWTC)
915 15th Street N.W.
5th Floor
Washington, DC 20005
202-783-0870

Health Insurance Association of America (HIAA)
1025 Connecticut Avenue N.W.
Suite 1200
Washington, DC 20036
202-223-7780

Independent Insurance Agents of America (IIAA)
127 South Peyton
Alexandria, VA 22314
703-683-4422

Institute for Certification of Computer Professionals (ICCP)
2200 East Deveon Avenue
Suite 268
Des Plaines, IL 60018
212-299-4270

Institute of Certified Travel Agents (ICTA)
P.O. Box 812059
148 Linden Street
Wellesley, MA 02181
617-237-0280

Institute of Environmental Sciences (IES)
940 East Northwest Highway
Mt. Prospect, IL 60056
312-255-1561

Institute of Internal Auditors (IIA)
249 Maitland Avenue
Altamonte Springs, FL 32701
305-830-7600

International Association of Business Communicators (IABC)
1 Hallidie Plaza
Suite 600
San Francisco, CA 94102
415-433-3400

International Chiropractors Association (ICA)
1110 North Glenbe Road
Suite 1000
Arlington, VA 22201
703-528-5000

International Dance-Exercise Association (IDEA)
6190 Cornerstone Court E.
San Diego, CA 92121
619-535-8979

International Society for Clinical Laboratory Technology (ISCLT)
818 Olive Street
Suite 918
St. Louis, MO 63101
314-241-1445

JETS-Guidance, Accreditation Board for Engineering and Technology (GABET)
1420 King Street
Suite 405
Alexandria, VA 22314
703-548-JETS

Joint Review Committee For Respiratory Therapy Education (JRCRTE)
1701 West Euless Boulevard
Suite 200
Euless, TX 76040
817-283-2835

Law School Admissions Service (LSAS)
P.O. Box 40
Newtown, PA 18940
215-968-1101

Mail Advertising Service Association (MASA)
1421 Prince Street
Suite 200
Alexandria, VA 22314
703-836-9200

Marketing Research Association (MRA)
2189 Silas Deane Highway
Suite 5
Rocky Hill, CT 06067
203-257-4008

Medical Group Management Association (MGMA)
104 Inverness Terrace East
Engelwood, CO 80112
303-799-1111

Microcomputer Software Association (MSA)
C/O ADAPSO
1616 North Fort Meyer Drive
Suite 1300
Arlington, VA 22209
703-522-5055

National Accrediting Commission of Cosmetology Arts and Sciences (NACCAS)
901 North Stuart Street
No. 900
Arlington, VA 22203
703-527-7600

National Alliance of Cardiovascular Technologists (NACT)
120 Falcon Drive
Fredricksburg, VA 22408
703-891-0079

National Association For Homecare
(NAH)
519 C Street N.E.
Washington, DC 20002
202-547-7424

National Association for Music
Therapy, Inc. (NAMT)
8455 Colesville Road
Suite 930
Silver Spring, MD 20910
301-589-3300

National Association for Practical
Nurse Education and Service, Inc.
(NAPNES)
1400 Spring Street
Suite 310
Silver Spring, MD 20910
301-588-2491

National Association of Accountants
(NAA)
10 Paragon Drive
Montvale, NJ 07645
201-573-9000

National Association of Accredited
Cosmetology Schools, Inc.
(NAACS)
901 North Washington Street
Suite 206
Alexandria, VA 22314
703-845-1333

National Association of Activity
Professionals (NAAP)
1225 Eye Street N.W.
Suite 300
Washington, DC 20005
202-889-0722

National Association of Alcoholism
and Drug Abuse Counselors
(NAADAC)
3717 Columbia Pike
Suite 300
Arlington, VA 22204
703-920-4644

National Association of Boards
of Pharmacy (NABP)
700 Busse Highway
Park Ridge, IL 60068
312-698-6227

National Association of Broadcast
Employees and Technicians
(NABET)
501 3rd street N.W.
8th Floor
Washington, Dc 20001
202-434-1254

National Association of Broadcasters
(NAB)
1771 N Street N.W.
Washington, DC 20036
202-429-5300

National Association of County
Training and Employment Professionals (NACTEP)
440 First Street N.W.
Washington, DC 20001
203-393-6226

National Association of Emergency
Medical Technicians (NAEMT)
102 West Leake Street
CLinton, MS 39056
601-924-7744

National Association of Environmental Professionals (NAEP)
5165 MacArthur Boulevard N.W.
Washington, DC 20016
202-966-1500

National Association of Government
Employees (NAGE)
2011 Crystal Drive
Suite 206
Arlington, VA 22202
703-979-0290

National Association of Health
Underwriters (NAHU)
1000 Connecticut Avenue
Suite 111
Washington, DC 20036
202-223-5533

National Association of Home Based
Businesses
P.O. Box 30220
Baltimore, MD 21270
410-363-3698

National Association of Legal
Assistants, Inc. (NALA)
1516 South Boston
Suite 200
Tulsa, OK 74119
918-587-6828

National Association of Legal
Secretaries International (NALS)
2250 East 73rd. Street
Suite 550
Tulsa, OK 74136
918-493-3540

National Association of Life Underwriters (NALU)
1922 F Street N.W.
Washington, DC 20006
203-331-6000

National Association of Professional
Geriatric Care Managers
(NAPGCM)
1604 North Country Club Road
Tucson, AZ 85716
602-881-8008

National Association of Professional
Insurance Agents (NAPIA)
400 North Washington Street
Alexandria, VA 22314
703-836-9340

National Association of Professional
Word Processing Technicians
110 West Byberry Road
Philadelphia, PA 19116
610-698-8525

National Association of Realtors
(NAR)
430 North Michigan Avenue
Chicago, IL 60611
312-329-8200

National Association of Social
Workers
750 First Street N.W.
Suite 700
Washington, DC 20002
202-408-8600

National Association of Substance
Abuse Trainers and Educators
(NASATE)
1521 Hillary Street
New Orleans, LA 70118
504-861-4756

National Association of Trade and
Technical Schools (NATTS)
750 1st Street N.E.
Suite 900
Washington, DC 20002
202-336-6700

National Board for Certified
Counselors (NBCC)
3-D Terrace Way
Greensboro, NC 27403
910-547-0607

National Board for Respiratory
Care, Inc. (NBRC)
8310 Nieman Road
Lenaxa, KS 66214
913-599-4200

National Certification Agency
for Medical Laboratory Personnel
(NCAMLP)
7910 Woodmont Avenue
Suite 1301
Bethesda, MD 20814
301-654-1622

National Child Care Association
(NCCA)
1501 Benning Road N.E.
Washington, DC 20002
202-397-3800

National Commission on Certification of Physician Assistants, Inc.
(NCCPA)
2845 Henderson Mill Road, N.E.
Atlanta, GA 30341
404-493-9100

National Cosmetology Association,
Inc. (NCA)
3510 Olive Street
St. Louis, MO 63103
314-534-7980

National Council for Accreditation
of Teacher Education (NCATE)
2010 Massachusetts Avenue S.W.
Suite 500
Washington, DC 20036
202-466-7496

National Council for Therapeutic
Recreation Certification (NCTRC)
479 Theills
Spring Valley, NY 10984
914-947-4346

National Education Association
(NEA)
1201 16th Street N.W.
Washington, DC 20036
202-833-4000

National Environmental Health
Association (NEHA)
720 South Colorado Boulevard
Suite 970-South Tower
Denver, CO 80222
303-756-9090

National Federation of Federal
Employees (NFFE)
1016 16th Street N.W.
Washington, DC 20005
202-862-4400

National Federation of Licensed
Practical Nurses, Inc. (NFLPN)
1418 Aversboro Road
Garaner, NC 27529
919-779-0046

National Federation of Paralegal
Associations (NFPA)
P.O. Box 33108
Kansas City, MO 64114
816-941-4000

National Health Council (NHC)
1730 M Street N.W.
Suite 500
Washington, DC 20036
202-785-3910

National Lawyers Guild (NLG)
55 6th Avenue
New York, NY 10013
212-966-5000

National League For Nursing (NLN)
350 Hudson Street
New York, NY 10014
212-989-9393

National Newspaper Association
(NNA)
1525 Wilson Boulevard
Suite 550
Arlington, VA 22209
703-907-7900

National Oceanic and Atmospheric
Administration Personnel Office
253 Monticello Avenue
Norfolk, VA 23510
804-827-6876

National Paralegal Association
(NPA)
Box 406
Solesbury, PA 18963
215-297-8333

National Retail Merchants
Association (NRMA)
325 7th Street N.W.
Suite 1000
Washington, DC 20004
202-783-7971

National Society of Cardiovascular
Technology/National Society
of Pulmonary Technology
(NSCT/NSPT)
120 Falcon Drive
Fredricksburg, VA 22408
703-891-0079

National Society of Fund Raising
Executives (NSFRE)
1101 King Street
Suite 3000
Alexandria, VA 22314
703-684-0410

National Society of Professional
Engineers (NSPE)
1420 King Street
Alexandria, VA 22314
703-684-2800

National Society of Public
Accountants (NSPA)
1010 North Fairfax Street
Alexandria, VA 22314
703-549-6400

National Student Nurses'
Association (NSSA)
555 West 57th Street
Suite 1325
New York, NY 10019
212-581-2211

National Therapeutic Recreation
Society (NTRS)
2775 South Quincy Street
Suite 300
Arlington, VA 22206
703-5678-5548

National Weather Service
400 North Capitol Street
Suite 357
Washington, DC 20001
202-783-3131

Nuclear Medicine Technology
Certification Board (NMTCB)
2970 Clairmont Road Suite 610
Atlanta,GA 30329
404-315-1739

Opticians Association of America
(OAA)
10341 Democracy Lane
P.O. Box 10110
Fairfax, VA 22030
703-691-8355

Professional Secretaries International
(PSI)
10502 NW Ambassador Drive
P.O. Box 20404
Kansas City, MO 64195
816-891-6600

Promotion Marketing Association of America (PMAA)
257 Park Avenue South
11th Floor
New York, NY 10001
212-420-1100

Public Relations Society of America (PRSA)
33 Irving Place
15th and 16th Streets
New York, NY 10003
212-995-2230

Radio and Advertising Bureau (RAB)
304 Park Avenue South
New York, NY 10010
212-387-2100

Robotics International of SME(RISME)
P.O Box 0930
1 SME Drive
Dearborn, MI 48121
313-271-1500

Sales and Marketing Executives International (SMEI)
Statler Office Tower
Suite 977
Cleveland, OH 44115
216-771-6650

Small Business Administration (SBA)
1441 L Street N.W.
Washington, DC 20416
202-653-6832

Society for Technical Communications, Inc. (STC)
901 North Stuart Street
suite 904
Arlington, VA 22203
703-522-4114

Society of Actuaries (SOA)
475 North Martingale Road
Suite 800
Schaumburg, IL 60173
708-706-3500

Society of Diagnostic Medical Sonographers (SDMS)
12770 Voit Road
Suite 508
Dallas, TX 75251
214-239-7367

Society of Illustrators (SOI)
128 East 63rd Street
New York, N.Y. 10021
212-838-2560

Society of Nuclear Medicine (SNM)
1850 Samuel Morse Drive
Reston, VA 22090
703-708-9000

Society of Women Engineer
120 Wall Street
11th Floor
New York, NY 10005
212-509-9577

Soil Science Society of America (SSSA)
677 South Segoe Road
Madison, WI 53711
608-273-8080

Television Bureau of Advertising (TBA)
850 3rd Avenue
10th Floor
New York, NY 10022
212-486-1111

The Newspaper Guild (TNG)
8611 Second Avenue
Silver Spring, MD 20912
301-585-2990

The One Club
3 West 18th Street, 3rd Floor
New York, NY 10011
212-255-7070

**Transport Workers Union
of America (TWUA)**
80 West End Avenue
New York, NY 10023
212-873-6000

**United Food and Commercial
Workers International Union
(UFCWIU)**
Suffridge Building
1775 K Street N.W.
Washington, DC 20006
202-223-3111

**United States Department
of Agriculture**
14th Street &
Independence Avenue S.W.
Washington, DC 20250
202-447-2791

United States Department of Labor
200 Constitution Avenue, N.W.
Washington, DC 20210
202-523-6255

**U.S. Office of Personnel
Management and the Veterans
Administration (VA)**
1900 E Street N.W.
Washington, DC 20541
202-632-5491

Veterans Administration
810 Vermont Avenue
Washington, DC 20420
202-233-2741

**Water Pollution Control Federation
(WPCF)**
601 Wythe Street
Alexandria, VA 22314
703-684-2400

**Women In Communications, Inc.
(WIC)**
3717 Columbia Pike
No. 310
Arrlington, VA 22204
703-528-4200

**Writers Guild of America East
(WGA)**
555 W. 57th Street
New York, NY 10019
212-767-7800

**Writers Guild of America West
(WGA)**
8955 Beverly Blvd.
West Hollywood, CA 90048
310-550-1000